The
Practical Guide to
CELESTIAL NAVIGATION

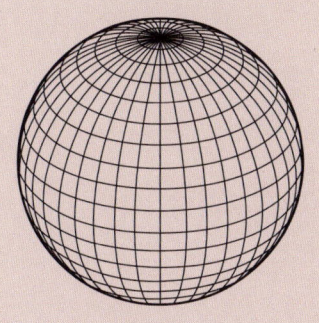

The Practical Guide to
CELESTIAL NAVIGATION

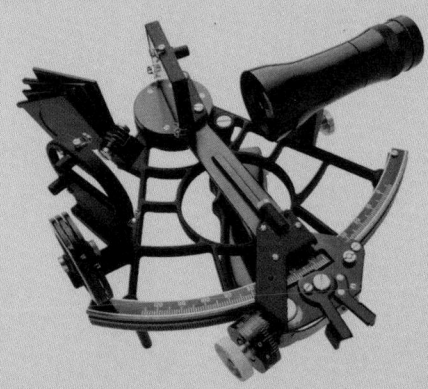

Step-by-step instructions
for when you've lost the plot

PHIL SOMERVILLE

ADLARD COLES

LONDON · OXFORD · NEW YORK · NEW DELHI · SYDNEY

ADLARD COLES
Bloomsbury Publishing Plc
50 Bedford Square, London, WC1B 3DP, UK
29 Earlsfort Terrace, Dublin 2, Ireland

BLOOMSBURY, ADLARD COLES and the Adlard Coles logo are trademarks of
Bloomsbury Publishing Plc

First published in Great Britain 2021

Copyright © Phil Somerville, 2021
Illustrations © Phil Somerville, 2021
Re-rendered by Dave Saunders

Phil Somerville has asserted his right under the Copyright, Designs and Patents Act, 1988, to be identified as Author of this work

For legal purposes the Acknowledgements on p.viii constitute an extension of this copyright page

All rights reserved. No part of this publication may be reproduced or transmitted in any form or by any means, electronic or mechanical, including photocopying, recording, or any information storage or retrieval system, without prior permission in writing from the publishers

Bloomsbury Publishing Plc does not have any control over, or responsibility for, any third-party websites referred to or in this book. All internet addresses given in this book were correct at the time of going to press. The author and publisher regret any inconvenience caused if addresses have changed or sites have ceased to exist, but can accept no responsibility for any such changes

A catalogue record for this book is available from the British Library

Library of Congress Cataloguing-in-Publication data has been applied for

ISBN: HB: 978-1-4729-8758-7; ePUB: 978-1-4729-8759-4; ePDF: 978-1-4729-8760-0

2 4 6 8 10 9 7 5 3 1

Typeset in Source Serif by Carr Design Studio
Printed and bound in India by Replika Press Pvt. Ltd

ACKNOWLEDGEMENTS

This product has been derived in part from material obtained from the UK Hydrographic Office with the permission of the UK Hydrographic Office and Her Majesty's Stationery Office. © British Crown Copyright, 2021. All rights reserved.

Yachtmaster™ is a trademark of the Royal Yachting Association registered in the United Kingdom and selected marketing territories. For information on RYA qualifications and RYA approved training courses for both power and sail please visit the website: www.rya.org.uk/training, email: training@rya.org.uk, telephone: +44 (0) 2380 604 181 or write to: RYA Training, RYA House, Ensign Way, Hamble, Hants SO31 4YA

To find out more about our authors and books visit www.bloomsbury.com and sign up for our newsletters

Contents

- For **practical learning**, read this book in order
- For **theory only**, follow chapters **1**, **2**, **5**, **6** and **14**
- For a **Quick Start refresher**, follow chapters **9**, **11** and **12**

About the author	vii
Acknowledgements	viii

Introduction — 1

A bit of history	1
Why bother?	2
A bit about this book	2

Chapter 1 The basics — 5

Latitude and longitude	5
Earth rotation	6
Great circles	8

Chapter 2 Foundation of celestial navigation and the geographical position — 11

Geographical position (GP)	11
Position lines and lines of position	14

Chapter 3 Defining the geographical position — 21

Declination	21
Greenwich Hour Angle (GHA)	22
Obtaining the sun's GP	23
Proforma introduction	26

Chapter 4 Sextant corrections — 33

Index error	34
Height of eye (dip)	34
Altitude correction	35
Applying the corrections: example	36

Chapter 5 The PZX triangle — 39

A bit of background	40

Chapter 6 The intercept method — 43

Chapter 7 Sight Reduction Tables — 47
The four keys — 48

Chapter 8 Undertaking a full sight reduction — 51
Resources — 51
Sight Reduction — 52

Chapter 9 Sun sight reduction – Quick Start and recap — 69
Resources — 69
Completing a sun sight reduction — 70

Chapter 10 Meridian passage — 73
How we take the sight — 75
Worked example — 75
Resources — 76

Chapter 11 Meridian passage – Quick Start and recap — 83
Resources — 83
Completing a meridian passage sight — 84

Chapter 12 Plotting — 87
Sun Run Sun: morning sun sight and meridian passage — 88
Plotting a Sun Run Sun — 90
Sun Run Sun: morning sight and afternoon sight — 105
Sun Run Sun: meridian passage and afternoon sight — 106

Chapter 13 Compass checking — 109
Variation — 109
Deviation — 110
Sight reduction for compass checking — 110
Checking for deviation — 111
Worked example — 112

Chapter 14 Time — 115
Time zones — 115
Chronometer — 117
A practical solution for accurate timekeeping — 117
International Date Line — 118

Chapter 15 Sextant: Practical aspects of sight taking — 119
Overview — 121
Errors — 121
Undertaking a sight — 125
Reading the sextant — 126
Sextant care — 126

Chapter 16 Troubleshooting — 127

Appendices — 129
1. Sun sight proforma — 130
2. Sun sight proforma guide — 131
3. Meridian passage proforma — 132
4. Meridian passage proforma guide — 133
5. Plotting sheet — 134
6. Plotting guide — 135
7. Longitude scale plotting — 136
8. Z versus Zn — 137
9. Assumed longitude — 139
10. Adding and subtracting of 60ths — 141
11. Polaris — 142

Glossary — 144

Index — 150

About the author

Originally from Derby, at the age of seven, Phil Somerville was bought a model sailing yacht by his grandfather. Even now, many decades later, the years have not faded the memory of that afternoon when the two of them took this small yacht down to a local boating lake together. It ignited a world of imagination and wonderment that has lasted a lifetime.

Phil went on to train and become a qualified marine electrical and electronics engineer. However, it wasn't long before the call of the sea became too strong to resist.

That was the start of an almost perpetual train of studies that has led Phil to become an RYA Yachtmaster Instructor and Examiner in both Power and Sail, and holder of an MCA Master 200gt unlimited certificate of competence.

Across Europe, Phil now teaches MCA Masters Celestial, RYA Ocean, MCA Masters Stability and the ten-day GMDSS communications course. As if that's not enough, he finds time to get involved in practical work opportunities

Phil is pictured here skippering the *Silurian*, a research vessel of the Hebridean Whale & Dolphin Trust (HWDT)

wherever possible. This has led to a diverse range of experience over the years, from the construction of wind turbines in Germany to working aboard Skip Novak's *Pelagic Australis* in the Southern Hemisphere.

Acknowledgements

Thanks go to all of those who have made the production of this book possible, in particular: Lily Somerville, Jason Rowe, Bill Merry, Mel Lapacho, Peter Senior, Anna Jacob, Annie Mellor and the team at Yacht Haven Quay Plymouth. Also to Earl Sepalla for providing the world with his great online celestial resource in the form of www.thenauticalalmanac.com. Extracts from which have been used extensively throughout this publication.

Extra special thanks go to my friend and colleague Alan Denham. Many people have experienced his contagious passion and inspiration in this subject and not least me. Alan has opened up many opportunities for me over the years, for which I am eternally grateful.

PHOTO CREDITS

All photos by the author except for the following:

ii Thorsten Lass/EyeEm/Getty Images
iii and 1 C Squared Studios/Getty Images
vii Anna Jacob
3 Ainara Vera
6 VMJones/Getty Images
7 Oli Scarff/Getty Images
9 Martin Zwick/REDA&CO/Universal Images Group via Getty Images
18 Jingying Zhao/Getty Images
20 Design Pics/SICI/Getty Images
26 Gary John Norman/Getty Images
32 Glenn Whalan/Getty Images
38 Hiu Fung Cheung/EyeEm/Getty Images
41 Tim Trzoska/EyeEm/Getty Images
42 SEBASTIEN SALOM GOMIS/AFP via Getty Images
43 Thierry Dosogne/Getty Images
49 Achilleas Chiras/NurPhoto via Getty Images
50 Jean-François Monnot/EyeEm/Getty Images
68 Colin Anderson Productions pty ltd/Getty Images
72 Daniel Montesi/EyeEm/Getty Images
75 Tom Grill/Getty Images
79 piola666/Getty Images
83 © 2019 FOTOGRIN/Shutterstock
86 Martin Zwick/REDA&CO/Universal Images Group via Getty Images
87 Onne van der Wal/Getty Images
88 Richard Hamilton Smith/Getty Images
98 Thierry Dosogne/Getty Images
108 Image Source/Getty Images
113 (top left) James Goddard
    (bottom) DAMIEN MEYER/AFP via Getty Images
114 © 2021 Alex Stemmer/Shutterstock.
118 Sharpshooters/VWPics/Universal Images Group via Getty Images
124 (bottom) stevecoleimages/Getty Images
128 Victor Dyomin/Getty Images
142 Tetra Images/Getty Images

Introduction

I remember only too well wrestling with the fundamentals of celestial navigation. 'I'm not stupid,' I thought, 'I'm reasonably well educated, why is this so difficult?'

I spent months wading through book after book, trying to grasp the principles that made it work. Sure, I could go through the motions and come up with a position, but it was all done mechanically and without a grasp of how it really worked.

Then, one evening, parked up in the mountains of southern Spain, I had the eureka moment. The relief and excitement I felt that evening was beyond words.

Thankfully, that was a long time ago and I now have years of teaching the subject to RYA Ocean and MCA Master students behind me. Over the years I've used my learning experience to dissect the subject and deliver it in proven, logical building blocks of understanding. Learning this timeless skill is not going to be a walk in the park and you should be prepared to put in some graft. The book will do the rest.

A BIT OF HISTORY

Before we talk further about the book, let's look at a bit of history.

Prior to a few centuries ago, there was no way of accurately fixing position at sea. The

mariners of old could obtain their latitude fairly easily (you'll discover how later on), but longitude was difficult. In fact, those mariners of old used dead reckoning (speed, direction and time), but this was less than ideal.

Then an event changed things for ever. Possibly the most pivotal of all British maritime disasters occurred in 1707. Sir Cloudesley Shovell was returning his fleet of 21 ships to the British Isles from a campaign in the Mediterranean. I won't go into much detail, but the lack of accurate position fixing led to four ships running aground in the Isles of Scilly, and the loss of between 1,400 and 2,000 men.

This event rocked the foundation of Great Britain as a maritime nation, and led the parliament of the time to issue the 'Longitude Prize'. A huge sum of money was on offer for the person who could solve the problem of obtaining longitude at sea. Eventually, and after many years, this was solved using John Harrison's H4 clock. It must be remembered in that age, pendulum clocks could keep time to a second a day (not bad considering there are 86,400 seconds a day), but pocket watches were terribly inaccurate, a loss or gain of three or four minutes a day was considered the norm. In fact, in those days, it was a common sight to see people correcting their watches many times a day whenever they could. Harrison's story and that of the Longitude Prize is fascinating in its own right, one that revolutionised navigation on the world's oceans.

WHY BOTHER?

But why bother today? For a start, understanding this incredible relationship comes with a great sense of achievement, not least because armed with just a sextant (an accurate angle-measuring device), a few publications and an accurate watch, you can fix your position anywhere in the world.

Having a secondary and independent means of fixing position should not be dismissed. This skill, understandably, is still required by the RYA, MCA and many maritime organisations around the world for mariners wishing to expand their ventures away from coastal waters. Reliance on on-board GPS firstly requires a dependable electrical system. Then there's GPS signal blocking, whether that be pirate attack or military intervention. (Only a few years ago, sailing a marine research vessel in the Western Isles of Scotland, a navigation warning was issued to all mariners that satellite navigation was going down for the entire area of the Minch. And it did, we lost all electronic navigation.) The priority of any military in times of war must surely be to compromise their opponent's ability to navigate. Then there are the concerns of sunspot activity and associated electromagnetic interference. The list goes on…

A BIT ABOUT THIS BOOK

Celestial navigation is a vast subject and many books try to cover it all in one sitting. This means the often disjointed concepts put forward get lost on the readers who are trying to understand the entirety of this subject in one go – and they give up. I know this only too well because it's a common story brought into the classroom by students.

This book is aiming to achieve three things:

- Teach you to fix your position using the biggest, most easily recognised and most freely available celestial object in the sky – the sun.

- Give you the underlying knowledge and fundamentals so you will gain an understanding into how it works.

- Give you a solid platform from which you can expand your knowledge to include the other celestial objects such as the stars, planets and the moon, if you desire.

It will not teach you to fix your position using planets, stars and the moon.

Now, I know the mention of celestial navigation probably conjures up romantic images of standing on the deck of a boat at night, staring up at the night sky taking sights. However, there are complexities with the stars, planets and the moon that for a secondary or emergency backup means of navigation (which for most of us is what celestial navigation will be used for) is perhaps taking things too far. For most of us, even if we do master the concepts and use of these twilight celestial objects, we will use the technique so infrequently that the skill will be lost in between.

These twilight objects have a limited 'window' of sight-taking opportunity each day. They require it to be dark enough to see them, while at the same time the sun needs to be just below the horizon, giving the observer a nice crisp image of the horizon. And, of course, you need to be able to identify them in the first place. I'm not saying don't take your learning there, I'm just suggesting that we park those objects for the future.

One final point that you should be aware of: celestial navigation is a vast subject. Each time one delves into an aspect of the subject and peels away a layer, it's common to find many more layers beneath. Indeed, it's this very nature that keeps so many people fascinated by the subject. However, for others, faced with busy lives and multiple pressures, it can feel like an incomprehensible, bottomless pit.

In teaching circles there is a mnemonic called MOSCOW, it stands for must know, should know and could know. If someone is presented purely with the must-know aspects, the learning experience can be very dry, lack context and be very difficult to understand. At the other end of the spectrum is the situation where one is presented with everything, the

Friend and colleague Alan Denham sight taking.

must, the should and the could. The result is a totally overwhelming experience.

Therefore, the challenge is to deliver the must know with just enough of the should know, to make things interesting and with enough context to make learning easier.

With this in mind, the concepts used in this book often depart from traditional formats:

- **Alternative concepts are adopted where it is considered that they are more logical and easier to grasp.**

- **Omissions are made where concepts serve little purpose or cloud the bigger picture.**

An example that won't make much sense if you're new to celestial navigation is the complete absence of reference to the celestial sphere in this book. This is a concept where we imagine the earth to be situated inside a bubble. Instead of celestial objects being situated somewhere out in space at varying distances, we imagine them to be superimposed on this sphere. There are aspects of celestial navigation where this conceptual celestial sphere can be of assistance. However, in the early stages of learning, it's been my overwhelming experience that it detracts from understanding and muddies the water.

Don't be concerned that you'll be presented with a format that has no relevance though. As already mentioned, the format adopted will give a firm foundation and act as a stepping stone for the future, should you wish to delve deeper.

This book looks at the theory of celestial navigation and its practical application.

We will see that, just as radar can be used to determine the distance from a known object, celestial navigation uses the sextant to determine the distance from a theoretical but nevertheless definable position on the earth's surface.

Then, using tables, we can obtain the same distance from our dead reckoning (or a position close by) to this same theoretical position. The difference between the two is used to determine a position line. Obtaining more than one position line enables us to fix our position.

In the absence of GPS, dead reckoning is used to approximate our position on the world's oceans. Dead reckoning, being based on distance and direction travelled, is by its nature not very accurate. However, the process of celestial navigation compensates for this lack of accuracy. In fact, the famous ocean sailor Bernard Moitessier had this to say:

> *In working a celestial sight, one can base the calculation on an estimated position that is completely absurd; the position line will bring the boat back to her true location. If the intercept is too long one need only redo the calculation using the new estimated position, which will be more accurate than that shown by the log, especially after a meridian sight. Just for fun, I have sometimes deliberately picked a position 600 miles off. In two calculations (easily done with the HO 249 tables) the boat took her true position on the chart.*
>
> – Bernard Moitessier, *The Long Way* (1971)

CHAPTER ONE

The basics

Before we head into the realms of this subject, something needs pointing out. The science of celestial navigation is founded on a number of very clever principles linked to the relationship between angles and distances, which, in order to comprehend, requires the understanding of several apparently unconnected relationships. They're not really unconnected, they wouldn't be included if they were, but they will appear to be unrelated until you have the full picture. Many publications perhaps fail on this score. You read one chapter of said publication, you understand it. You then move on to the next chapter, fail to make any links and give up – an all too familiar story.

These relationships will be looked at in the following pages. Take them at face value, park them and move on. Only as you move through the book will all these pieces of the jigsaw fit together, and hopefully, with enough time spent pondering the concepts, you too will get that eureka moment.

LATITUDE AND LONGITUDE

In this day and age of electronic navigation aids (GPS and chart plotters), you'd be forgiven for thinking that latitude is just a horizontal line on a chart and longitude just a vertical one. We're not going back to basics for nothing here, the experience of teaching this subject has proven that this is a common misconception. So, we must remember what they're really based on. In Figure 1, we have an illustration of the earth. The red line is the equator and the green line the Greenwich Meridian. We'll be keeping these colours as we build future pictures as it saves lots of labelling and helps with understanding.

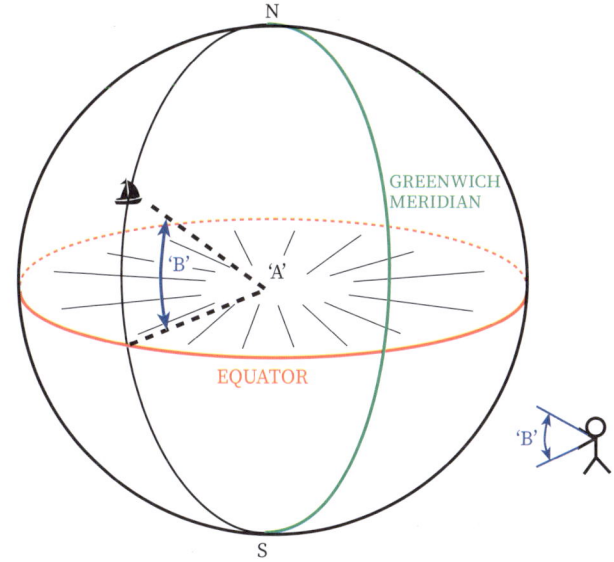

Figure 1

Imagine standing at point A, the centre of the earth. If we were to hold out our arms, pointing one at the vessel and one at the equator, the angle between our arms will be the vessel's latitude. To put this in more correct terms, the vertical angle subtended between the equator and our vessel is our latitude (somewhere between 0° and 90°, which is why we denote the degrees of latitude with two digits, eg **50°** 34.3' North).

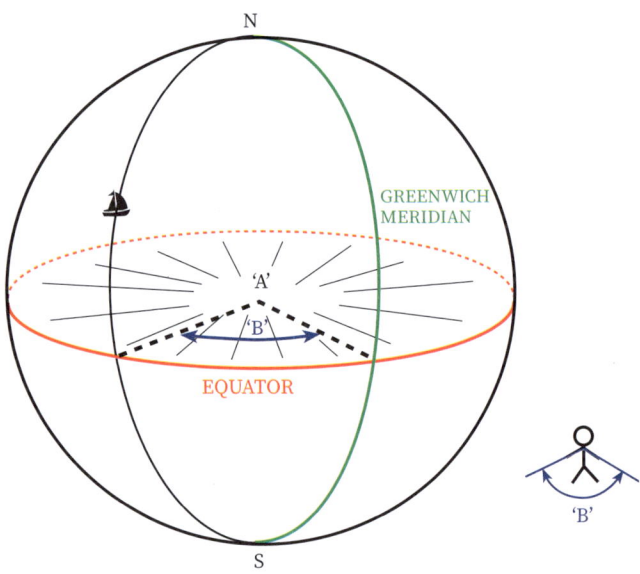

Figure 2

Similarly, looking at Figure 2, if we point horizontally between the Greenwich Meridian and the meridian of the vessel, the angle between our arms is the vessel's longitude (in this case the longitude is west). It will be somewhere between 0° and 180° east or west. Here the degrees have three digits, because the longitude, unlike latitude, can go to three digits, eg **050°** 44.7' East.

EARTH ROTATION

Now that we're getting the idea of these angles subtended at the centre of the earth, let's have a look at its rotation.

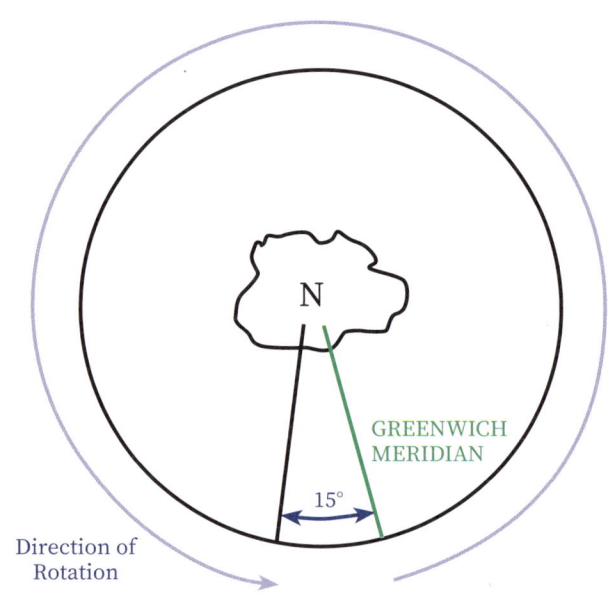

Figure 3

Figure 3 is a 'top down' view of the earth. In other words, we're looking down at the North Pole. So, we know the earth takes 24 hours to rotate through a complete revolution (actually it takes 23 hours and 56 minutes, but let's forget about that for these purposes). Table

1 shows this revolution. It takes 24 hours to rotate through 360 degrees. Perhaps a lesser known fact is that during that 24 hours, someone standing on the equator will have travelled 21,600nm (ignoring the earth travelling through space). Or to put it another way, the circumference of the earth is 21,600nm (The earth in actual fact is not completely round, it is slightly squashed at the poles and is known as an oblate ellipsoid or spheroid. This deformation is, however, too small to be of concern to us.)

ANGLE	TIME	DISTANCE
360°	24hr	21,600nm
15°	1hr	900nm
1°	4min	60nm
60'	4min	60nm
15'	1min	15nm
1'	4sec	1nm

Table 1

Looking down, we see it takes one hour for the earth to rotate through 15 degrees, covering a distance of 900nm at the equator. In other words, a person stood on the equator is travelling at 900 miles per hour.

One degree takes four minutes and covers a distance of 60nm.

60 minutes (which is, of course, a degree) also takes four minutes and a distance of 60nm.

Carrying on down, it takes the earth one minute to rotate through 15 minutes of angle and cover a distance of 15nm.

And finally, and importantly, we see it takes four seconds to rotate through one minute of angle and cover one mile. Two things are of importance here with this last one:

- Every four seconds of inaccuracy in our timekeeping is going to result in an error of 1nm.

- We're back to a relationship we should know where 1 minute of angle = 1 nautical mile. Interesting!

The Marine Timekeeper 'H4' watch made by John Harrison in 1759.

GREAT CIRCLES

Now, great circles are normally something mentioned when sailing great circle routes rather than sailing rhumb lines. If that doesn't make sense to you don't worry. But we do need to understand what a great circle is, because it's fundamental to understanding celestial navigation. So what is a great circle? Let's look at two possible definitions.

DEFINITION 1

A great circle is any circle on the surface of the earth that shares its centre with the centre of the earth. The equator is a great circle, as shown in Figures 4 & 4a. What other great circles do we know of?

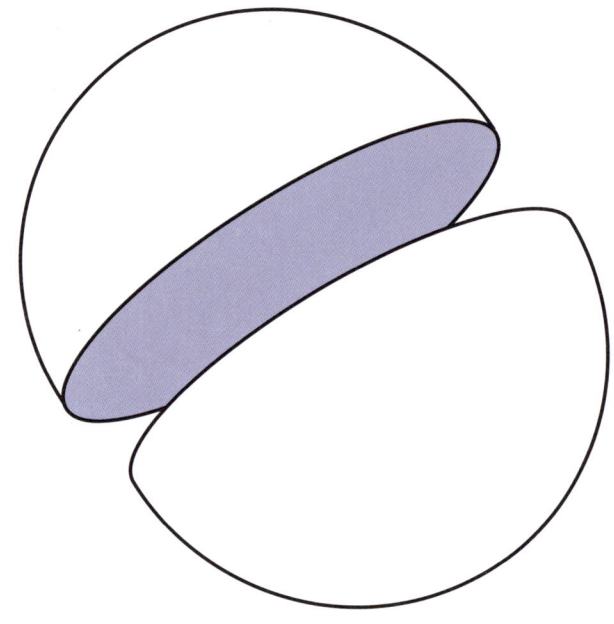

Figure 4

Maybe you said the Greenwich Meridian and, indeed, this is a great circle but so is every other meridian of longitude. But why is this important? Because every great circle shares the same angle versus distance relationship, as seen in Table 1, ie 360° = 21,600nm, 15° = 900nm and we can drill down until 1 minute of angle = 1nm. This is why on a chart we always measure on the latitude scale, because we're measuring along a meridian and therefore measuring along a great

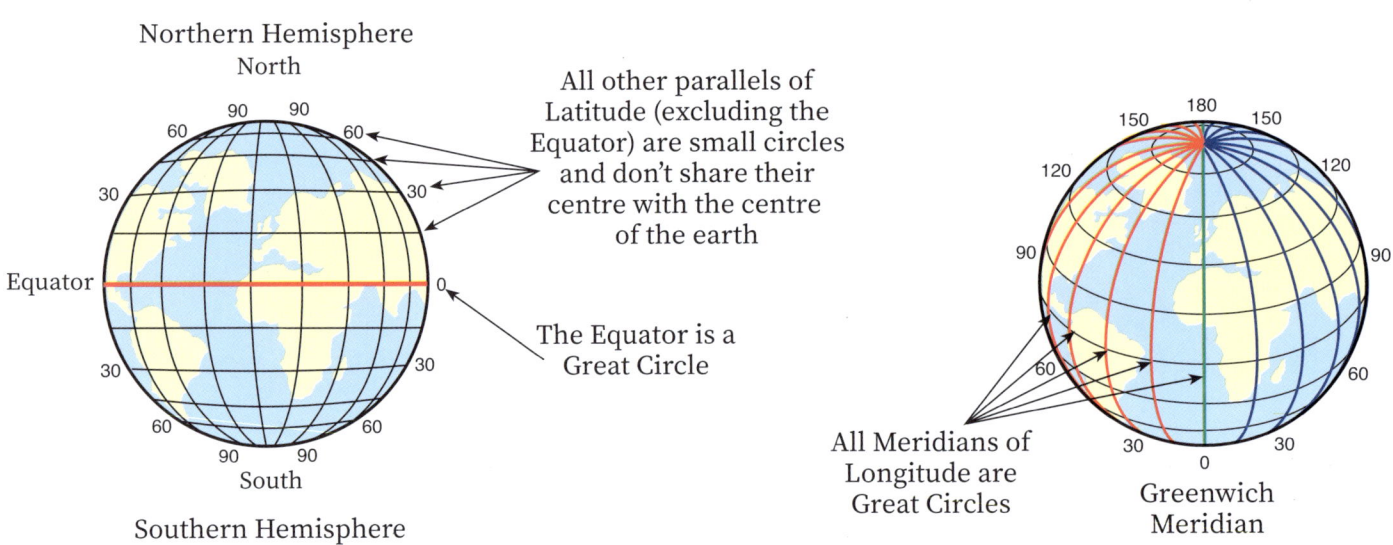

Figure 4a

circle where this angle versus distance relationship exists.

To confirm our understanding look at Figure 5. Imagine this is a great circle. If we take a 15° angle subtended at the centre of the circle, the distance on the surface would be 900nm. This is true of any great circle on the surface of the earth, be it the equator or any of the meridians.

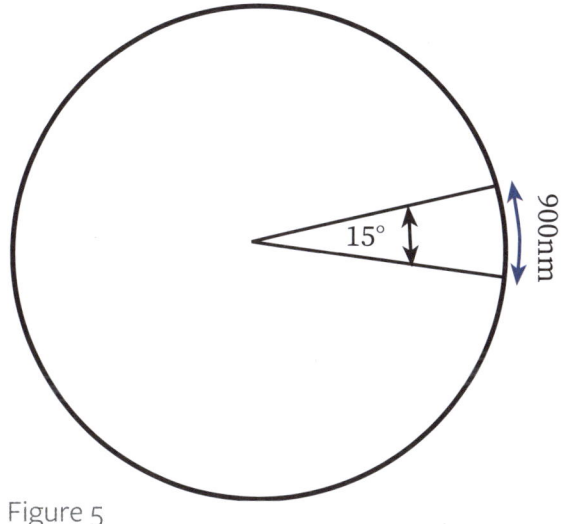

Figure 5

Sailing ship in the Uunartoq Fjord, Greenland.

DEFINITION 2

For the purpose of celestial navigation, we need to expand our use of great circles and this leads on to the second definition:

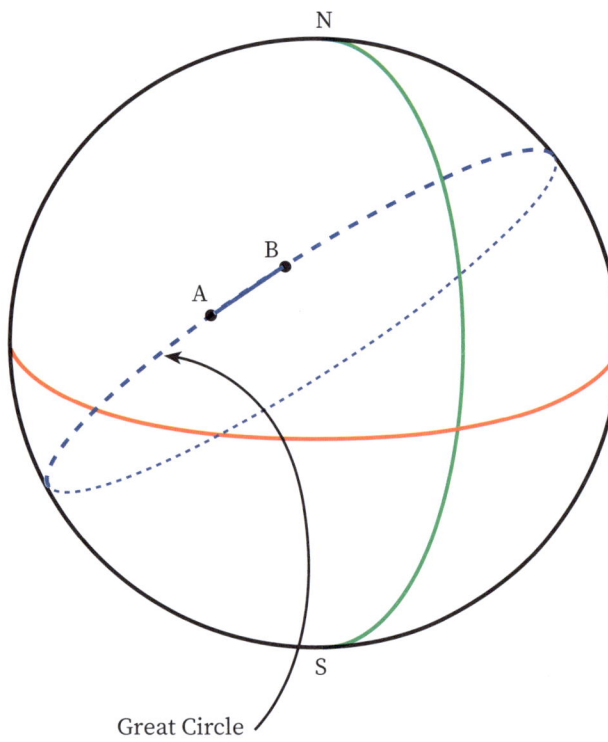

Figure 6

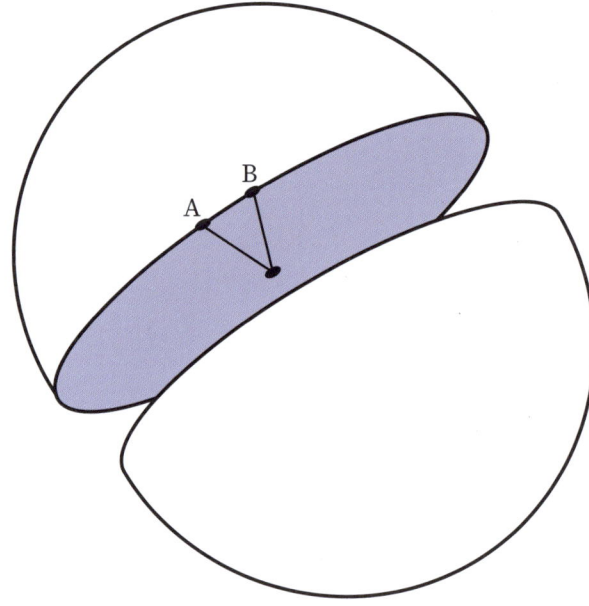

Figure 6a

If we take any two points on the surface of the earth, say point 'A' and point 'B', and draw a line between them using the shortest possible distance, we will have created part of a great circle. If we were to extend that line all the way around the earth, we would produce a great circle, a great circle that has the same relationship between angles subtended in the centre versus distance around its circumference.

You can try this on a globe. It's a very important concept on your road to understanding the big picture.

Now, before we move on, it's imperative that the great circle relationship is grasped, as it is fundamental to overall understanding. Of course, this relationship between angle and distance is no accident. The relationship of one minute of angle to one nautical mile upward is completely deliberate, in fact it's the basis on which the nautical mile is founded.

Just a thought to ponder – if you know your latitude, you can now work out your distance from the equator.

CHAPTER TWO

Foundation of celestial navigation and the geographical position

As we carry on building the picture, we must first introduce a few terms and definitions. As with any new subject matter, there's new jargon and three-letter abbreviations (TLAs) to learn, and celestial navigation is no exception, in fact it has them in bucketloads.

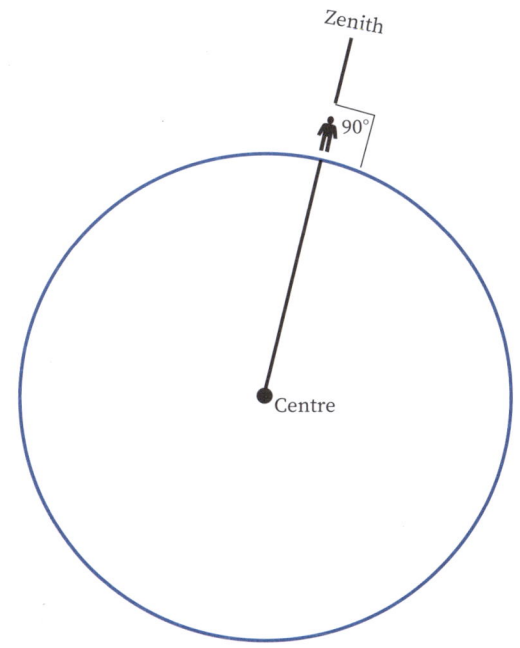

Figure 7

Imagine standing somewhere on the earth's surface, as shown in Figure 7. If you were to draw a straight line starting at the centre of the earth up through yourself and up into the space above you, that point above you would be known as your zenith. Your zenith has no finishing point or length, it could be a few metres above you or 1,000 miles.

GEOGRAPHICAL POSITION (GP)

The sun emits light in all directions, similar to a light bulb. However, because the sun is so far away, we imagine the rays of light hitting the earth's surface to be travelling parallel to each other. Of course, this isn't quite true but because the earth is such a small dot in the scheme of things, the rays are pretty much parallel (as they aren't quite parallel, a 'parallax' correction is made during calculations) and it helps us with the geometrical picture shown in Figure 8.

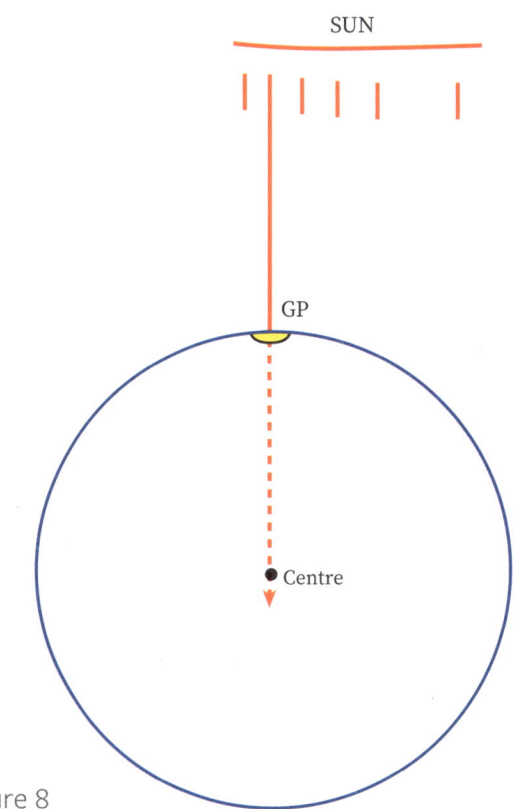

Figure 8

Now imagine the earth is transparent. One of those rays of light, just one single ray, would travel through the centre of the earth. In doing so, it would have to pass through a single point on the surface of the earth. This point is known as the geographical position or GP. Of course, the earth is rotating, both around its own axis and through space revolving around the sun, so the GP is a constantly moving point (more about that later).

Next, imagine that you have a frozen moment in time when the earth has stopped rotating. And in this frozen moment, shown in Figure 9, imagine that you go and stand on the GP. In this moment the sun is your zenith.

We haven't talked about the sextant yet, but in essence it is just an accurate angle-measuring device. Imagine you take out your sextant and measure the angle between the sun and the horizon, what angle would you observe?

Well, you have probably correctly replied that it would be 90°. Let's call that by its correct name of sextant altitude (SA). You can also think of it as sextant angle if you wish, the terms altitude and angle are often interchangeable in the world of celestial navigation. In fact, the sextant altitude would be 90° in whatever direction you faced.

Now you are going to leave the GP while still in this frozen moment of time and travel 900nm away. Thinking back to the great circle, we said if we draw the shortest line between two points on the surface of the earth, a great circle is formed. This is shown in Figures 10a, 10b and 10c.

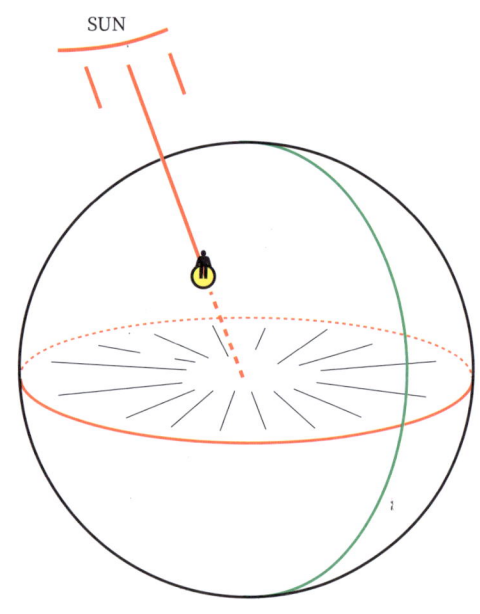

Figure 9

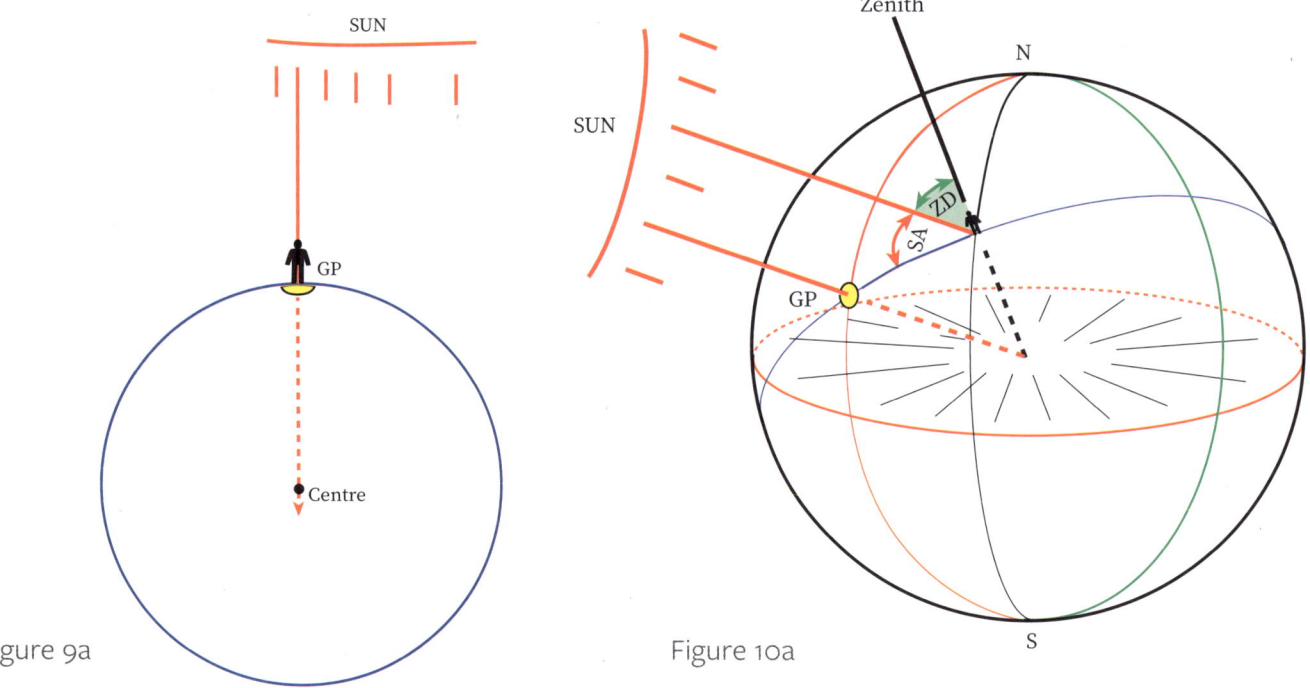

Figure 9a

Figure 10a

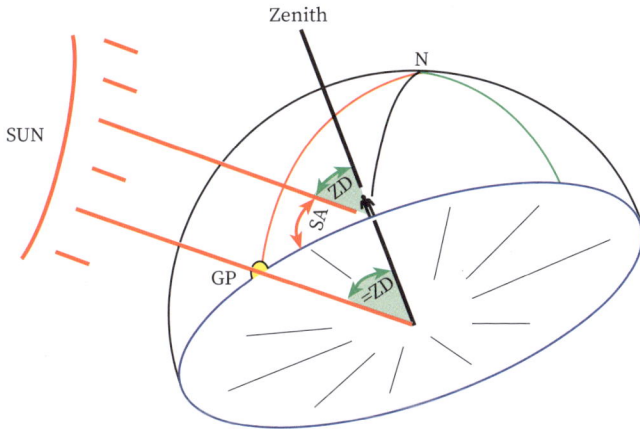

Figure 10b

The angle between your zenith and the horizon is 90°.

Therefore, all of the following are true:

$$ZD + SA = 90°$$
$$ZD = 90° - SA$$
$$SA = 90° - ZD$$

What SA would we now observe, given that we've moved 900nm?

In order to solve the puzzle, let's 'reverse engineer' the picture for a moment. As we've said, we are on a great circle, and we have a distance on the surface of the earth of 900nm. Referring back to Table 1, what would be the angle subtended at the centre of the earth? Let's develop the picture in Figure 11.

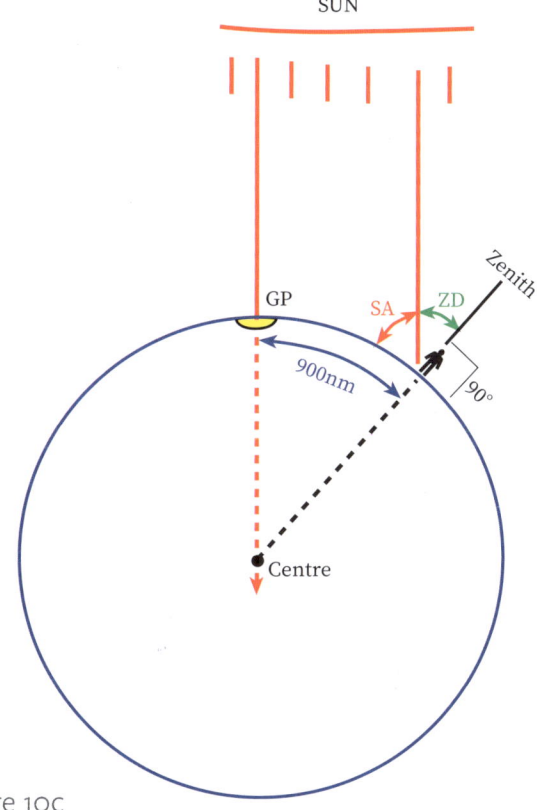

Figure 10c

As you travel away from the sun's GP, the angle of the sun to the horizon will start to drop below 90°. As you move away from the GP and as the sextant altitude (SA) decreases, a new angle is formed and starts to increase. This is called the zenith distance (ZD) and it's perhaps the most important angle of all. You're probably thinking 'Why is this called a distance when it's clearly an angle?' Just park that thought for a few minutes.

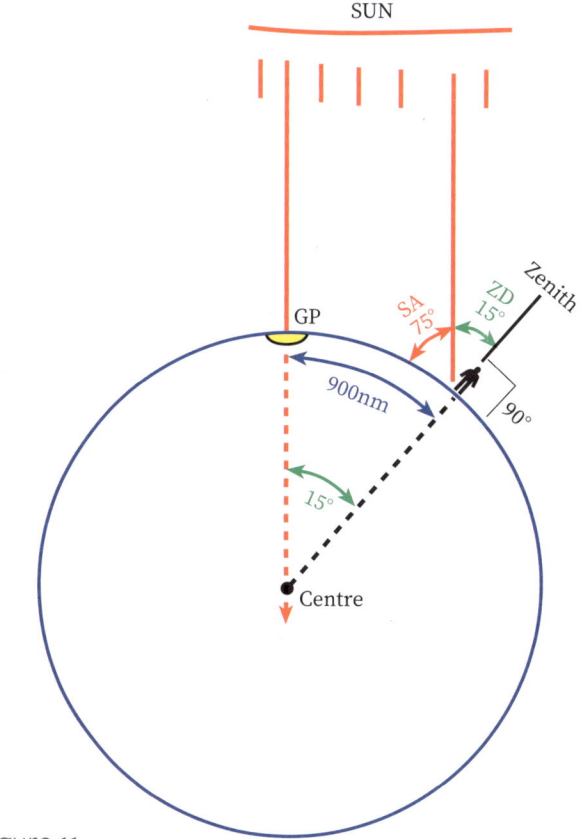

Figure 11

The angle subtended at the centre of the earth would be 15°.

Due to the assumed parallel rays from the sun, we have a geometrical picture in Figure 11 where the angle subtended at the centre of the earth and the ZD are the same. This is very significant! Before we see why, let's complete the numbers. If the angle subtended at the centre of the earth is 15°, then the ZD must also be 15°. Therefore, the SA must be 75° (because SA = 90° − ZD).

In other words, because of the great circle angle–distance relationship, we can use the sextant as a 'range finder', it can tell us how far away we are from the GP. But it's not the sextant altitude (SA) that's important. It's actually the zenith distance (ZD) that's important. Now we get the idea why it's called zenith distance – because of its relationship with the distance from the geographical position (GP).

POSITION LINES AND LINES OF POSITION

Before we continue, let's look at other areas of navigation where we might use range-based positioning. This will help us develop our understanding and introduce some more terminology.

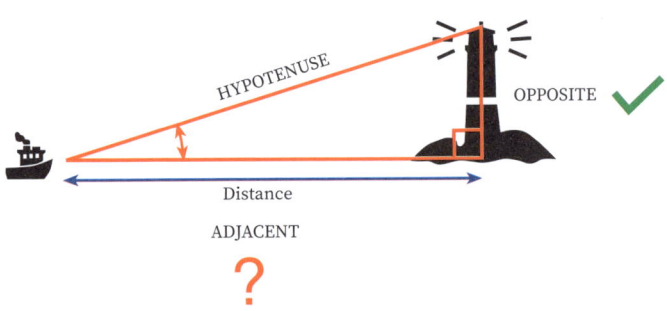

Figure 12

Now we're not saying we actually use the lighthouse scenario shown in Figure 12 in day-to-day navigation, but we could. Cast your mind back to the trigonometry lessons you probably did at school (they were the lessons where you were most likely putting all your efforts into staying awake, never mind taking it in). Don't worry if you can't remember, just as long as you can accept that there is a relationship between sides and angles of a right-angle triangle that trigonometry uses, it will do for the purpose of this exercise.

In Figure 12 we have a lighthouse. This lighthouse is like Eddystone Lighthouse off Plymouth, it's standing on an isolated rock surrounded by water. If we wanted to obtain our range (distance) from the lighthouse, we could do this using trigonometry. Without going unnecessarily into the depths of the mathematics, we know the height (from the Almanac) and what we want to obtain is the length of the adjacent side of the triangle (our range or distance from the lighthouse). If we were to measure the angle between the base and the top of the lighthouse, we could dig out some old tangent tables (or most likely use a scientific calculator) which would enable us to calculate this distance away.

Let's say we calculated that we were 3nm away. We don't at this point know exactly where we are, only that we are 3nm away. Therefore we are somewhere around the lighthouse on a circle with a radius of 3nm as shown in Figure 13. We call this a *position circle*.

Figure 13

Now in reality, we would probably approach our position fixing scenario as follows:

First, we would take out our hand-bearing compass and obtain our bearing to the

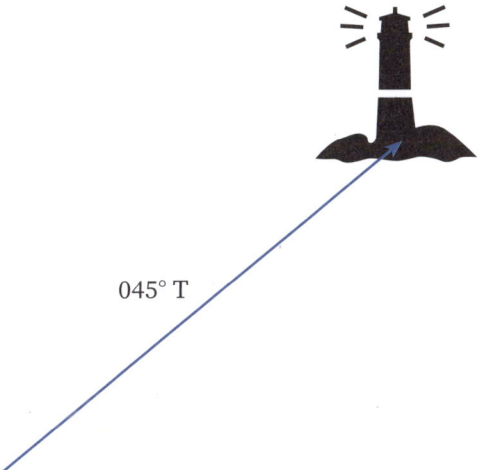

Figure 14

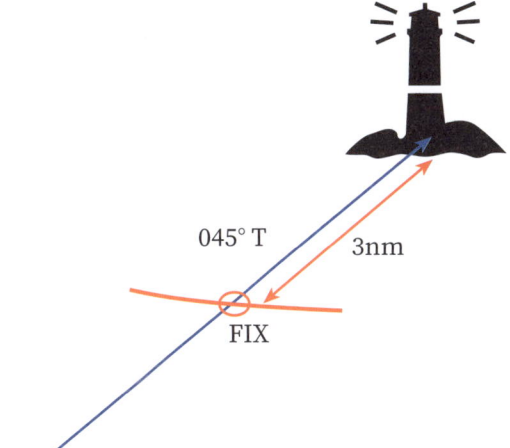

Figure 15

lighthouse and plot this on to our chart as shown in Figure 14. Let's say it's 045° T.

We now know we are somewhere on that blue line.

Secondly, we would obtain our distance away or range (3nm as before) and plot this as shown in Figure 15.

There's no need to draw the full circle because we already know we're somewhere on the blue line, so we can draw just a part of the full

position circle in red. Where the two intercept is our position or *fix*.

Let's look at the terminology we're going to be using. In Figure 16, strictly speaking, both the red and blue lines are position lines. However, the blue is a *bearing*-based position line, and the red is a *range*-based position line. So, in order to differentiate them we're going to adopt the following terminology. We'll be calling the blue

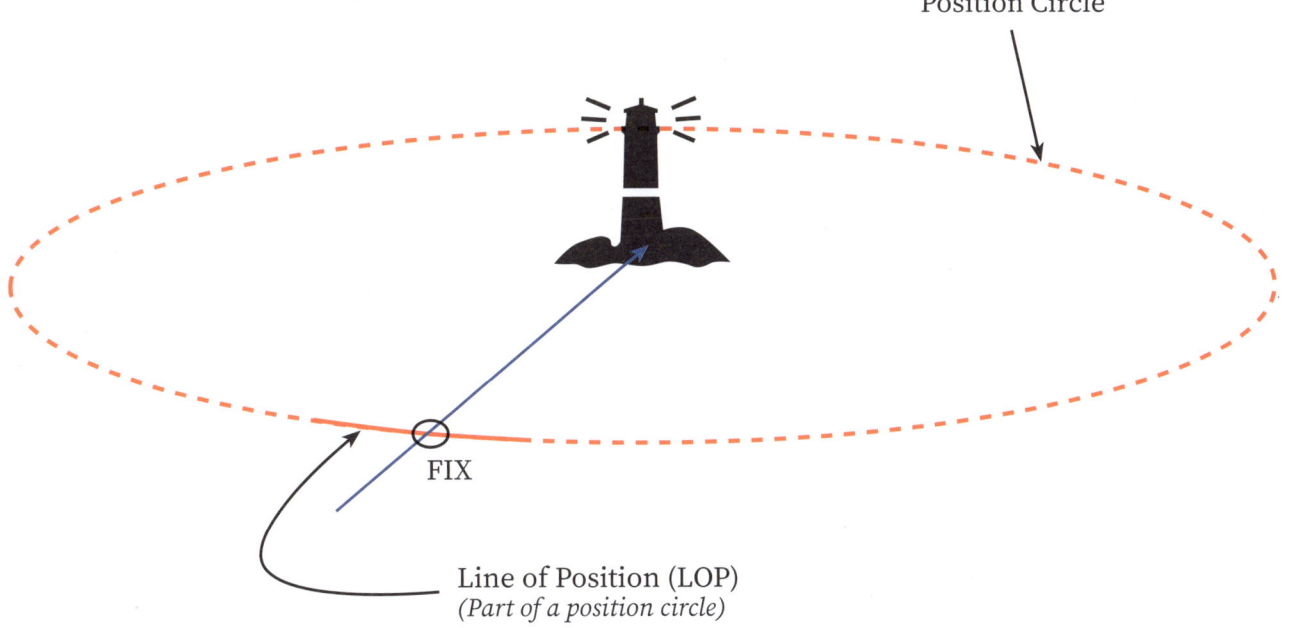

Figure 16

(bearing-based position line) a position line. But the red we'll be referring to as a *line of position* (LOP), which is only part of our position circle. As previously stated, in this scenario, our fix would be at the point where the position line (blue) and the line of position (red) intercept.

When we looked at the sextant's ability to range find we saw that we only obtain a range or distance away. So the sextant (or more to the point, the ZD) gives us a position circle or a line of position.

How can we fix our position using only range-based lines of position? To answer this, let's look at radar.

In the days before radar was integrated into chart plotters we had something that looked like Figure 17. They were probably aligned to ship's head (the top of the screen showing what's in front of the vessel) and let's assume they didn't have a compass input. In any case, bearings from radar can be subject to errors. (Things like bearing discrimination, alignment of the antenna and compass input have the potential to create inaccuracies in bearing readings.) However, range is very accurate. The radar pings out a signal and listens for a reflection of its own transmission. Using the speed of light (or radio which is the same) at 300,000,000 m/sec, it calculates the distance of a given object. Using the variable range marker (VRM) on the radar screen we can accurately obtain the distance to observed features.

Let's imagine the scenario in Figure 18. We are out at sea and identify two features on land, A and B, that we can identify on the radar.

On the radar screen we observe that feature

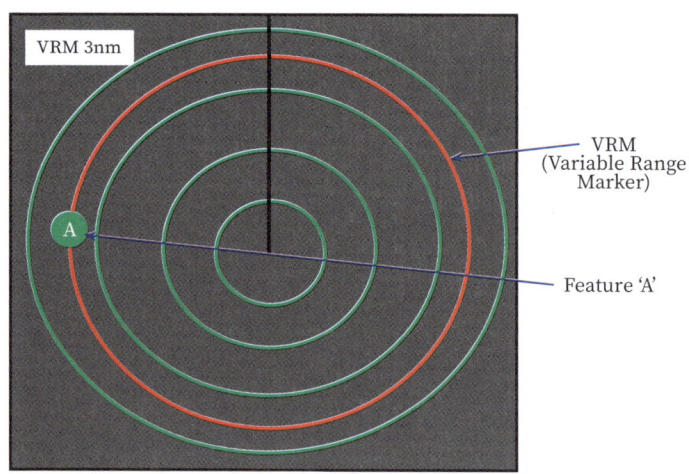

Figure 17

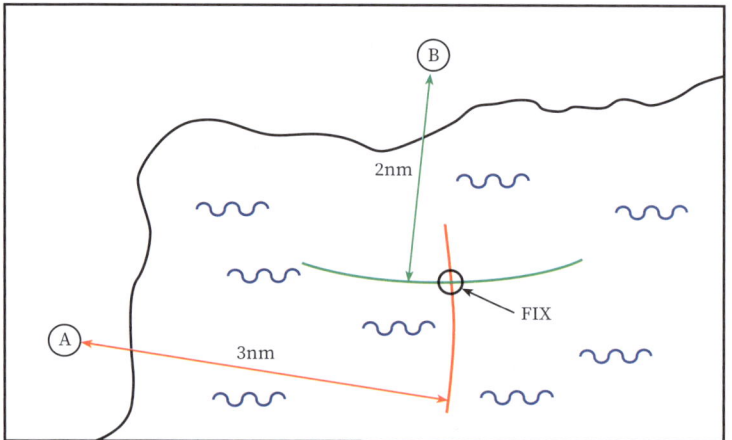

Figure 18

A is 3nm away from us. On our chart we plot an LOP (part of a position circle). We then observe feature B to be 2nm away, and we plot that in the form of a second LOP. We have now obtained a two-point fix. Unlike the three-point fix we may be familiar with in traditional navigation (which is based on bearing-based position lines), here we have obtained a two-point fix based on range-based lines of position. This, in essence, is the basis of how celestial navigation works. However, instead of establishing our range using a radar, we use the sextant to establish our distance from the geographical position (GP).

The radar example in Figure 18 had two features so a fix could be obtained in 'one go'. If we were

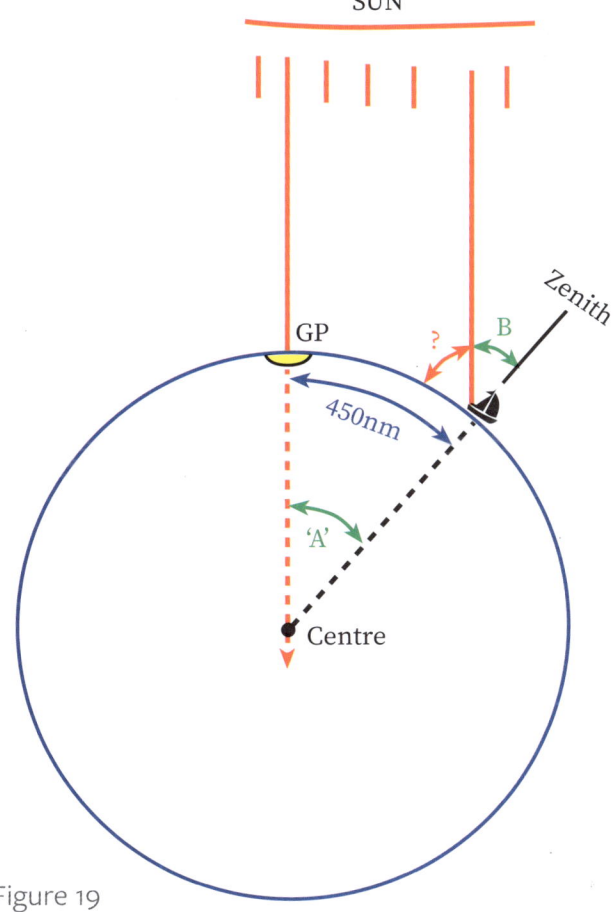

Figure 19

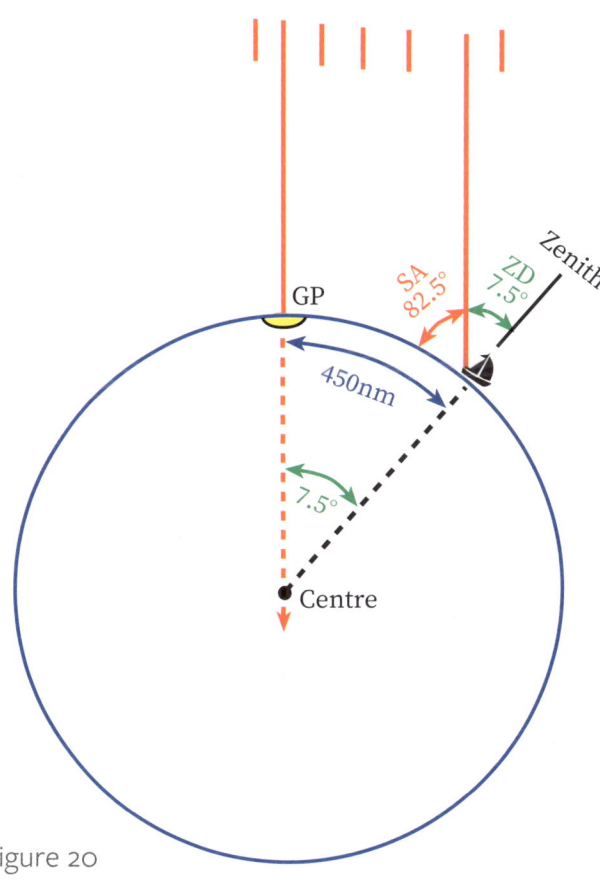

Figure 20

looking at stars and planets (which we're not), that would be the advantage to using them instead of the sun: two twilight objects could be chosen, and a two-point fix (or three objects and a three-point fix) could be obtained in the 'one go'. However, we have only one sun, therefore we take a sight of it, then we wait for a suitable amount of time for the sun to move, and then a second sight is taken. This is where the term *Sun Run Sun* comes from, which will be the basis on which we'll be fixing our position as we move through the book. The run part is factoring in where the boat has been travelling between the two sights.

Revisiting this great circle relationship before we move on, have a look at Figure 19 and see if you can work out what the sextant altitude (SA) would be. The answer is given in Figure 20.

A distance of 450nm on the surface of a great circle would equate to a subtended angle in the centre 'A' of 7.5°.

The ZD 'B' would also be 7.5° because they are the same.

The SA would = 90° − ZD
= 90° − 7.5°
= 82.5° or 82° 30.0'

What about the other way around? Have a look at Figure 21 and see if you can calculate your distance from the GP. The answer is given in Figure 22.

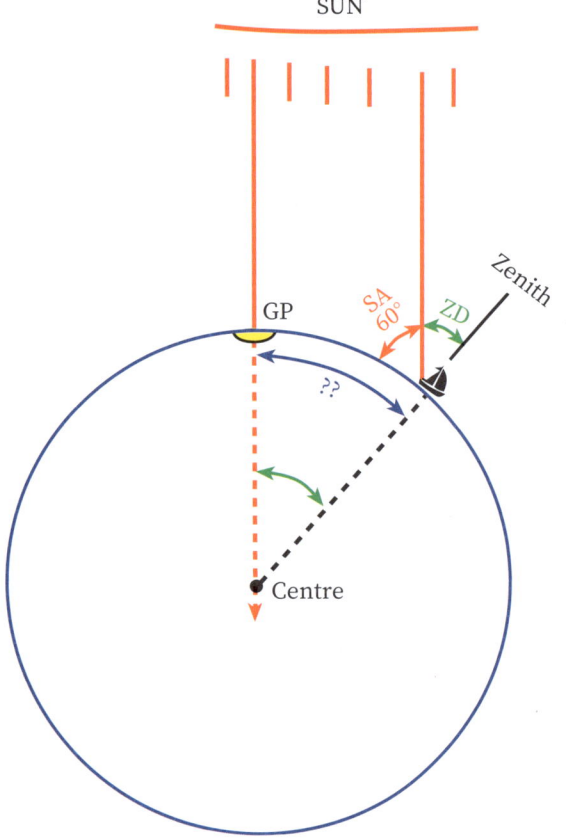

Figure 21

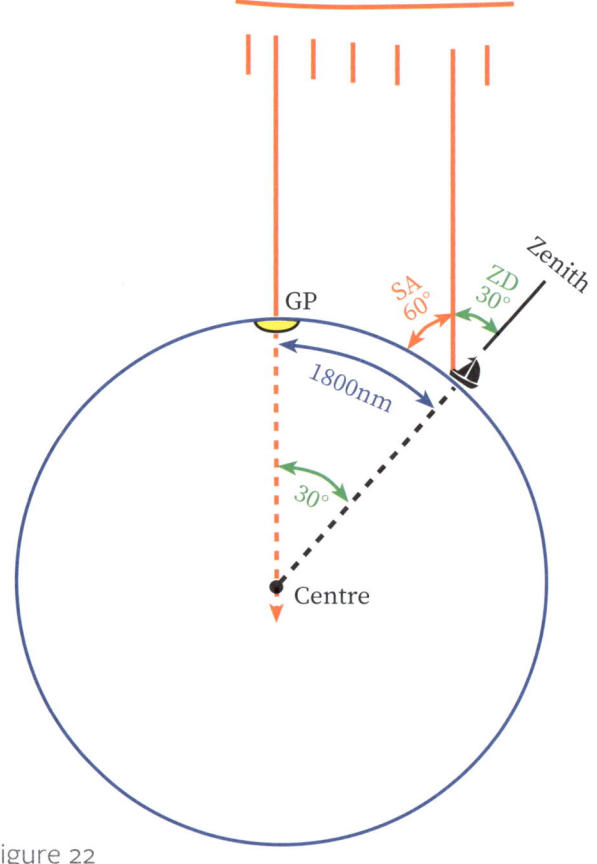

Figure 22

An SA of 60° 00.0' would give us a ZD of 30° 00.0' (ZD = 90°- SA)

The angle subtended at the centre of the earth = 30° 00.0' (same as ZD)

An angle of 30° 00.0' would give a distance on the surface of 1,800nm
(great circle relationship – see table 1)

So, that's it, from one perspective anyway! You have now seen how celestial navigation works.

In Figure 23, we could obtain the GP of the sun from a nautical almanac (which gives us the position of the sun for every hour, day and month of a given year). We could then plot the GP of the sun on a chart and draw around it a position circle with a radius of 1,800nm.

In reality, we would have to undertake two sights (having waited for the sun to move) in order to obtain two (second in green) position circles.

This scenario does not take into account any movement of our vessel, only the movement of the sun as it tracks from east to west. Although there are two intercepts (or fixes), in reality, it's unlikely on this scale that you wouldn't know which one of the two was correct.

This would indeed work in a crude way, but unfortunately, we have a couple of issues:

What if we had an SA of 15° 00.0'? That would give us a ZD of 75° and a distance from the GP of 4,500nm. Even if we could find a chart big enough, think of the scale, our pencil line would probably be 20nm thick. It would work, but it wouldn't give us the accuracy of 3 or 4nm that we ideally want.

We therefore need a different approach (based on the fundamentals of everything we've covered so far) that enables us to obtain much more accuracy.

We'll be developing this from Chapter 5 onwards. Before we do that, let's look at how we obtain the GP of the sun and a bit about the sextant and the necessary corrections we must apply to it.

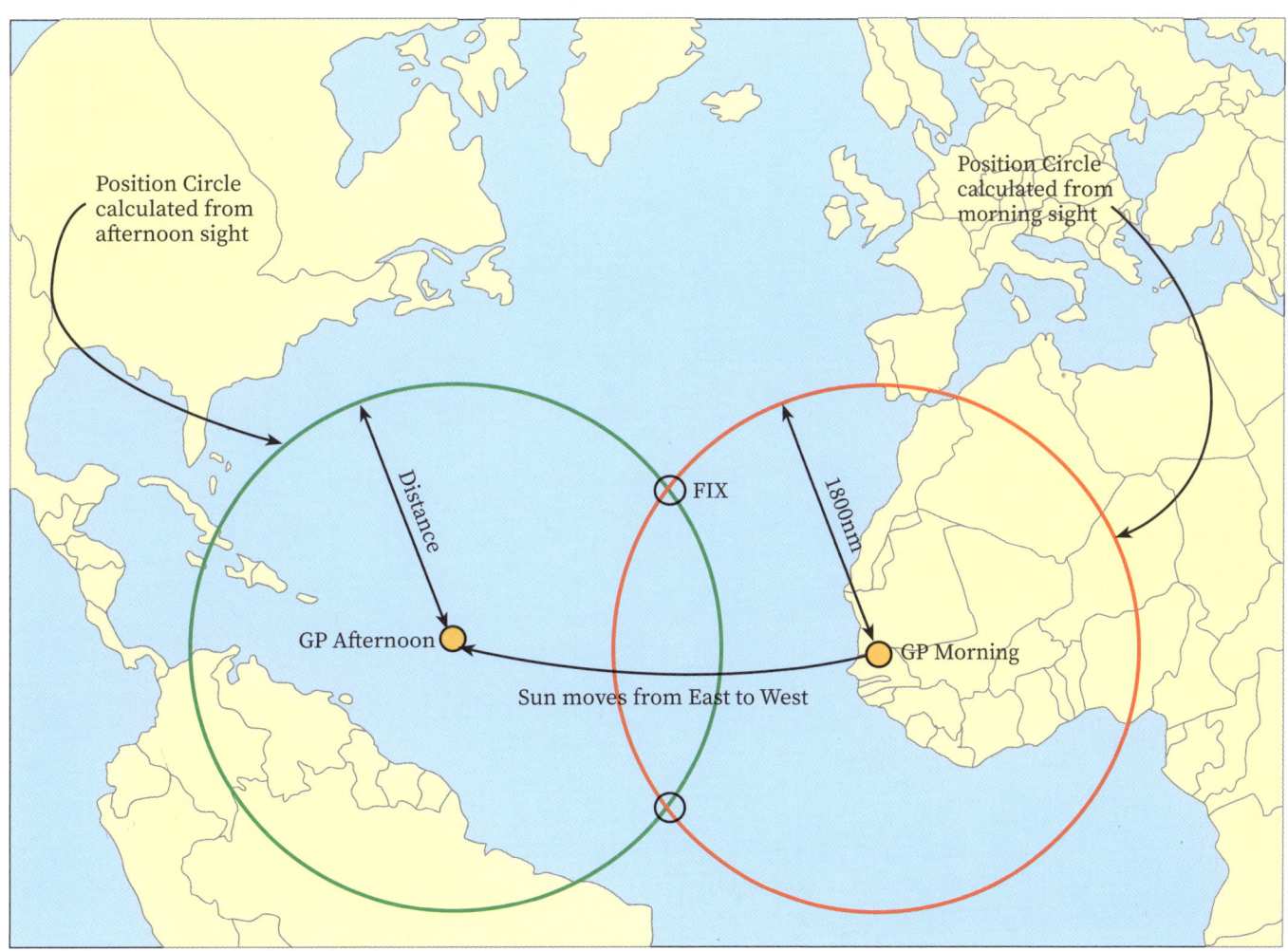

Figure 23

CHAPTER THREE

Defining the geographical position

In this chapter, we're going to look at how we define the sun's GP and where we obtain its position for any given moment of time.

Just as a reminder, when we talked about the GP earlier, we imagined that the earth was transparent. Alongside all the other rays of light coming from the sun, one ray would pass through the centre of the earth. In doing so, that ray of light would have to pass through a point on the earth's surface (see Figure 8).

We also mentioned that this is a definable position, which could be obtained from a nautical almanac and plotted on a chart, although in reality we don't do this.

Just as we do for our position on the surface of the earth, we could almost define the GP in terms of its latitude and longitude. Instead, these are given different names, and there is a slight difference when looking at the GP's 'longitude'.

DECLINATION

Declination (Dec.) is the term given to the sun's north/south aspect. In reality, it could be thought of as the sun's latitude. When looking at the sun's declination throughout the year, we will see that it changes between approximately 23.5° North and 23.5° South. This is due to the relationship of the earth's axis compared with

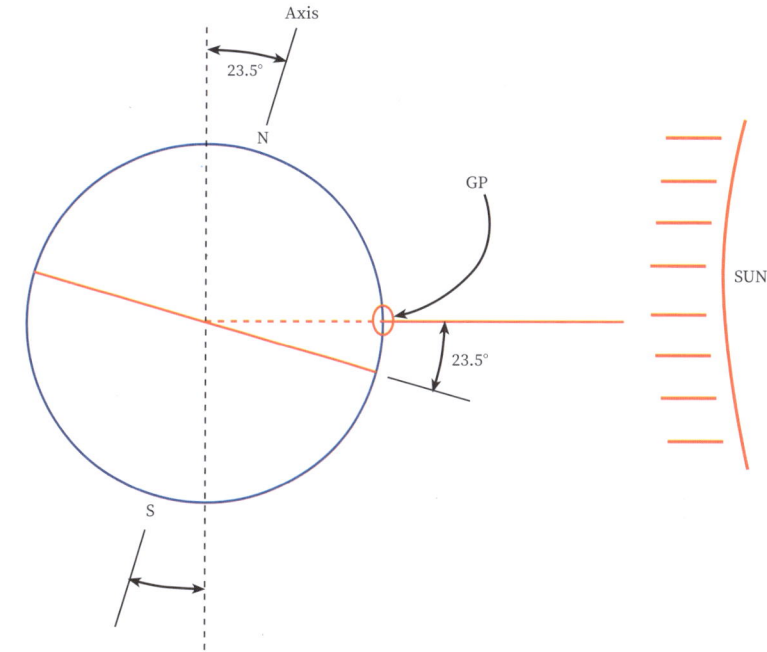

Figure 24

the location of the sun. If the axis was at right angles to the sun, there would be no declination because the sun's GP would never leave the equator.

Figure 24 is a scenario of the sun's GP in the northern hemisphere, representing northern hemisphere summer. The most northerly point of travel here is represented on globes and charts as the Tropic of Cancer.

Figure 25 shows the same scenario from a similar perspective to that used when we discussed latitude.

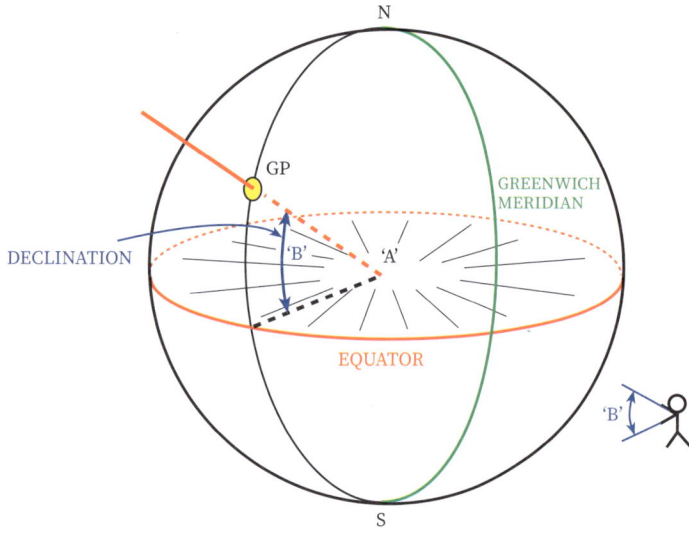

Figure 25

GREENWICH HOUR ANGLE (GHA)

The Greenwich Hour Angle (GHA) is the term given to the sun's east/west aspect and could be thought of as the sun's longitude, although there is a subtle difference between longitude and GHA.

When we first looked at the rotation of the earth in Chapter 1, we saw from Table 1 that the earth revolves at 15° per hour. It therefore follows on logically that the sun's GHA also moves at 15° per hour. Whereas the sun's declination moves slowly and in line with seasonal variation, the GHA moves quickly (at 15° per hour). And, if you think of the rotation of the earth, it moves constantly in a westerly direction (since the sun rises in the east and sets in the west).

Figure 26 shows the earth's track as it orbits around the sun throughout the year, leading to the declination tracking between 23.5° North and 23.5° South. The left-hand image is the same one we looked at in Figure 24 above.

We'll move on to where we find the sun's declination shortly, but before we do, let's look at the other parameter.

We've said that GHA is similar to longitude, as in that it is the horizontal angle subtended between the Greenwich Meridian and the sun's GP, as shown in Figure 27. Imagine, just as we did when discussing longitude, that you are

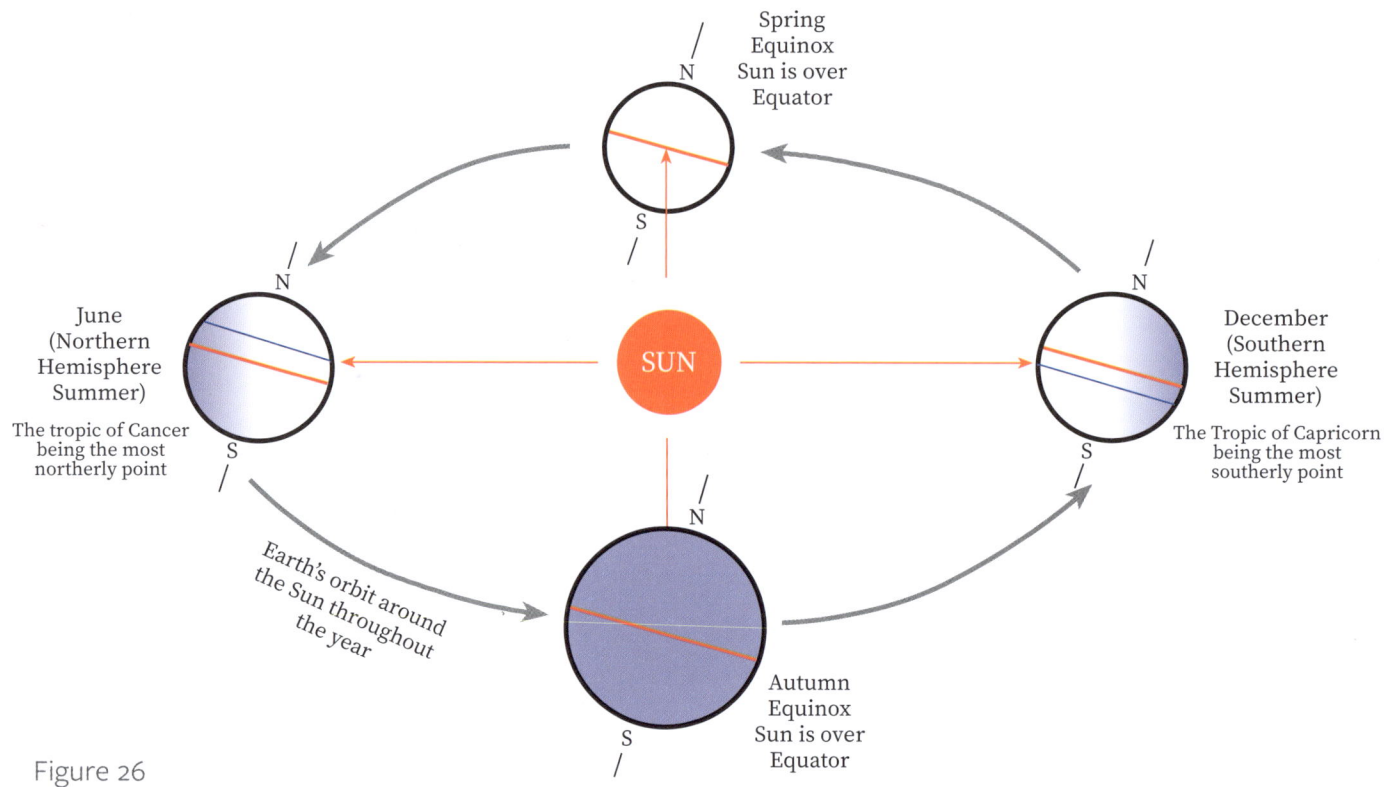

Figure 26

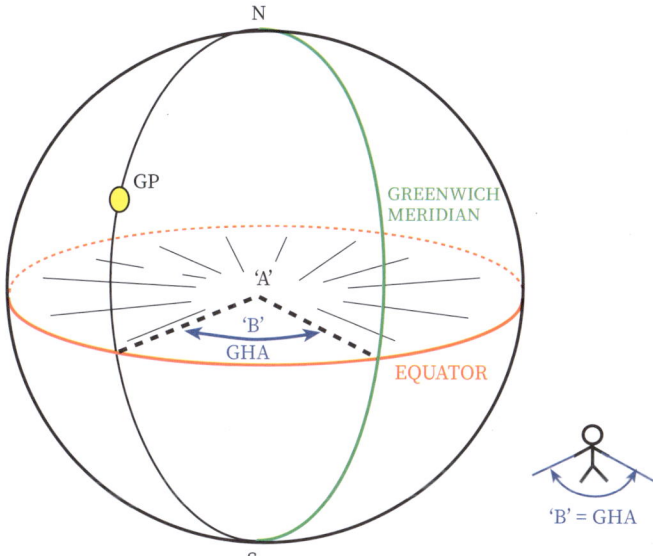

Figure 27

standing in the centre of the earth, pointing both at the meridian of the sun and the Greenwich Meridian. The angle between your arms would represent the GHA.

There is a subtle difference between longitude and GHA. Whereas longitude is measured between 0° and 180° East or West, GHA is measured from 0° to 360° in a westerly going direction. Figure 28 shows a view from above the North Pole. Here, we see that the GHA is around 200°, ie it's greater than 180°.

If you think about it, because of the Earth's direction of rotation, the GHA is always increasing in value, which simplifies matters later on.

In summary, the sun's geographical position is made up of Declination (Dec.) and Greenwich Hour Angle (GHA), as shown in Figure 29.

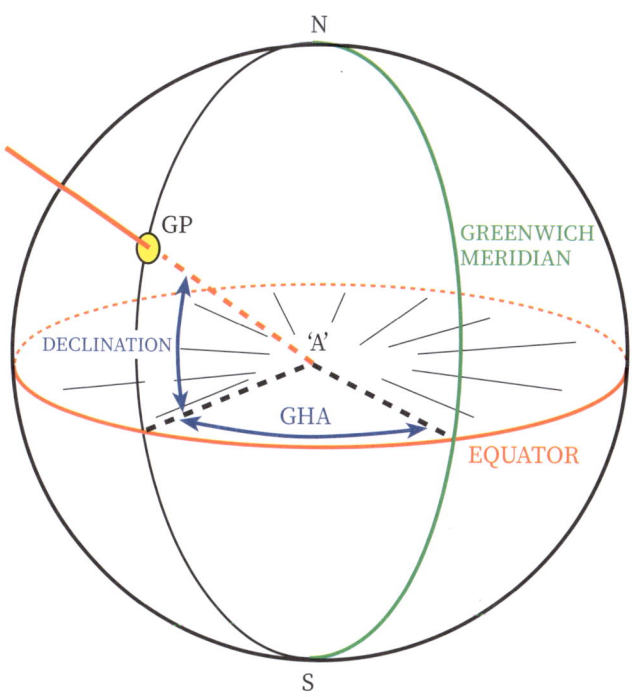

Figure 29

Figure 28

OBTAINING THE SUN'S GP

Just like our position consists of latitude and longitude, the sun's GP is made up of two parameters – declination and GHA. Let's look at how we obtain this information.

Figure 30 shows an extract from a nautical almanac. Here we are using extracts from *Reeds 2020 Almanac*. Different publications may have a slightly different layout and values will change slightly between publications. For alternatives, go to www.philsomerville.com. In addition to supporting information, the almanac contains

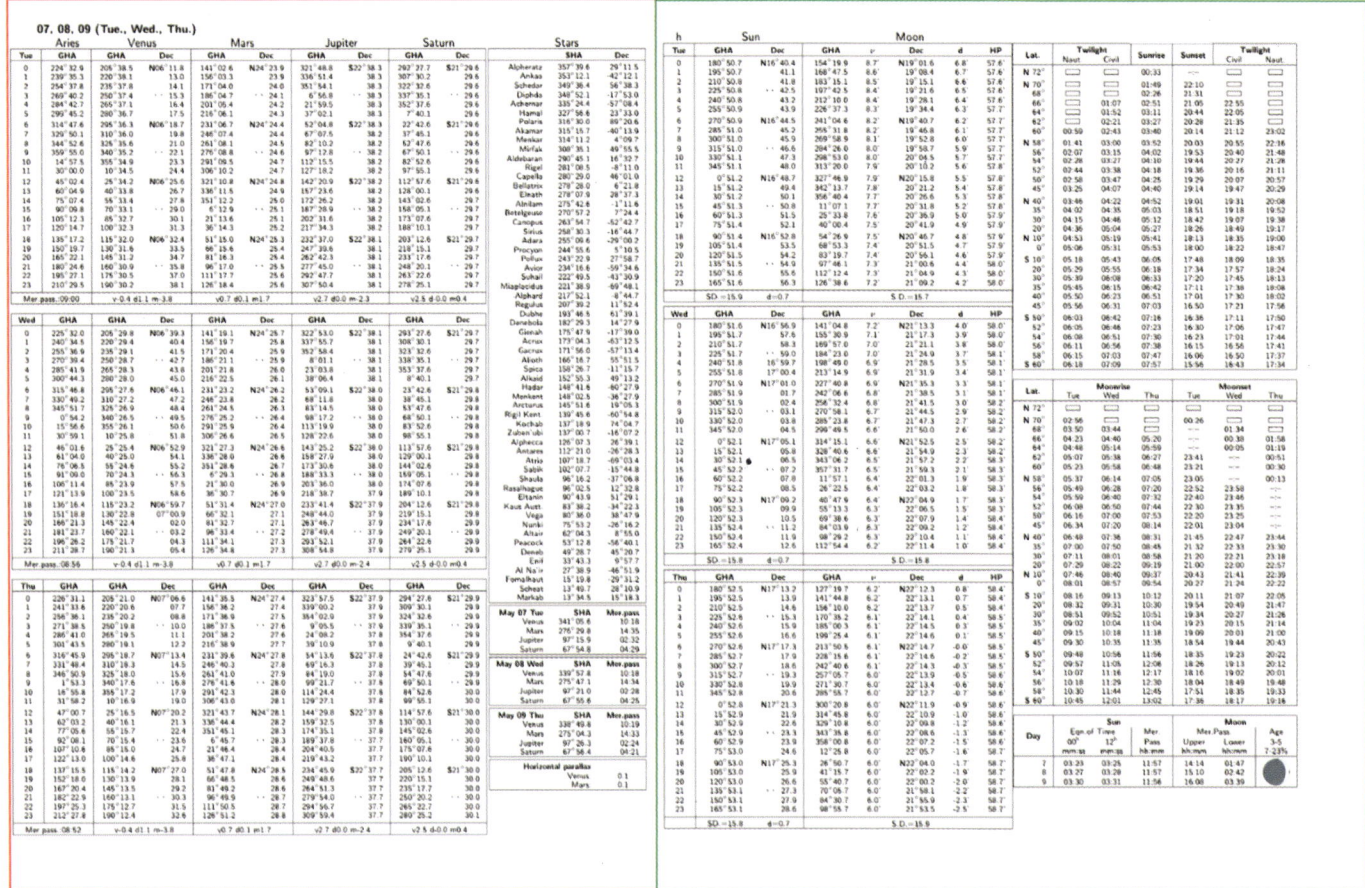

Figure 30

pages like this for every day of a given year (so a new almanac is required annually). These pages are referred to as the 'Daily Pages'. As you can see, this extract contains three days (Tues 7th, Wed 8th and Thurs 9th). The information for these three days is spread across two pages in the almanac, the red box representing the left-hand page and the green one representing the right-hand page.

We're not going to be using any of the information on the left-hand page, but for interest's sake we'll include an overview. Moving down the left-hand column, we can see the three days broken down hour by hour. Moving across the top we see:

ARIES

This is a 'reference point' used when using star sights.

VENUS, MARS, JUPITER AND SATURN

The four planets of use to us in celestial navigation.

STARS

These are the 57 'selected' stars which, depending on the 'sight reduction tables' we use (we'll be looking at these tables later on), can be of use to us for star sights.

The right-hand page is the one we'll be using for position fixing with the sun. Figure 31 is an enlarged view of the right-hand page.

Looking down the left-hand column, we see the same three days broken down by the hour.

Moving across the top, we see the sun and the moon and then the right half of the page gives us information on sunrise, moonrise, sunset and moonset. There's also some other information

h	Sun		Moon				Lat.	Twilight		Sunrise	Sunset	Twilight	
Tue	GHA	Dec	GHA	v	Dec	d	HP		Naut.	Civil			Civil	Naut.
0	180°50.7	N16°40.4	154°19.9	8.7	N19°01.6	6.8	57.6	N 72°	☐	☐	00:33	☐	☐	☐
1	195°50.7	41.1	168°47.5	8.6	19°08.4	6.7	57.6	N 70°	☐	☐	01:49	22:10	☐	☐
2	210°50.8	41.8	183°15.1	8.5	19°15.1	6.6	57.6	68°	☐	01:07	02:26	21:31	☐	☐
3	225°50.8	42.5	197°42.5	8.4	19°21.6	6.5	57.6	66°	☐	01:07	02:51	21:05	22:55	☐
4	240°50.8	43.2	212°10.0	8.4	19°28.1	6.4	57.6	64°	☐	01:52	03:11	20:44	22:05	☐
5	255°50.9	43.9	226°37.3	8.3	19°34.4	6.3	57.7	62°	☐	02:21	03:27	20:28	21:35	☐
6	270°50.9	N16°44.5	241°04.6	8.2	N19°40.7	6.2	57.7	60°	00:59	02:43	03:40	20:14	21:12	23:02
7	285°51.0	45.2	255°31.8	8.2	19°46.8	6.1	57.7	N 58°	01:41	03:00	03:52	20:03	20:55	22:16
8	300°51.0	45.9	269°58.9	8.1	19°52.8	6.0	57.7	56°	02:07	03:15	04:02	19:53	20:40	21:48
9	315°51.0	46.6	284°26.0	8.0	19°58.7	5.9	57.7	54°	02:28	03:27	04:10	19:44	20:27	21:28
10	330°51.1	47.3	298°53.0	8.0	20°04.5	5.7	57.7	52°	02:44	03:38	04:18	19:36	20:16	21:11
11	345°51.1	48.0	313°20.0	7.9	20°10.2	5.6	57.8	50°	02:58	03:47	04:25	19:29	20:07	20:57
12	0°51.2	N16°48.7	327°46.9	7.9	N20°15.8	5.5	57.8	45°	03:25	04:07	04:40	19:14	19:47	20:29
13	15°51.2	49.4	342°13.7	7.8	20°21.2	5.4	57.8	N 40°	03:46	04:22	04:52	19:01	19:31	20:08
14	30°51.2	50.1	356°40.4	7.7	20°26.6	5.3	57.8	35°	04:02	04:35	05:03	18:51	19:18	19:52
15	45°51.3	50.8	11°07.1	7.7	20°31.8	5.2	57.8	30°	04:15	04:46	05:12	18:42	19:07	19:38
16	60°51.3	51.5	25°33.8	7.6	20°36.9	5.0	57.9	20°	04:36	05:04	05:27	18:26	18:49	19:17
17	75°51.4	52.1	40°00.4	7.5	20°41.9	4.9	57.9	N 10°	04:53	05:19	05:41	18:13	18:35	19:00
18	90°51.4	N16°52.8	54°26.9	7.5	N20°46.7	4.8	57.9	0°	05:06	05:31	05:53	18:00	18:22	18:47
19	105°51.4	53.5	68°53.3	7.4	20°51.5	4.7	57.9	S 10°	05:18	05:43	06:05	17:48	18:09	18:35
20	120°51.5	54.2	83°19.7	7.4	20°56.1	4.6	57.9	20°	05:29	05:55	06:18	17:34	17:57	18:24
21	135°51.5	54.9	97°46.1	7.3	21°00.6	4.4	58.0	30°	05:39	06:08	06:33	17:20	17:45	18:13
22	150°51.6	55.6	112°12.4	7.3	21°04.9	4.3	58.0	35°	05:45	06:15	06:42	17:11	17:38	18:08
23	165°51.6	56.3	126°38.6	7.2	21°09.2	4.2	58.0	40°	05:50	06:23	06:51	17:01	17:30	18:02
	S.D.=15.9	d=0.7			S.D.=15.7			45°	05:56	06:31	07:03	16:50	17:21	17:56
Wed	GHA	Dec	GHA	v	Dec	d	HP	S 50°	06:03	06:42	07:16	16:36	17:11	17:50
0	180°51.6	N16°56.9	141°04.8	7.2	N21°13.3	4.0	58.0	52°	06:05	06:46	07:23	16:30	17:06	17:47
1	195°51.7	57.6	155°30.9	7.1	21°17.3	3.9	58.0	54°	06:08	06:51	07:30	16:23	17:01	17:44
2	210°51.7	58.3	169°57.0	7.0	21°21.1	3.8	58.0	56°	06:11	06:56	07:38	16:15	16:56	17:41
3	225°51.7	59.0	184°23.0	7.0	21°24.9	3.7	58.1	58°	06:15	07:03	07:47	16:06	16:50	17:37
4	240°51.8	16°59.7	198°49.0	6.9	21°28.5	3.5	58.1	S 60°	06:18	07:09	07:57	15:56	16:43	17:34
5	255°51.8	17°00.4	213°14.9	6.9	21°31.9	3.4	58.1							
6	270°51.9	N17°01.0	227°40.8	6.9	N21°35.3	3.3	58.1	Lat.	Moonrise			Moonset		
7	285°51.9	01.7	242°06.6	6.8	21°38.5	3.1	58.1		Tue	Wed	Thu	Tue	Wed	Thu
8	300°51.9	02.4	256°32.4	6.8	21°41.5	3.0	58.2	N 72°	☐	☐	☐	☐	☐	☐
9	315°52.0	03.1	270°58.1	6.7	21°44.5	2.9	58.2	N 70°	02:56	☐	☐	00:26	☐	☐
10	330°52.0	03.8	285°23.8	6.7	21°47.3	2.7	58.2	68°	03:50	03:44	☐	--:--	01:34	☐
11	345°52.0	04.5	299°49.5	6.6	21°50.0	2.6	58.2	66°	04:23	04:40	05:20	--:--	00:38	01:58
12	0°52.1	N17°05.1	314°15.1	6.6	N21°52.5	2.5	58.2	64°	04:48	05:14	05:59	--:--	00:05	01:19
13	15°52.1	05.8	328°40.6	6.6	21°54.9	2.3	58.2	62°	05:07	05:38	06:27	23:41	--:--	00:51
14	30°52.1	06.5	343°06.2	6.5	21°57.2	2.2	58.3	60°	05:23	05:58	06:48	23:21	--:--	00:30
15	45°52.2	07.2	357°31.7	6.5	21°59.3	2.1	58.3	N 58°	05:37	06:14	07:05	23:05	--:--	00:13
16	60°52.2	07.8	11°57.1	6.4	22°01.3	1.9	58.3	56°	05:49	06:28	07:20	22:52	23:58	--:--
17	75°52.2	08.5	26°22.5	6.4	22°03.2	1.8	58.3	54°	05:59	06:40	07:32	22:40	23:46	--:--
18	90°52.3	N17°09.2	40°47.9	6.4	N22°04.9	1.7	58.3	52°	06:08	06:50	07:44	22:30	23:35	--:--
19	105°52.3	09.9	55°13.3	6.3	22°06.5	1.5	58.3	50°	06:16	07:00	07:53	22:20	23:25	--:--
20	120°52.3	10.5	69°38.6	6.3	22°07.9	1.4	58.4	45°	06:34	07:20	08:14	22:01	23:04	--:--
21	135°52.4	11.2	84°03.9	6.3	22°09.2	1.2	58.4	N 40°	06:48	07:36	08:31	21:45	22:47	23:44
22	150°52.4	11.9	98°29.2	6.3	22°10.4	1.1	58.4	35°	07:00	07:49	08:45	21:32	22:33	23:30
23	165°52.4	12.6	112°54.4	6.2	22°11.4	1.0	58.4	30°	07:11	08:01	08:58	21:20	22:21	23:18
	S.D.=15.8	d=0.7			S.D.=15.8			20°	07:29	08:22	09:19	21:00	22:00	22:57
Thu	GHA	Dec	GHA	v	Dec	d	HP	N 10°	07:46	08:40	09:37	20:43	21:41	22:39
0	180°52.5	N17°13.2	127°19.7	6.2	N22°12.3	0.8	58.4	0°	08:01	08:57	09:54	20:27	21:24	22:22
1	195°52.5	13.9	141°44.8	6.2	22°13.1	0.7	58.4	S 10°	08:16	09:13	10:12	20:11	21:07	22:05
2	210°52.5	14.6	156°10.0	6.2	22°13.7	0.5	58.4	20°	08:32	09:31	10:30	19:54	20:49	21:47
3	225°52.6	15.3	170°35.2	6.1	22°14.1	0.4	58.5	30°	08:51	09:52	10:51	19:34	20:27	21:26
4	240°52.6	15.9	185°00.3	6.1	22°14.5	0.3	58.5	35°	09:02	10:04	11:04	19:23	20:15	21:14
5	255°52.6	16.6	199°25.4	6.1	22°14.6	0.1	58.5	40°	09:15	10:18	11:18	19:09	20:01	21:00
6	270°52.7	N17°17.3	213°50.5	6.1	N22°14.7	-0.0	58.5	45°	09:30	10:35	11:35	18:54	19:44	20:43
7	285°52.7	17.9	228°15.6	6.1	22°14.6	-0.2	58.5	S 50°	09:48	10:56	11:56	18:35	19:23	20:22
8	300°52.7	18.6	242°40.6	6.1	22°14.3	-0.3	58.5	52°	09:57	11:05	12:06	18:26	19:13	20:12
9	315°52.7	19.3	257°05.7	6.0	22°13.9	-0.5	58.6	54°	10:07	11:16	12:17	18:16	19:02	20:01
10	330°52.8	19.9	271°30.7	6.0	22°13.4	-0.6	58.6	56°	10:18	11:29	12:30	18:04	18:49	19:48
11	345°52.8	20.6	285°55.7	6.0	22°12.7	-0.7	58.6	58°	10:30	11:44	12:45	17:51	18:35	19:33
12	0°52.8	N17°21.3	300°20.8	6.0	N22°11.9	-0.9	58.6	S 60°	10:45	12:01	13:02	17:36	18:17	19:16
13	15°52.9	21.9	314°45.8	6.0	22°10.9	-1.0	58.6		Sun			Moon		
14	30°52.9	22.6	329°10.8	6.0	22°09.8	-1.2	58.6	Day	Eqn. of Time		Mer.	Mer. Pass.		Age
15	45°52.9	23.3	343°35.8	6.0	22°08.6	-1.3	58.6		00h	12h	Pass	Upper	Lower	3-5
16	60°52.9	23.9	358°00.8	6.0	22°07.2	-1.5	58.7		mm:ss	mm:ss	hh:mm	hh:mm	hh:mm	7-23%
17	75°53.0	24.6	12°25.8	6.0	22°05.7	-1.6	58.7	7	03:23	03:25	11:57	14:14	01:47	
18	90°53.0	N17°25.3	26°50.7	6.0	N22°04.0	-1.7	58.7	8	03:27	03:28	11:57	15:10	02:42	
19	105°53.0	25.9	41°15.7	6.0	22°02.2	-1.9	58.7	9	03:30	03:31	11:56	16:08	03:39	●
20	120°53.0	26.6	55°40.7	6.0	22°00.2	-2.0	58.7							
21	135°53.1	27.3	70°05.7	6.0	21°58.1	-2.2	58.7							
22	150°53.1	27.9	84°30.7	6.0	21°55.9	-2.3	58.7							
23	165°53.1	28.6	98°55.7	6.0	21°53.5	-2.5	58.7							
	S.D.=15.8	d=0.7			S.D.=15.9									

Figure 31

of interest to us at the bottom of the right-hand page, which we'll look at in due course.

For now, we're interested in the data contained within the red box. Looking at the top you'll see we have columns for GHA (Greenwich Hour Angle) and Dec. (declination). Note that the values for GHA and Dec. are given hour by hour.

We will look at GHA first. When we talked about the GHA (see Figure 29), we stated that because the earth rotates at 15° per hour, the GHA also increases by 15° per hour.

If we look at Tuesday at 1200, we see the GHA = 000° 51.2'. An hour later at 1300, the GHA = 15° 51.2'. An hour later at 1400, the GHA = 30° 51.2' etc. As you can see the tables reflect the earth's rotation compared with the sun. If we follow the table down, we see the GHA increasing up to 345° (at 1100 on Wednesday) before going back to zero.

Let's take a look at declination. This value does not change quickly. It's linked to the seasons and therefore moves quite slowly. In actual fact, the hourly change speeds up and slows down depending on the time of year. As we'll see, at most the declination only changes by one minute of angle per hour.

Something to remember before moving on, is that the tables often try to be economic with printing. If we look at 0600 on Tuesday, we see a value of N16° 44.5'. At 0700 the value is N16° 45.2'. Note though, that the 'N16' is omitted.

Another point to note is that the declination tracks between 23.5° N and 23.5° S. Therefore, hour by hour, the angle of declination can be increasing or decreasing, depending on the time of year.

Let's have a look at 1800 on Thursday:
GHA = 090° 53.0'
Dec. = 17° 25.3'

That's fine if we happen to require the sun's position exactly on the hour, but the reality, of course, is that this is unlikely.

PROFORMA INTRODUCTION

At this point let's introduce the proforma we'll be using. This is a very important tool in our toolbox. It helps us with the sight reduction process. This is the name of the process that takes an observed sextant altitude and transforms it into a line of position on a chart. It's relatively easy to learn the sight reduction process if all of your efforts are focused on achieving this; indeed with ongoing practice no proforma is required. However, the challenge is to have the tools available in the future, so that in six months or a year you'll still be able to fix your position after a *Quick Start* refresher. This is perhaps one of the biggest challenges to overcome. After all, there's no point learning something if you won't be able to use it when it counts.

Appendix 1 (see page 130) is a proforma that has been developed for this purpose. It may look quite complex, but please park any concerns you may have. We'll be breaking it down step by step. Spending the time learning it now will pay dividends in the future. To enable you to undertake the *Quick Start* refresher in the future, Appendix 2 on page 131 will serve as a proforma reminder and guide. (There are other proforma available in circulation.)

When considering the proforma and the sight reduction process it may help to liken it to playing a platform video game such as Super Mario. In these multi-level games one might have to obtain gold coins, keys or pieces of information that are required in the next tier of the game. In a sense, the sight reduction process is the same. We obtain *key* pieces of information during the process that help us unlock tables. These tables then give us answers or more keys that are needed later in the process. The proforma and the plotting process mirror this progression.

Now, we have seen that a nautical almanac only gives the GHA and Dec. *on* the hour. If the tables were broken down to the minute, they would have to be 60 times the size. And, if they were broken down to the minute and the second, they would have to be another 60 times the size. Because the time in between each hour has a linear and constant relationship, there is no need to include them in the Daily Pages. Instead, to find out these *incremental* values, we use an area of the tables called *Increments and Corrections* (more about them shortly).

Referring back to the proforma, for the purpose of determining the GHA and Dec. for the appropriate time, we use the section outlined in red in Figure 32.

Sun Sight Pro forma

DATE _____

DR LATITUDE __ __ ° __ __ . __ ' N/S

DR LONGITUDE __ __ ° __ __ . __ ' W/E

SHIPS CLOCK __ __ : __ __

ZONE TIME WEST (+) / EAST (−) __ __

__ __ : __ __ UT

DATE IN GREENWICH _____

CHRONOMETER __ H __ __ M __ __ S

CORRECTION PLUS (+) / MINUS (−) __ __ M __ __ S

UT __ __ H __ __ M __ __ S ⟶ A

SEXTANT ◯ __ __ ° __ __ . __ '

INDEX ERROR On arc = SUBTRACT / Off arc = ADD __ . __ '

HEIGHT OF EYE __ . __ m SUBTRACT __ . __ '

APPARENT ALTITUDE __ __ ° __ __ . __ '

ALTITUDE CORRECTION SUBTRACT / ADD __ . __ '

TRUE SEXTANT ALTITUDE (Ho) __ __ ° __ __ . __ ' ⟶ B

A ⟶ __ __ H __ __ M __ __ S

GHA	DEC
__ __ ° __ __ . __ '	__ __ ° __ __ . __ ' N/S d __ . __ (+)/(−)
ADD __ ° __ __ . __ '	__ . __ ' ← v and d corrections
GHA = __ __ ° __ __ . __ '	DEC = __ __ ° __ __ . __ '

If we are WEST SUBTRACT ASSUMED LONG FROM GHA
If we are EAST ADD ASSUMED TO GHA (add 360 to GHA if req'd)
If LHA is > 360 subtract 360

ASSUMED LONGITUDE __ __ ° __ __ . __ '

LHA = __ __ __ ° 0 0 . 0 ' ⟶ C

⟶ D

ASSUMED LATITUDE __ __ ° N/S ⟶ C   **LHA** __ __ __ °   **DEC** __ __ ° ⟶ D N/S   SAME or CONTRARY

NB - Chosen Latitude = D.R. Latitude rounded UP or DOWN

Using ASSUMED LAT, DEC, SAME/CONTRARY & LHA in the SIGHT REDUCTION TABLES VOL 2 or 3 look up the Hc, d correction and the Azimuth (Z)

Hc __ __ ° __ __ . 0 '   d __ . __ (+)/(−)   **Z** __ __ __ °

CORRECTION __ __ . 0 ' ← TABLE 5

CALCULATED SEXTANT ALTITUDE Hc __ __ ° __ __ . 0 '

N. Lat. { L.H.A. greater than 180° ..... Zn=Z
         { L.H.A. less than 180° .... Zn=360°−Z

S. Lat. { L.H.A. greater than 180° ..... Zn=180°−Z
         { L.H.A. less than 180° .... Zn=180°+Z

B ⟶ **TRUE SEXTANT ALTITUDE Ho** __ __ ° __ __ . __ '

INTERCEPT __ __ . __ '   TOWARDS / AWAY   **Zn** __ __ __ °

Figure 32

Finding the GP using the proforma

The easiest way to see how this works is to do an example. Using Figure 31 let's find the GP (GHA & Dec.) on Tuesday at 10hr 35min 43sec (in practice, this would be the time when you took a sight of the sun with your sextant).
Note that all times in the nautical almanac are in Universal Time (UT), otherwise known as Greenwich Mean Time (GMT).

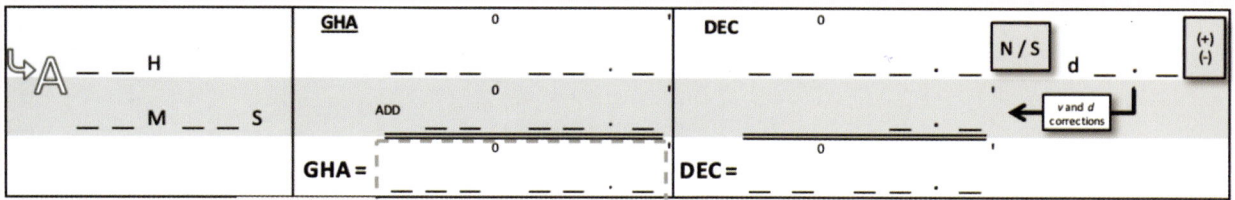

Figure 33

Looking at Figure 33, you'll see three boxes: Time, GHA and Dec.
Looking at the time box, you'll see the time is broken down into rows (light grey = hours, dark grey = minutes and seconds).

Step 1 (Figure 34) Input the time

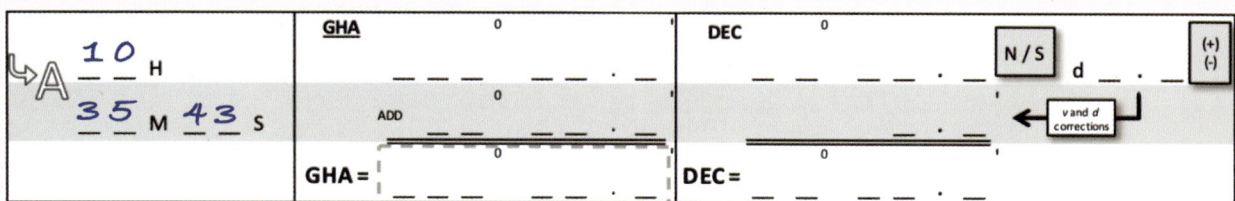

Figure 34

Step 2 (Figure 35) Looking at the Daily Pages (Figure 31 in red box), extract the GHA and Dec for 1000hr.

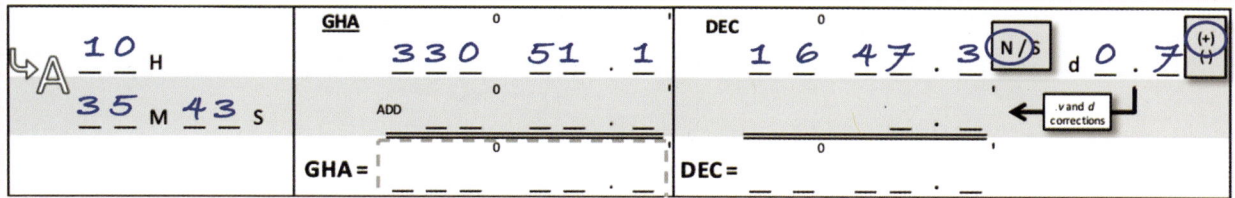

Figure 35

Note: When looking up the Dec. we also extract the d value and we must determine if the declination is increasing or decreasing. We do this by looking down the declination column to see if the value is increasing or decreasing. If it is increasing, we circle the + symbol. If it's decreasing, we circle the – symbol.
  (The d value is given at the end of each day in this almanac. It is the amount the declination is changing by per hour. Here the declination is changing by 0.7' per hour. The + or – that follows tells us if the declination is increasing 0.7' per hour or decreasing by 0.7' per hour.)

Now we have the GHA and Dec. for 1000hr. However, we now need to account for the minutes and seconds. In order to do that, we use the table *Increments and Corrections* – think of it as catering for the increments of each hour. These tables are found at the back of the nautical almanac.

Increments and Corrections

m 33	Sun Plan.	Aries	Moon	v and d corr		
0	8°15.0	8°16.4	7°52.5	0.0 - 0.0	6.0 - 3.4	12.0 - 6.7
1	8°15.2	8°16.6	7°52.7	0.1 - 0.1	6.1 - 3.4	12.1 - 6.8
2	8°15.5	8°16.9	7°52.9	0.2 - 0.1	6.2 - 3.5	12.2 - 6.8
3	8°15.7	8°17.1	7°53.2	0.3 - 0.2	6.3 - 3.5	12.3 - 6.9
4	8°16.0	8°17.4	7°53.4	0.4 - 0.2	6.4 - 3.6	12.4 - 6.9
5	8°16.3	8°17.6	7°53.6	0.5 - 0.3	6.5 - 3.6	12.5 - 7.0
6	8°16.5	8°17.9	7°53.9	0.6 - 0.3	6.6 - 3.7	12.6 - 7.0
7	8°16.8	8°18.1	7°54.1	0.7 - 0.4	6.7 - 3.7	12.7 - 7.1
8	8°17.0	8°18.4	7°54.4	0.8 - 0.4	6.8 - 3.8	12.8 - 7.1
9	8°17.2	8°18.6	7°54.6	0.9 - 0.5	6.9 - 3.9	12.9 - 7.2
10	8°17.5	8°18.9	7°54.8	1.0 - 0.6	7.0 - 3.9	13.0 - 7.3
11	8°17.7	8°19.1	7°55.1	1.1 - 0.6	7.1 - 4.0	13.1 - 7.3
12	8°18.0	8°19.4	7°55.3	1.2 - 0.7	7.2 - 4.0	13.2 - 7.4
13	8°18.3	8°19.6	7°55.6	1.3 - 0.7	7.3 - 4.1	13.3 - 7.4
14	8°18.5	8°19.9	7°55.8	1.4 - 0.8	7.4 - 4.1	13.4 - 7.5
15	8°18.8	8°20.1	7°56.0	1.5 - 0.8	7.5 - 4.2	13.5 - 7.5
16	8°19.0	8°20.4	7°56.3	1.6 - 0.9	7.6 - 4.2	13.6 - 7.6
17	8°19.2	8°20.6	7°56.5	1.7 - 0.9	7.7 - 4.3	13.7 - 7.6
18	8°19.5	8°20.9	7°56.7	1.8 - 1.0	7.8 - 4.4	13.8 - 7.7
19	8°19.8	8°21.1	7°57.0	1.9 - 1.1	7.9 - 4.4	13.9 - 7.8
20	8°20.0	8°21.4	7°57.2	2.0 - 1.1	8.0 - 4.5	14.0 - 7.8
21	8°20.3	8°21.6	7°57.5	2.1 - 1.2	8.1 - 4.5	14.1 - 7.9
22	8°20.5	8°21.9	7°57.7	2.2 - 1.2	8.2 - 4.6	14.2 - 7.9
23	8°20.7	8°22.1	7°57.9	2.3 - 1.3	8.3 - 4.6	14.3 - 8.0
24	8°21.0	8°22.4	7°58.2	2.4 - 1.3	8.4 - 4.7	14.4 - 8.0
25	8°21.2	8°22.6	7°58.4	2.5 - 1.4	8.5 - 4.7	14.5 - 8.1
26	8°21.5	8°22.9	7°58.7	2.6 - 1.5	8.6 - 4.8	14.6 - 8.2
27	8°21.8	8°23.1	7°58.9	2.7 - 1.5	8.7 - 4.9	14.7 - 8.2
28	8°22.0	8°23.4	7°59.1	2.8 - 1.6	8.8 - 4.9	14.8 - 8.3
29	8°22.3	8°23.6	7°59.4	2.9 - 1.6	8.9 - 5.0	14.9 - 8.3
30	8°22.5	8°23.9	7°59.6	3.0 - 1.7	9.0 - 5.0	15.0 - 8.4
31	8°22.7	8°24.1	7°59.8	3.1 - 1.7	9.1 - 5.1	15.1 - 8.4
32	8°23.0	8°24.4	8°00.1	3.2 - 1.8	9.2 - 5.1	15.2 - 8.5
33	8°23.2	8°24.6	8°00.3	3.3 - 1.8	9.3 - 5.2	15.3 - 8.5
34	8°23.5	8°24.9	8°00.6	3.4 - 1.9	9.4 - 5.2	15.4 - 8.6
35	8°23.8	8°25.1	8°00.8	3.5 - 2.0	9.5 - 5.3	15.5 - 8.7
36	8°24.0	8°25.4	8°01.0	3.6 - 2.0	9.6 - 5.4	15.6 - 8.7
37	8°24.3	8°25.6	8°01.3	3.7 - 2.1	9.7 - 5.4	15.7 - 8.8
38	8°24.5	8°25.9	8°01.5	3.8 - 2.1	9.8 - 5.5	15.8 - 8.8
39	8°24.7	8°26.1	8°01.8	3.9 - 2.2	9.9 - 5.5	15.9 - 8.9
40	8°25.0	8°26.4	8°02.0	4.0 - 2.2	10.0 - 5.6	16.0 - 8.9
41	8°25.2	8°26.6	8°02.2	4.1 - 2.3	10.1 - 5.6	16.1 - 9.0
42	8°25.5	8°26.9	8°02.5	4.2 - 2.3	10.2 - 5.7	16.2 - 9.0
43	8°25.8	8°27.1	8°02.7	4.3 - 2.4	10.3 - 5.8	16.3 - 9.1
44	8°26.0	8°27.4	8°02.9	4.4 - 2.5	10.4 - 5.8	16.4 - 9.2
45	8°26.3	8°27.6	8°03.2	4.5 - 2.5	10.5 - 5.9	16.5 - 9.2
46	8°26.5	8°27.9	8°03.4	4.6 - 2.6	10.6 - 5.9	16.6 - 9.3
47	8°26.7	8°28.1	8°03.7	4.7 - 2.6	10.7 - 6.0	16.7 - 9.3
48	8°27.0	8°28.4	8°03.9	4.8 - 2.7	10.8 - 6.0	16.8 - 9.4
49	8°27.3	8°28.6	8°04.1	4.9 - 2.7	10.9 - 6.1	16.9 - 9.4
50	8°27.5	8°28.9	8°04.4	5.0 - 2.8	11.0 - 6.1	17.0 - 9.5
51	8°27.8	8°29.1	8°04.6	5.1 - 2.8	11.1 - 6.2	17.1 - 9.5
52	8°28.0	8°29.4	8°04.9	5.2 - 2.9	11.2 - 6.3	17.2 - 9.6
53	8°28.2	8°29.6	8°05.1	5.3 - 3.0	11.3 - 6.3	17.3 - 9.7
54	8°28.5	8°29.9	8°05.3	5.4 - 3.0	11.4 - 6.4	17.4 - 9.7
55	8°28.7	8°30.1	8°05.6	5.5 - 3.1	11.5 - 6.4	17.5 - 9.8
56	8°29.0	8°30.4	8°05.8	5.6 - 3.1	11.6 - 6.5	17.6 - 9.8
57	8°29.3	8°30.6	8°06.1	5.7 - 3.2	11.7 - 6.5	17.7 - 9.9
58	8°29.5	8°30.9	8°06.3	5.8 - 3.2	11.8 - 6.6	17.8 - 9.9
59	8°29.8	8°31.1	8°06.5	5.9 - 3.3	11.9 - 6.6	17.9 - 10.0

m 34	Sun Plan.	Aries	Moon	v and d corr		
0	8°30.0	8°31.4	8°06.8	0.0 - 0.0	6.0 - 3.4	12.0 - 6.9
1	8°30.2	8°31.6	8°07.0	0.1 - 0.1	6.1 - 3.5	12.1 - 7.0
2	8°30.5	8°31.9	8°07.2	0.2 - 0.1	6.2 - 3.6	12.2 - 7.0
3	8°30.7	8°32.1	8°07.5	0.3 - 0.2	6.3 - 3.6	12.3 - 7.1
4	8°31.0	8°32.4	8°07.7	0.4 - 0.2	6.4 - 3.7	12.4 - 7.1
5	8°31.3	8°32.6	8°08.0	0.5 - 0.3	6.5 - 3.7	12.5 - 7.2
6	8°31.5	8°32.9	8°08.2	0.6 - 0.3	6.6 - 3.8	12.6 - 7.2
7	8°31.8	8°33.1	8°08.4	0.7 - 0.4	6.7 - 3.9	12.7 - 7.3
8	8°32.0	8°33.4	8°08.7	0.8 - 0.5	6.8 - 3.9	12.8 - 7.4
9	8°32.2	8°33.7	8°08.9	0.9 - 0.5	6.9 - 4.0	12.9 - 7.4
10	8°32.5	8°33.9	8°09.2	1.0 - 0.6	7.0 - 4.0	13.0 - 7.5
11	8°32.7	8°34.2	8°09.4	1.1 - 0.6	7.1 - 4.1	13.1 - 7.5
12	8°33.0	8°34.4	8°09.6	1.2 - 0.7	7.2 - 4.1	13.2 - 7.6
13	8°33.3	8°34.7	8°09.9	1.3 - 0.7	7.3 - 4.2	13.3 - 7.6
14	8°33.5	8°34.9	8°10.1	1.4 - 0.8	7.4 - 4.3	13.4 - 7.7
15	8°33.8	8°35.2	8°10.3	1.5 - 0.9	7.5 - 4.3	13.5 - 7.8
16	8°34.0	8°35.4	8°10.6	1.6 - 0.9	7.6 - 4.4	13.6 - 7.8
17	8°34.2	8°35.7	8°10.8	1.7 - 1.0	7.7 - 4.4	13.7 - 7.9
18	8°34.5	8°35.9	8°11.1	1.8 - 1.0	7.8 - 4.5	13.8 - 7.9
19	8°34.8	8°36.2	8°11.3	1.9 - 1.1	7.9 - 4.5	13.9 - 8.0
20	8°35.0	8°36.4	8°11.5	2.0 - 1.1	8.0 - 4.6	14.0 - 8.0
21	8°35.3	8°36.7	8°11.8	2.1 - 1.2	8.1 - 4.7	14.1 - 8.1
22	8°35.5	8°36.9	8°12.0	2.2 - 1.3	8.2 - 4.7	14.2 - 8.2
23	8°35.7	8°37.2	8°12.3	2.3 - 1.3	8.3 - 4.8	14.3 - 8.2
24	8°36.0	8°37.4	8°12.5	2.4 - 1.4	8.4 - 4.8	14.4 - 8.3
25	8°36.2	8°37.7	8°12.7	2.5 - 1.4	8.5 - 4.9	14.5 - 8.3
26	8°36.5	8°37.9	8°13.0	2.6 - 1.5	8.6 - 4.9	14.6 - 8.4
27	8°36.8	8°38.2	8°13.2	2.7 - 1.6	8.7 - 5.0	14.7 - 8.5
28	8°37.0	8°38.4	8°13.4	2.8 - 1.6	8.8 - 5.1	14.8 - 8.5
29	8°37.3	8°38.7	8°13.7	2.9 - 1.7	8.9 - 5.1	14.9 - 8.6
30	8°37.5	8°38.9	8°13.9	3.0 - 1.7	9.0 - 5.2	15.0 - 8.6
31	8°37.7	8°39.2	8°14.2	3.1 - 1.8	9.1 - 5.2	15.1 - 8.7
32	8°38.0	8°39.4	8°14.4	3.2 - 1.8	9.2 - 5.3	15.2 - 8.7
33	8°38.2	8°39.7	8°14.6	3.3 - 1.9	9.3 - 5.3	15.3 - 8.8
34	8°38.5	8°39.9	8°14.9	3.4 - 2.0	9.4 - 5.4	15.4 - 8.9
35	8°38.8	8°40.2	8°15.1	3.5 - 2.0	9.5 - 5.5	15.5 - 8.9
36	8°39.0	8°40.4	8°15.4	3.6 - 2.1	9.6 - 5.5	15.6 - 9.0
37	8°39.3	8°40.7	8°15.6	3.7 - 2.1	9.7 - 5.6	15.7 - 9.0
38	8°39.5	8°40.9	8°15.8	3.8 - 2.2	9.8 - 5.6	15.8 - 9.1
39	8°39.7	8°41.2	8°16.1	3.9 - 2.2	9.9 - 5.7	15.9 - 9.1
40	8°40.0	8°41.4	8°16.3	4.0 - 2.3	10.0 - 5.8	16.0 - 9.2
41	8°40.2	8°41.7	8°16.5	4.1 - 2.4	10.1 - 5.8	16.1 - 9.3
42	8°40.5	8°41.9	8°16.8	4.2 - 2.4	10.2 - 5.9	16.2 - 9.3
43	8°40.8	8°42.2	8°17.0	4.3 - 2.5	10.3 - 5.9	16.3 - 9.4
44	8°41.0	8°42.4	8°17.3	4.4 - 2.5	10.4 - 6.0	16.4 - 9.4
45	8°41.3	8°42.7	8°17.5	4.5 - 2.6	10.5 - 6.0	16.5 - 9.5
46	8°41.5	8°42.9	8°17.7	4.6 - 2.6	10.6 - 6.1	16.6 - 9.5
47	8°41.7	8°43.2	8°18.0	4.7 - 2.7	10.7 - 6.2	16.7 - 9.6
48	8°42.0	8°43.4	8°18.2	4.8 - 2.8	10.8 - 6.2	16.8 - 9.7
49	8°42.3	8°43.7	8°18.5	4.9 - 2.8	10.9 - 6.3	16.9 - 9.7
50	8°42.5	8°43.9	8°18.7	5.0 - 2.9	11.0 - 6.3	17.0 - 9.8
51	8°42.8	8°44.2	8°18.9	5.1 - 2.9	11.1 - 6.4	17.1 - 9.8
52	8°43.0	8°44.4	8°19.2	5.2 - 3.0	11.2 - 6.4	17.2 - 9.9
53	8°43.2	8°44.7	8°19.4	5.3 - 3.0	11.3 - 6.5	17.3 - 9.9
54	8°43.5	8°44.9	8°19.7	5.4 - 3.1	11.4 - 6.6	17.4 - 10.0
55	8°43.7	8°45.2	8°19.9	5.5 - 3.2	11.5 - 6.6	17.5 - 10.1
56	8°44.0	8°45.4	8°20.1	5.6 - 3.2	11.6 - 6.7	17.6 - 10.1
57	8°44.3	8°45.7	8°20.4	5.7 - 3.3	11.7 - 6.7	17.7 - 10.2
58	8°44.5	8°45.9	8°20.6	5.8 - 3.3	11.8 - 6.8	17.8 - 10.2
59	8°44.8	8°46.2	8°20.8	5.9 - 3.4	11.9 - 6.8	17.9 - 10.3

m 35	Sun Plan.	Aries	Moon	v and d corr		
0	8°45.0	8°46.4	8°21.1	0.0 - 0.0	6.0 - 3.5	12.0 - 7.1
1	8°45.2	8°46.7	8°21.3	0.1 - 0.1	6.1 - 3.6	12.1 - 7.2
2	8°45.5	8°46.9	8°21.6	0.2 - 0.1	6.2 - 3.7	12.2 - 7.2
3	8°45.7	8°47.2	8°21.8	0.3 - 0.2	6.3 - 3.7	12.3 - 7.3
4	8°46.0	8°47.4	8°22.0	0.4 - 0.2	6.4 - 3.8	12.4 - 7.3
5	8°46.3	8°47.7	8°22.3	0.5 - 0.3	6.5 - 3.8	12.5 - 7.4
6	8°46.5	8°47.9	8°22.5	0.6 - 0.4	6.6 - 3.9	12.6 - 7.5
7	8°46.8	8°48.2	8°22.8	0.7 - 0.4	6.7 - 4.0	12.7 - 7.5
8	8°47.0	8°48.4	8°23.0	0.8 - 0.5	6.8 - 4.0	12.8 - 7.6
9	8°47.2	8°48.7	8°23.2	0.9 - 0.5	6.9 - 4.1	12.9 - 7.6
10	8°47.5	8°48.9	8°23.5	1.0 - 0.6	7.0 - 4.1	13.0 - 7.7
11	8°47.7	8°49.2	8°23.7	1.1 - 0.7	7.1 - 4.2	13.1 - 7.8
12	8°48.0	8°49.4	8°23.9	1.2 - 0.7	7.2 - 4.3	13.2 - 7.8
13	8°48.3	8°49.7	8°24.2	1.3 - 0.8	7.3 - 4.3	13.3 - 7.9
14	8°48.5	8°49.9	8°24.4	1.4 - 0.8	7.4 - 4.4	13.4 - 7.9
15	8°48.8	8°50.2	8°24.7	1.5 - 0.9	7.5 - 4.4	13.5 - 8.0
16	8°49.0	8°50.4	8°24.9	1.6 - 0.9	7.6 - 4.5	13.6 - 8.0
17	8°49.2	8°50.7	8°25.1	1.7 - 1.0	7.7 - 4.6	13.7 - 8.1
18	8°49.5	8°50.9	8°25.4	1.8 - 1.1	7.8 - 4.6	13.8 - 8.2
19	8°49.8	8°51.2	8°25.6	1.9 - 1.1	7.9 - 4.7	13.9 - 8.2
20	8°50.0	8°51.4	8°25.9	2.0 - 1.2	8.0 - 4.7	14.0 - 8.3
21	8°50.3	8°51.7	8°26.1	2.1 - 1.2	8.1 - 4.8	14.1 - 8.3
22	8°50.5	8°52.0	8°26.3	2.2 - 1.3	8.2 - 4.9	14.2 - 8.4
23	8°50.7	8°52.2	8°26.6	2.3 - 1.4	8.3 - 4.9	14.3 - 8.5
24	8°51.0	8°52.5	8°26.8	2.4 - 1.4	8.4 - 5.0	14.4 - 8.5
25	8°51.2	8°52.7	8°27.0	2.5 - 1.5	8.5 - 5.0	14.5 - 8.6
26	8°51.5	8°53.0	8°27.3	2.6 - 1.5	8.6 - 5.1	14.6 - 8.6
27	8°51.8	8°53.2	8°27.5	2.7 - 1.6	8.7 - 5.1	14.7 - 8.7
28	8°52.0	8°53.5	8°27.8	2.8 - 1.7	8.8 - 5.2	14.8 - 8.8
29	8°52.3	8°53.7	8°28.0	2.9 - 1.7	8.9 - 5.3	14.9 - 8.8
30	8°52.5	8°54.0	8°28.2	3.0 - 1.8	9.0 - 5.3	15.0 - 8.9
31	8°52.7	8°54.2	8°28.5	3.1 - 1.8	9.1 - 5.4	15.1 - 8.9
32	8°53.0	8°54.5	8°28.7	3.2 - 1.9	9.2 - 5.4	15.2 - 9.0
33	8°53.2	8°54.7	8°29.0	3.3 - 2.0	9.3 - 5.5	15.3 - 9.1
34	8°53.5	8°55.0	8°29.2	3.4 - 2.0	9.4 - 5.6	15.4 - 9.1
35	8°53.8	8°55.2	8°29.4	3.5 - 2.1	9.5 - 5.6	15.5 - 9.2
36	8°54.0	8°55.5	8°29.7	3.6 - 2.1	9.6 - 5.7	15.6 - 9.2
37	8°54.3	8°55.7	8°29.9	3.7 - 2.2	9.7 - 5.7	15.7 - 9.3
38	8°54.5	8°56.0	8°30.2	3.8 - 2.2	9.8 - 5.8	15.8 - 9.3
39	8°54.7	8°56.2	8°30.4	3.9 - 2.3	9.9 - 5.9	15.9 - 9.4
40	8°55.0	8°56.5	8°30.6	4.0 - 2.4	10.0 - 5.9	16.0 - 9.5
41	8°55.2	8°56.7	8°30.9	4.1 - 2.4	10.1 - 6.0	16.1 - 9.5
42	8°55.5	8°57.0	8°31.1	4.2 - 2.5	10.2 - 6.0	16.2 - 9.6
43	8°55.8	8°57.2	8°31.3	4.3 - 2.5	10.3 - 6.1	16.3 - 9.6
44	8°56.0	8°57.5	8°31.6	4.4 - 2.6	10.4 - 6.2	16.4 - 9.7
45	8°56.3	8°57.7	8°31.8	4.5 - 2.7	10.5 - 6.2	16.5 - 9.8
46	8°56.5	8°58.0	8°32.1	4.6 - 2.7	10.6 - 6.3	16.6 - 9.8
47	8°56.7	8°58.2	8°32.3	4.7 - 2.8	10.7 - 6.3	16.7 - 9.9
48	8°57.0	8°58.5	8°32.5	4.8 - 2.8	10.8 - 6.4	16.8 - 9.9
49	8°57.3	8°58.7	8°32.8	4.9 - 2.9	10.9 - 6.4	16.9 - 10.0
50	8°57.5	8°59.0	8°33.0	5.0 - 3.0	11.0 - 6.5	17.0 - 10.1
51	8°57.8	8°59.2	8°33.3	5.1 - 3.0	11.1 - 6.6	17.1 - 10.1
52	8°58.0	8°59.5	8°33.5	5.2 - 3.1	11.2 - 6.6	17.2 - 10.2
53	8°58.2	8°59.7	8°33.7	5.3 - 3.1	11.3 - 6.7	17.3 - 10.2
54	8°58.5	9°00.0	8°34.0	5.4 - 3.2	11.4 - 6.7	17.4 - 10.3
55	8°58.7	9°00.2	8°34.2	5.5 - 3.3	11.5 - 6.8	17.5 - 10.4
56	8°59.0	9°00.5	8°34.4	5.6 - 3.3	11.6 - 6.9	17.6 - 10.4
57	8°59.3	9°00.7	8°34.7	5.7 - 3.4	11.7 - 6.9	17.7 - 10.5
58	8°59.5	9°01.0	8°34.9	5.8 - 3.4	11.8 - 7.0	17.8 - 10.5
59	8°59.8	9°01.2	8°35.2	5.9 - 3.5	11.9 - 7.0	17.9 - 10.6

Figure 36

Figure 36 is an extract from the *Increments and Corrections* tables.

The tables cater for 60 minutes (0 to 60). Here, in an extract from the tables, we have a page with three minutes on it: 33 minutes (red box), 34 minutes (green box) and 35 minutes (orange box).

We are interested in 35 minutes so let's focus on that.

Figures 37 and 37a show the same extract for 35 minutes. We are interested in two areas, the red box (sun) and the light blue box.

Focusing on the red box (sun), we

m 35	Sun Plan.	Aries	Moon	v and d corr		
0	8°45.0	8°46.4	8°21.1	0.0 - 0.0	6.0 - 3.5	12.0 - 7.1
1	8°45.2	8°46.7	8°21.3	0.1 - 0.1	6.1 - 3.6	12.1 - 7.2
2	8°45.5	8°46.9	8°21.6	0.2 - 0.1	6.2 - 3.7	12.2 - 7.2
3	8°45.7	8°47.2	8°21.8	0.3 - 0.2	6.3 - 3.7	12.3 - 7.3
4	8°46.0	8°47.4	8°22.0	0.4 - 0.2	6.4 - 3.8	12.4 - 7.3
5	8°46.3	8°47.7	8°22.3	0.5 - 0.3	6.5 - 3.8	12.5 - 7.4
6	8°46.5	8°47.9	8°22.5	0.6 - 0.4	6.6 - 3.9	12.6 - 7.5
7	8°46.8	8°48.2	8°22.8	0.7 - 0.4	6.7 - 4.0	12.7 - 7.5
8	8°47.0	8°48.4	8°23.0	0.8 - 0.5	6.8 - 4.0	12.8 - 7.6
9	8°47.2	8°48.7	8°23.2	0.9 - 0.5	6.9 - 4.1	12.9 - 7.6
10	8°47.5	8°48.9	8°23.5	1.0 - 0.6	7.0 - 4.1	13.0 - 7.7
11	8°47.7	8°49.2	8°23.7	1.1 - 0.7	7.1 - 4.2	13.1 - 7.8
12	8°48.0	8°49.4	8°23.9	1.2 - 0.7	7.2 - 4.3	13.2 - 7.8
13	8°48.3	8°49.7	8°24.2	1.3 - 0.8	7.3 - 4.3	13.3 - 7.9
14	8°48.5	8°49.9	8°24.4	1.4 - 0.8	7.4 - 4.4	13.4 - 7.9
15	8°48.8	8°50.2	8°24.7	1.5 - 0.9	7.5 - 4.4	13.5 - 8.0
16	8°49.0	8°50.4	8°24.9	1.6 - 0.9	7.6 - 4.5	13.6 - 8.0
17	8°49.2	8°50.7	8°25.1	1.7 - 1.0	7.7 - 4.6	13.7 - 8.1
18	8°49.5	8°50.9	8°25.4	1.8 - 1.1	7.8 - 4.6	13.8 - 8.2
19	8°49.8	8°51.2	8°25.6	1.9 - 1.1	7.9 - 4.7	13.9 - 8.2
20	8°50.0	8°51.4	8°25.9	2.0 - 1.2	8.0 - 4.7	14.0 - 8.3
21	8°50.3	8°51.7	8°26.1	2.1 - 1.2	8.1 - 4.8	14.1 - 8.3
22	8°50.5	8°52.0	8°26.3	2.2 - 1.3	8.2 - 4.9	14.2 - 8.4
23	8°50.7	8°52.2	8°26.6	2.3 - 1.4	8.3 - 4.9	14.3 - 8.5
24	8°51.0	8°52.5	8°26.8	2.4 - 1.4	8.4 - 5.0	14.4 - 8.5
25	8°51.2	8°52.7	8°27.0	2.5 - 1.5	8.5 - 5.0	14.5 - 8.6
26	8°51.5	8°53.0	8°27.3	2.6 - 1.5	8.6 - 5.1	14.6 - 8.6
27	8°51.8	8°53.2	8°27.5	2.7 - 1.6	8.7 - 5.1	14.7 - 8.7
28	8°52.0	8°53.5	8°27.8	2.8 - 1.7	8.8 - 5.2	14.8 - 8.8
29	8°52.3	8°53.7	8°28.0	2.9 - 1.7	8.9 - 5.3	14.9 - 8.8
30	8°52.5	8°54.0	8°28.2	3.0 - 1.8	9.0 - 5.3	15.0 - 8.9
31	8°52.7	8°54.2	8°28.5	3.1 - 1.8	9.1 - 5.4	15.1 - 8.9
32	8°53.0	8°54.5	8°28.7	3.2 - 1.9	9.2 - 5.4	15.2 - 9.0
33	8°53.2	8°54.7	8°29.0	3.3 - 2.0	9.3 - 5.5	15.3 - 9.1
34	8°53.5	8°55.0	8°29.2	3.4 - 2.0	9.4 - 5.6	15.4 - 9.1
35	8°53.8	8°55.2	8°29.4	3.5 - 2.1	9.5 - 5.6	15.5 - 9.2
36	8°54.0	8°55.5	8°29.7	3.6 - 2.1	9.6 - 5.7	15.6 - 9.2
37	8°54.3	8°55.7	8°29.9	3.7 - 2.2	9.7 - 5.7	15.7 - 9.3
38	8°54.5	8°56.0	8°30.2	3.8 - 2.2	9.8 - 5.8	15.8 - 9.3
39	8°54.7	8°56.2	8°30.4	3.9 - 2.3	9.9 - 5.9	15.9 - 9.4
40	8°55.0	8°56.5	8°30.6	4.0 - 2.4	10.0 - 5.9	16.0 - 9.5
41	8°55.2	8°56.7	8°30.9	4.1 - 2.4	10.1 - 6.0	16.1 - 9.5
42	8°55.5	8°57.0	8°31.1	4.2 - 2.5	10.2 - 6.0	16.2 - 9.6
43	8°55.8	8°57.2	8°31.3	4.3 - 2.5	10.3 - 6.1	16.3 - 9.6
44	8°56.0	8°57.5	8°31.6	4.4 - 2.6	10.4 - 6.2	16.4 - 9.7
45	8°56.3	8°57.7	8°31.8	4.5 - 2.7	10.5 - 6.2	16.5 - 9.8
46	8°56.5	8°58.0	8°32.1	4.6 - 2.7	10.6 - 6.3	16.6 - 9.8
47	8°56.7	8°58.2	8°32.3	4.7 - 2.8	10.7 - 6.3	16.7 - 9.9
48	8°57.0	8°58.5	8°32.5	4.8 - 2.8	10.8 - 6.4	16.8 - 9.9
49	8°57.3	8°58.7	8°32.8	4.9 - 2.9	10.9 - 6.4	16.9 - 10.0
50	8°57.5	8°59.0	8°33.0	5.0 - 3.0	11.0 - 6.5	17.0 - 10.1
51	8°57.8	8°59.2	8°33.3	5.1 - 3.0	11.1 - 6.6	17.1 - 10.1
52	8°58.0	8°59.5	8°33.5	5.2 - 3.1	11.2 - 6.6	17.2 - 10.2
53	8°58.2	8°59.7	8°33.7	5.3 - 3.1	11.3 - 6.7	17.3 - 10.2
54	8°58.5	9°00.0	8°34.0	5.4 - 3.2	11.4 - 6.7	17.4 - 10.3
55	8°58.7	9°00.2	8°34.2	5.5 - 3.3	11.5 - 6.8	17.5 - 10.4
56	8°59.0	9°00.5	8°34.4	5.6 - 3.3	11.6 - 6.9	17.6 - 10.4
57	8°59.3	9°00.7	8°34.7	5.7 - 3.4	11.7 - 6.9	17.7 - 10.5
58	8°59.5	9°01.0	8°34.9	5.8 - 3.4	11.8 - 7.0	17.8 - 10.5
59	8°59.8	9°01.2	8°35.2	5.9 - 3.5	11.9 - 7.0	17.9 - 10.6

Figure 37

m 35	Sun Plan.	Aries	Moon	v and d corr		
0	8°45.0	8°46.4	8°21.1	0.0 - 0.0	6.0 - 3.5	12.0 - 7.1
1	8°45.2	8°46.7	8°21.3	0.1 - 0.1	6.1 - 3.6	12.1 - 7.2
2	8°45.5	8°46.9	8°21.6	0.2 - 0.1	6.2 - 3.7	12.2 - 7.2
3	8°45.7	8°47.2	8°21.8	0.3 - 0.2	6.3 - 3.7	12.3 - 7.3
4	8°46.0	8°47.4	8°22.0	0.4 - 0.2	6.4 - 3.8	12.4 - 7.3
5	8°46.3	8°47.7	8°22.3	0.5 - 0.3	6.5 - 3.8	12.5 - 7.4
6	8°46.5	8°47.9	8°22.5	0.6 - 0.4	6.6 - 3.9	12.6 - 7.5
7	8°46.8	8°48.2	8°22.8	0.7 - 0.4	6.7 - 4.0	12.7 - 7.5
8	8°47.0	8°48.4	8°23.0	0.8 - 0.5	6.8 - 4.0	12.8 - 7.6
9	8°47.2	8°48.7	8°23.2	0.9 - 0.5	6.9 - 4.1	12.9 - 7.6
10	8°47.5	8°48.9	8°23.5	1.0 - 0.6	7.0 - 4.1	13.0 - 7.7
11	8°47.7	8°49.2	8°23.7	1.1 - 0.7	7.1 - 4.2	13.1 - 7.8
12	8°48.0	8°49.4	8°23.9	1.2 - 0.7	7.2 - 4.3	13.2 - 7.8
13	8°48.3	8°49.7	8°24.2	1.3 - 0.8	7.3 - 4.3	13.3 - 7.9
14	8°48.5	8°49.9	8°24.4	1.4 - 0.8	7.4 - 4.4	13.4 - 7.9
15	8°48.8	8°50.2	8°24.7	1.5 - 0.9	7.5 - 4.4	13.5 - 8.0
16	8°49.0	8°50.4	8°24.9	1.6 - 0.9	7.6 - 4.5	13.6 - 8.0
17	8°49.2	8°50.7	8°25.1	1.7 - 1.0	7.7 - 4.6	13.7 - 8.1
18	8°49.5	8°50.9	8°25.4	1.8 - 1.1	7.8 - 4.6	13.8 - 8.2
19	8°49.8	8°51.2	8°25.6	1.9 - 1.1	7.9 - 4.7	13.9 - 8.2
20	8°50.0	8°51.4	8°25.9	2.0 - 1.2	8.0 - 4.7	14.0 - 8.3
21	8°50.3	8°51.7	8°26.1	2.1 - 1.2	8.1 - 4.8	14.1 - 8.3
22	8°50.5	8°52.0	8°26.3	2.2 - 1.3	8.2 - 4.9	14.2 - 8.4
23	8°50.7	8°52.2	8°26.6	2.3 - 1.4	8.3 - 4.9	14.3 - 8.5
24	8°51.0	8°52.5	8°26.8	2.4 - 1.4	8.4 - 5.0	14.4 - 8.5
25	8°51.2	8°52.7	8°27.0	2.5 - 1.5	8.5 - 5.0	14.5 - 8.6
26	8°51.5	8°53.0	8°27.3	2.6 - 1.5	8.6 - 5.1	14.6 - 8.6
27	8°51.8	8°53.2	8°27.5	2.7 - 1.6	8.7 - 5.1	14.7 - 8.7
28	8°52.0	8°53.5	8°27.8	2.8 - 1.7	8.8 - 5.2	14.8 - 8.8
29	8°52.3	8°53.7	8°28.0	2.9 - 1.7	8.9 - 5.3	14.9 - 8.8
30	8°52.5	8°54.0	8°28.2	3.0 - 1.8	9.0 - 5.3	15.0 - 8.9
31	8°52.7	8°54.2	8°28.5	3.1 - 1.8	9.1 - 5.4	15.1 - 8.9
32	8°53.0	8°54.5	8°28.7	3.2 - 1.9	9.2 - 5.4	15.2 - 9.0
33	8°53.2	8°54.7	8°29.0	3.3 - 2.0	9.3 - 5.5	15.3 - 9.1
34	8°53.5	8°55.0	8°29.2	3.4 - 2.0	9.4 - 5.6	15.4 - 9.1
35	8°53.8	8°55.2	8°29.4	3.5 - 2.1	9.5 - 5.6	15.5 - 9.2
36	8°54.0	8°55.5	8°29.7	3.6 - 2.1	9.6 - 5.7	15.6 - 9.2
37	8°54.3	8°55.7	8°29.9	3.7 - 2.2	9.7 - 5.7	15.7 - 9.3
38	8°54.5	8°56.0	8°30.2	3.8 - 2.2	9.8 - 5.8	15.8 - 9.3
39	8°54.7	8°56.2	8°30.4	3.9 - 2.3	9.9 - 5.9	15.9 - 9.4
40	8°55.0	8°56.5	8°30.6	4.0 - 2.4	10.0 - 5.9	16.0 - 9.5
41	8°55.2	8°56.7	8°30.9	4.1 - 2.4	10.1 - 6.0	16.1 - 9.5
42	8°55.5	8°57.0	8°31.1	4.2 - 2.5	10.2 - 6.0	16.2 - 9.6
43	8°55.8	8°57.2	8°31.3	4.3 - 2.5	10.3 - 6.1	16.3 - 9.6
44	8°56.0	8°57.5	8°31.6	4.4 - 2.6	10.4 - 6.2	16.4 - 9.7
45	8°56.3	8°57.7	8°31.8	4.5 - 2.7	10.5 - 6.2	16.5 - 9.8
46	8°56.5	8°58.0	8°32.1	4.6 - 2.7	10.6 - 6.3	16.6 - 9.8
47	8°56.7	8°58.2	8°32.3	4.7 - 2.8	10.7 - 6.3	16.7 - 9.9
48	8°57.0	8°58.5	8°32.5	4.8 - 2.8	10.8 - 6.4	16.8 - 9.9
49	8°57.3	8°58.7	8°32.8	4.9 - 2.9	10.9 - 6.4	16.9 - 10.0
50	8°57.5	8°59.0	8°33.0	5.0 - 3.0	11.0 - 6.5	17.0 - 10.1
51	8°57.8	8°59.2	8°33.3	5.1 - 3.0	11.1 - 6.6	17.1 - 10.1
52	8°58.0	8°59.5	8°33.5	5.2 - 3.1	11.2 - 6.6	17.2 - 10.2
53	8°58.2	8°59.7	8°33.7	5.3 - 3.1	11.3 - 6.7	17.3 - 10.2
54	8°58.5	9°00.0	8°34.0	5.4 - 3.2	11.4 - 6.7	17.4 - 10.3
55	8°58.7	9°00.2	8°34.2	5.5 - 3.3	11.5 - 6.8	17.5 - 10.4
56	8°59.0	9°00.5	8°34.4	5.6 - 3.3	11.6 - 6.9	17.6 - 10.4
57	8°59.3	9°00.7	8°34.7	5.7 - 3.4	11.7 - 6.9	17.7 - 10.5
58	8°59.5	9°01.0	8°34.9	5.8 - 3.4	11.8 - 7.0	17.8 - 10.5
59	8°59.8	9°01.2	8°35.2	5.9 - 3.5	11.9 - 7.0	17.9 - 10.6

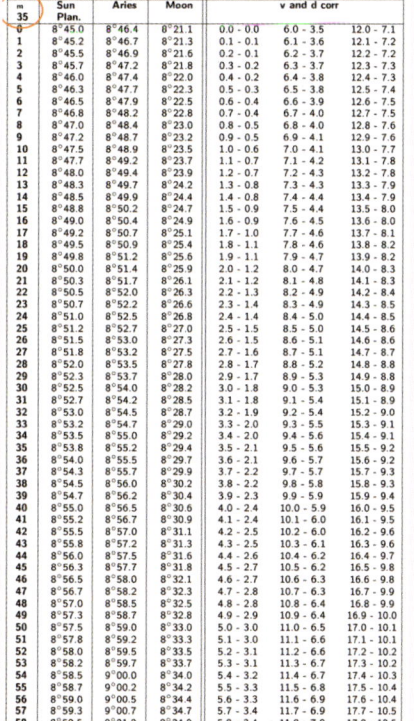

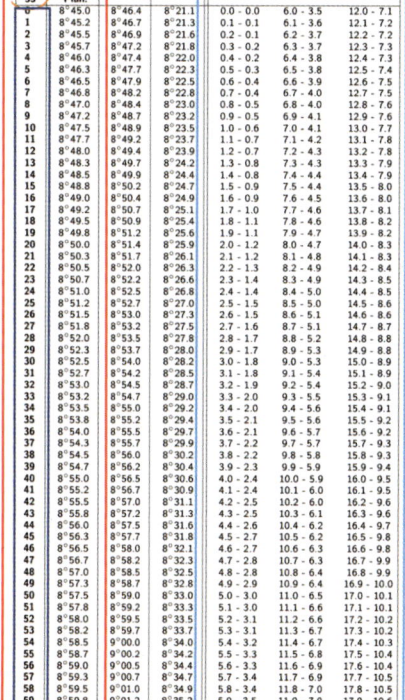

Figure 37a

see within the dark blue box there are the numbers 0 to 59, these are seconds. In other words, we are already on 35 minutes (the whole table here is for 35 minutes), and we then have 0 to 59 seconds down the first column (dark blue box). This is being emphasised because a common mistake made is to look for the correct 'minutes table', ie 35 minutes, and then, instead of looking up 43 seconds in the left-hand column, looking up 35 again. Staying within the red box, the second column is the change in GHA for 35 minutes, depending on however many seconds are chosen.

So we move down the first column until we find 43 seconds and select the corresponding value and enter it into our proforma as per Figure 38.

Step 3 (Figure 38) Accounting for the minutes and seconds using the *Increments and Corrections* table.

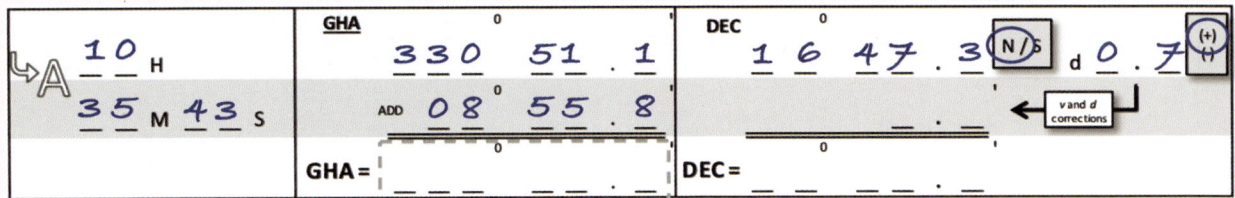

Figure 38

Now, what to do with the declination and the value of 0.7' we have? We've said this means the declination is changing by 0.7' per hour.

How much would it change by in 30 minutes? Well, of course, it would be 0.7' divided by 2 = 0.35'.

But how much would an hourly change of 0.7' equate over 35 minutes? Here, the maths is a little more difficult, and that's what this second part of the table does for us (it's the one entitled *v* and *d* corrections).

Quickly looking back at Figure 37a, the first part to note is that this second section (*v* and *d* corrections, light blue) is not connected with the left-hand section. In other words, the red box and light blue box are not connected, other than they are both related to the increment of 35 minutes.

Figure 39 is the *v* and *d* corrections table, the same right-hand section looked at as before, but it deserves some clarification because it's a common cause for confusion. As you can see, the table is split into three columns, A, B and C. Looking in the red box (A), we see the left-hand column contains numbers 0 to 5.9. The blue box (B) left-hand column then carries on from 6 to 11.9. And finally, the orange box (C) goes from 12 to 17.9. In other words, each column follows on from the last.

In essence, we choose a value in the left-hand column between 0 and 17.9 and the table returns a value based on 35 minutes. To put it another way, it divides the selected value by 60 and multiplies by 35.

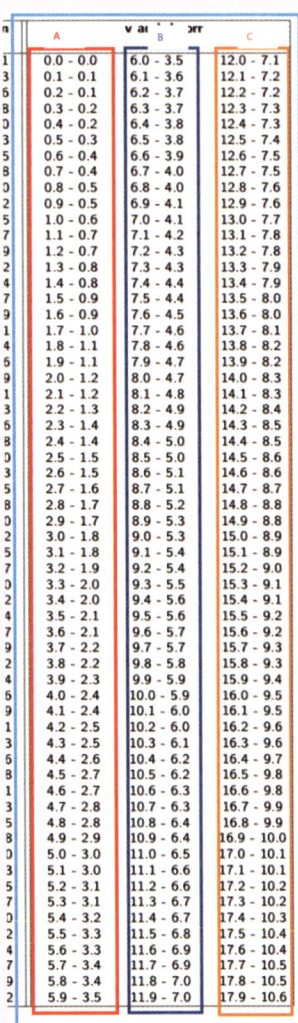

Figure 39

Back to the proforma. We want to know what value we should take for 0.7'. To do this, identify 0.7 in the table and put the corresponding value on to the proforma as shown in Figure 40.

Step 4 (Figure 40) Identify 0.7 in the table and put the corresponding value on to the proforma.

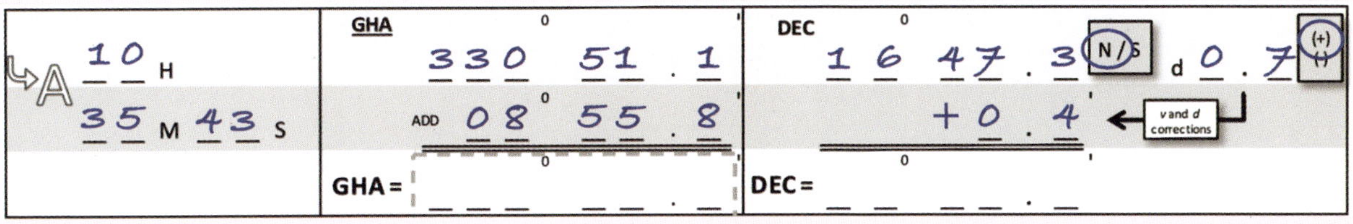

Figure 40

Step 5 (Figure 41)

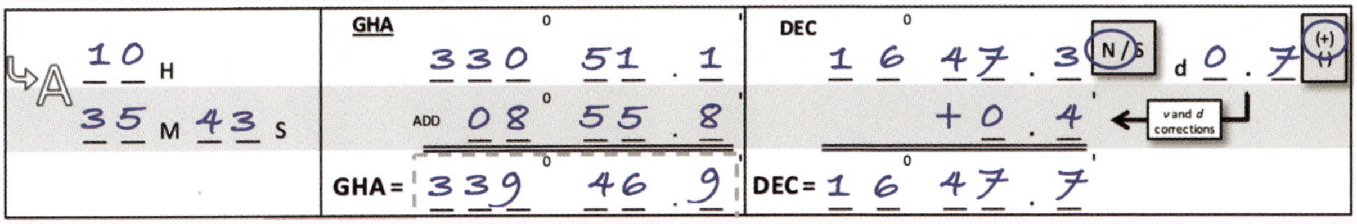

Figure 41

As shown in Figure 41, we now have the sun's GP for 10hr 35min 43sec, made up of GHA and declination. This is an actual position that could be plotted on a chart.

Note: As discussed on page 18, having taken a sextant sight, we *could* now calculate the ZD and, using the great circle angle versus distance relationship, calculate our distance from the GP established above. This wouldn't give a very accurate position circle but, in the absence of the more accurate solution we'll be moving on to, we could do so.

CHAPTER FOUR

Sextant corrections

In this chapter we'll be looking at the corrections we need to apply to an observed sextant altitude (ie an actual reading we've obtained from our sextant) before we can use its value. Chapter 15 looks at the practical aspects of sextant error checking and sight taking.

Before going any further, something's worth a mention. Many people think celestial navigation is all about the sextant. Of course, it's a fundamental part of the process. But, from a learning perspective, it's only a small part.

The sextant is an accurate measuring device. In celestial navigation it's used to measure the angle between the horizon and a celestial body, in our case the sun, as shown in Figure 42.

Figure 43 shows the components that make up a sextant.

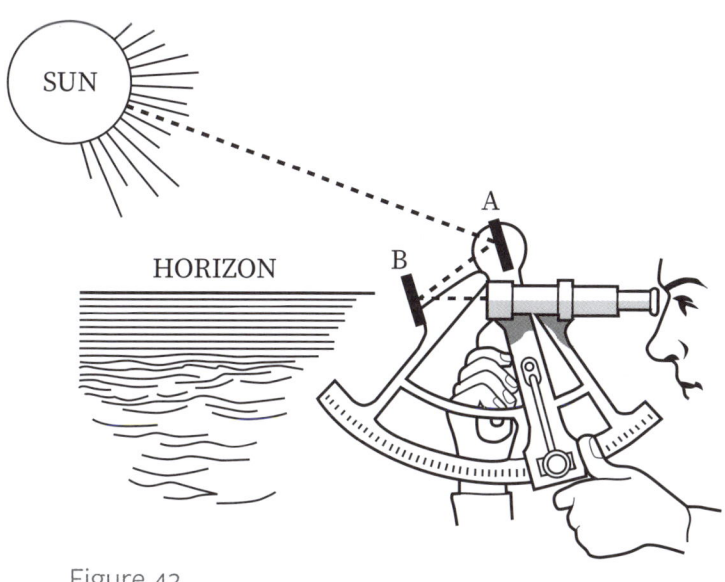

Figure 42

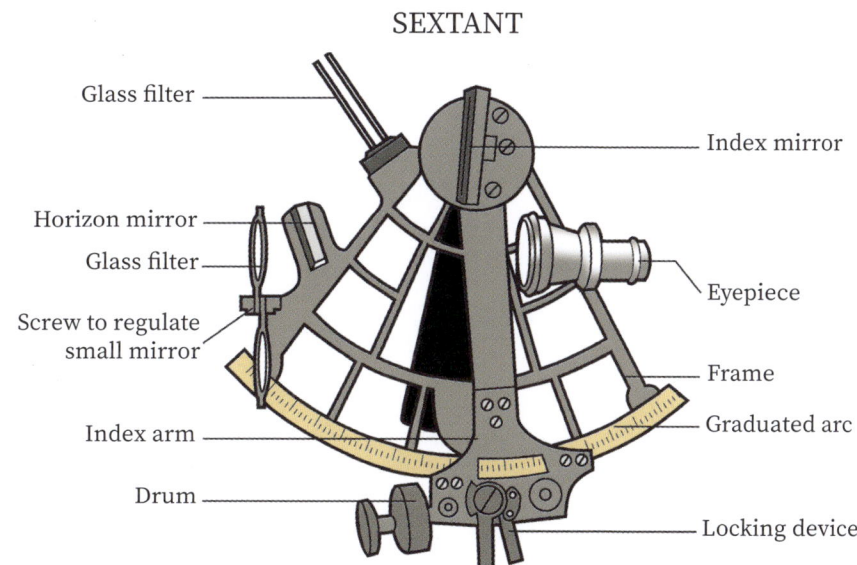

Figure 43

CHAPTER FOUR: SEXTANT CORRECTIONS

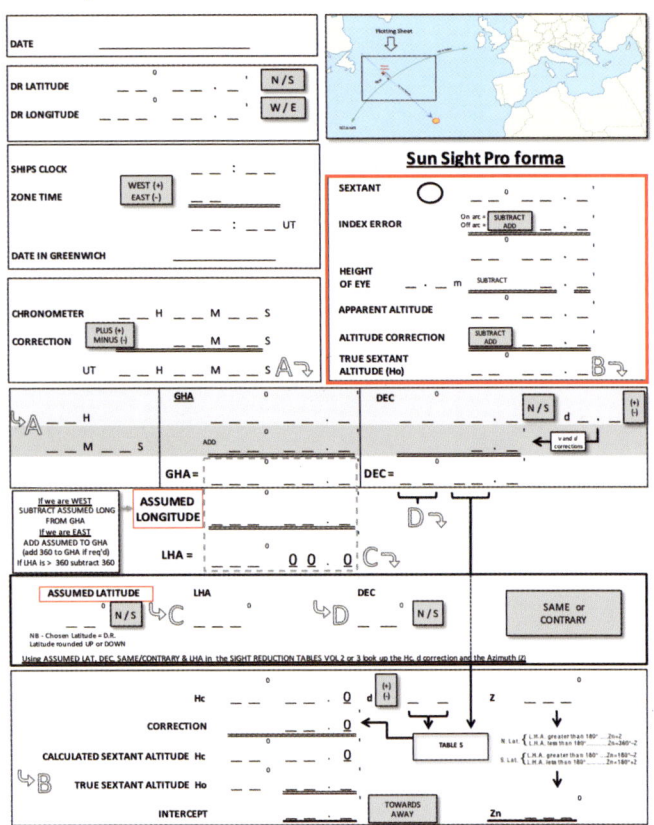

Figure 44

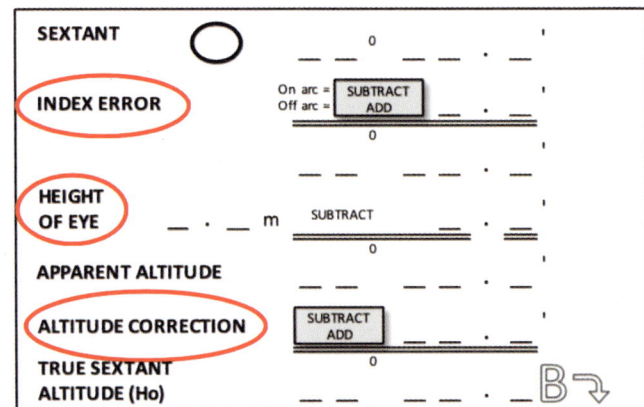

Figure 44a

Once we have undertaken a sight there are some corrections that have to be made before we can use the result. Figure 44 shows in red the part of the proforma that facilitates these corrections. Figure 44a expands this *sextant correction* area.

Before we look at how we undertake the corrections let's look at what they are:

INDEX ERROR

This is a residual error that's left on the sextant, after having undertaken the error corrections outlined in Chapter 15. In essence, it's an error that will mean our sextant will under- or over-read.

HEIGHT OF EYE (DIP)

Our height of eye, referred to as *dip*, has an effect on our observed sextant reading. Our resultant *true sextant altitude* needs to be at sea level and therefore a correction is needed to compensate for our height of eye when taking the sight. Figure 45 demonstrates the effect our height has. In red, our lower observer would have the horizon closer than our green observer (see dotted lines). This would result in the green observer obtaining a larger sextant altitude (SA).

Dip gets its name due to the fact the horizon seems to dip away as the observer's height of eye increases.

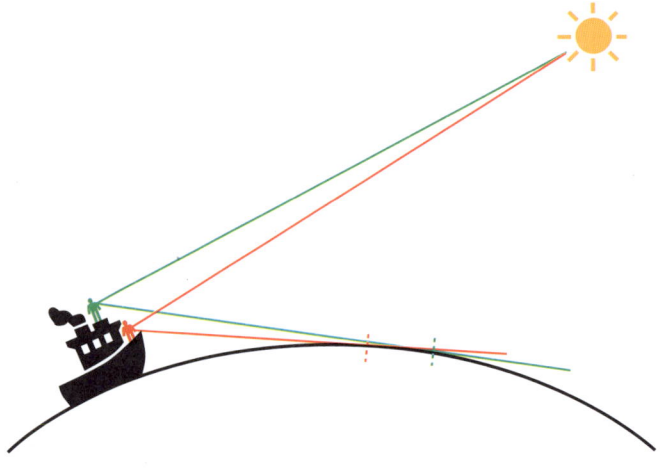

Figure 45

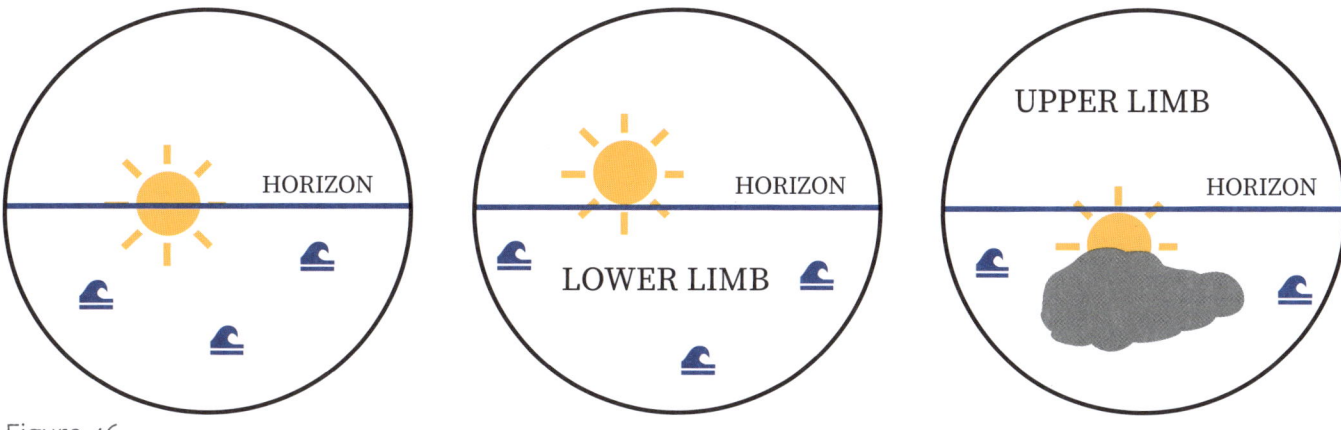

Figure 46

ALTITUDE CORRECTION

Altitude correction encompasses three further elements. It's not necessary to remember these, but it's worth having a look at what they are: semi-diameter, parallax and refraction.

SEMI-DIAMETER

In Figure 46, the left-hand image shows the sight we would ideally want to obtain from our sextant. However, aligning exactly with the centre of the sun is quite difficult to judge.

So instead we usually obtain the centre image where we bring the sun down to the horizon until the bottom of the sun just touches it. We call this the *lower limb* of the sun.

We wouldn't normally obtain the right-hand image unless the lower limb has been obscured. It's harder to judge this upper limb and therefore 90% of our sights will probably be lower limb.

The *Altitude Correction Table* takes account of this by adding or subtracting approximately 15' from our sextant altitude. (The sun's diameter is approximately 30'.)

PARALLAX

We've said that celestial navigation works on the assumption that the rays of light from the sun arrive in parallel to one another. Of course, this isn't quite so, therefore a correction is required to adjust for this slight error.

REFRACTION

This is a result of the different densities between outer space and the earth's atmosphere. When light from the sun arrives, it can bend as it enters the earth's atmosphere, as shown in Figure 47. If the sun is overhead there is no refraction, but as the sun moves towards the horizon, the refraction increases. This is the same when viewing a fish in a pool. If a hunter is trying to spear a fish, refraction must be accounted for. If overhead, the hunter would aim at the fish. But if an angle exists, the hunter must aim below where the fish appears to be in order to spear it.

The correction, at most, is around 5.5', so it's fairly small.

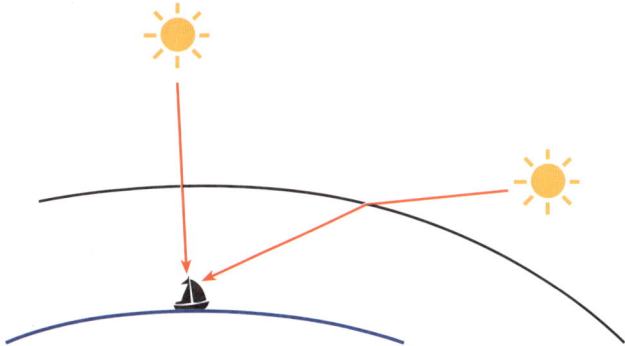

Figure 47

APPLYING THE CORRECTIONS: EXAMPLE

Having explained what the corrections are, let's look at where we get these corrections and how to apply them. The best way to do this is to work through an example.

Let's say we took a sight of the sun on:

- 24 April
- We took a sight of the lower limb
- Our height of eye was 4.3m above sea level
- SA 43° 45.6'

Figures 48 and 48a show the tables we require to make our corrections; these are usually found as a loose leaf within our nautical almanac. You'll see this extract covers the sun, stars and planets 10 ° to 90°. We wouldn't under normal circumstances take a sight below 10° as refraction becomes too significant.

ALTITUDE CORRECTION TABLES 10°-90°—SUN, STARS, PLANETS

OCT.—MAR. SUN App. Alt.	Lower Limb	Upper Limb	APR.—SEPT. SUN App. Alt.	Lower Limb	Upper Limb
° ′	′	′	° ′	′	′
9 34	+10.8	−21.5	9 39	+10.6	−21.2
9 45	+10.9	−21.4	9 51	+10.7	−21.1
9 56	+11.0	−21.3	10 03	+10.8	−21.0
10 08	+11.1	−21.2	10 15	+10.9	−20.9
10 21	+11.2	−21.1	10 27	+11.0	−20.8
10 34	+11.3	−21.0	10 40	+11.1	−20.7
10 47	+11.4	−20.9	10 54	+11.2	−20.6
11 01	+11.5	−20.8	11 08	+11.3	−20.5
11 15	+11.6	−20.7	11 23	+11.4	−20.4
11 30	+11.7	−20.6	11 38	+11.5	−20.3
11 46	+11.8	−20.5	11 54	+11.6	−20.2
12 02	+11.9	−20.4	12 10	+11.7	−20.1
12 19	+12.0	−20.3	12 28	+11.8	−20.0
12 37	+12.1	−20.2	12 46	+11.9	−19.9
12 55	+12.2	−20.1	13 05	+12.0	−19.8
13 14	+12.3	−20.0	13 24	+12.1	−19.7
13 35	+12.4	−19.9	13 45	+12.2	−19.6
13 56	+12.5	−19.8	14 07	+12.3	−19.5
14 18	+12.6	−19.7	14 30	+12.4	−19.4
14 42	+12.7	−19.6	14 54	+12.5	−19.3
15 06	+12.8	−19.5	15 19	+12.6	−19.2
15 32	+12.9	−19.4	15 46	+12.7	−19.1
15 59	+13.0	−19.3	16 14	+12.8	−19.0
16 28	+13.1	−19.2	16 44	+12.9	−18.9
16 59	+13.2	−19.1	17 15	+13.0	−18.8
17 32	+13.3	−19.0	17 48	+13.1	−18.7
18 06	+13.4	−18.9	18 24	+13.2	−18.6
18 42	+13.5	−18.8	19 01	+13.3	−18.5
19 21	+13.6	−18.7	19 42	+13.4	−18.4
20 03	+13.7	−18.6	20 25	+13.5	−18.3
20 48	+13.8	−18.5	21 11	+13.6	−18.2
21 35	+13.9	−18.4	22 00	+13.7	−18.1
22 26	+14.0	−18.3	22 54	+13.8	−18.0
23 22	+14.1	−18.2	23 51	+13.9	−17.9
24 21	+14.2	−18.1	24 53	+14.0	−17.8
25 26	+14.3	−18.0	26 00	+14.1	−17.7
26 36	+14.4	−17.9	27 13	+14.2	−17.6
27 52	+14.5	−17.8	28 33	+14.3	−17.5
29 15	+14.6	−17.7	30 00	+14.4	−17.4
30 46	+14.7	−17.6	31 35	+14.5	−17.3
32 26	+14.8	−17.5	33 20	+14.6	−17.2
34 17	+14.9	−17.4	35 17	+14.7	−17.1
36 20	+15.0	−17.3	37 26	+14.8	−17.0
38 36	+15.1	−17.2	39 50	+14.9	−16.9
41 08	+15.2	−17.1	42 31	+15.0	−16.8
43 59	+15.3	−17.0	45 31	+15.1	−16.7
47 10	+15.4	−16.9	48 55	+15.2	−16.6
50 46	+15.5	−16.8	52 44	+15.3	−16.5
54 49	+15.6	−16.7	57 02	+15.4	−16.4
59 23	+15.7	−16.6	61 51	+15.5	−16.3
64 30	+15.8	−16.5	67 17	+15.6	−16.2
70 12	+15.9	−16.4	73 16	+15.7	−16.1
76 26	+16.0	−16.3	79 43	+15.8	−16.0
83 05	+16.1	−16.2	86 32	+15.9	−15.9
90 00			90 00		

STARS AND PLANETS App Alt.	Corrⁿ
° ′	′
9 56	−5.3
10 08	−5.2
10 20	−5.1
10 33	−5.0
10 46	−4.9
11 00	−4.8
11 14	−4.7
11 29	−4.6
11 45	−4.5
12 01	−4.4
12 18	−4.3
12 35	−4.2
12 54	−4.1
13 13	−4.0
13 33	−3.9
13 54	−3.8
14 16	−3.7
14 40	−3.6
15 04	−3.5
15 30	−3.4
15 57	−3.3
16 26	−3.2
16 56	−3.1
17 28	−3.0
18 02	−2.9
18 38	−2.8
19 17	−2.7
19 58	−2.6
20 42	−2.5
21 28	−2.4
22 19	−2.3
23 13	−2.2
24 11	−2.1
25 14	−2.0
26 22	−1.9
27 36	−1.8
28 56	−1.7
30 24	−1.6
32 00	−1.5
33 45	−1.4
35 40	−1.3
37 48	−1.2
40 08	−1.1
42 44	−1.0
45 36	−0.9
48 47	−0.8
52 18	−0.7
56 11	−0.6
60 28	−0.5
65 08	−0.4
70 11	−0.3
75 34	−0.2
81 13	−0.1
87 03	0.0
90 00	

App. Alt.	Additional Corrⁿ
2003	
VENUS	
Jan. 1–Feb. 20	
°	′
0	+0.2
41	+0.1
76	
Feb. 21–Dec. 31	
°	′
0	+0.1
60	
MARS	
Jan. 1–May 2, Dec. 17–Dec. 31	
°	′
0	+0.1
60	
May 3–June 26, Oct. 26–Dec. 16	
°	′
0	+0.2
41	+0.1
76	
June 27–Aug. 1, Sept. 23–Oct. 25	
°	′
0	+0.3
34	+0.2
60	+0.1
80	
Aug. 2–Sept. 22	
°	′
0	+0.4
29	+0.3
51	+0.2
68	+0.1
83	

DIP Ht. of Eye	Corrⁿ	Ht. of Eye
m	′	ft.
2.4	−2.8	8.0
2.6	−2.9	8.6
2.8	−3.0	9.2
3.0	−3.1	9.8
3.2	−3.2	10.5
3.4	−3.3	11.2
3.6	−3.4	11.9
3.8	−3.5	12.6
4.0	−3.6	13.3
4.3	−3.7	14.1
4.5	−3.8	14.9
4.7	−3.9	15.7
5.0	−4.0	16.5
5.2	−4.1	17.4
5.5	−4.2	18.3
5.8	−4.3	19.1
6.1	−4.4	20.1
6.3	−4.5	21.0
6.6	−4.6	22.0
6.9	−4.7	22.9
7.2	−4.8	23.9
7.5	−4.9	24.9
7.9	−5.0	26.0
8.2	−5.1	27.1
8.5	−5.2	28.1
8.8	−5.3	29.2
9.2	−5.4	30.4
9.5	−5.5	31.5
9.9	−5.6	32.7
10.3	−5.7	33.9
10.6	−5.8	35.1
11.0	−5.9	36.3
11.4	−6.0	37.6
11.8	−6.1	38.9
12.2	−6.2	40.1
12.6	−6.3	41.5
13.0	−6.4	42.8
13.4	−6.5	44.2
13.8	−6.6	45.5
14.2	−6.7	46.9
14.7	−6.8	48.4
15.1	−6.9	49.8
15.5	−7.0	51.3
16.0	−7.1	52.8
16.5	−7.2	54.3
16.9	−7.3	55.8
17.4	−7.4	57.4
17.9	−7.5	58.9
18.4	−7.6	60.5
18.8	−7.7	62.1
19.3	−7.8	63.8
19.8	−7.9	65.4
20.4	−8.0	67.1
20.9	−8.1	68.8
21.4		70.5

DIP Ht. of Eye	Corrⁿ
m	′
1.0	−1.8
1.5	−2.2
2.0	−2.5
2.5	−2.8
3.0	−3.0
See table ←	
m	′
20	−7.9
22	−8.3
24	−8.6
26	−9.0
28	−9.3
30	−9.6
32	−10.0
34	−10.3
36	−10.6
38	−10.8
40	−11.1
42	−11.4
44	−11.7
46	−11.9
48	−12.2
ft.	′
2	−1.4
4	−1.9
6	−2.4
8	−2.7
10	−3.1
See table ←	
ft.	′
70	−8.1
75	−8.4
80	−8.7
85	−8.9
90	−9.2
95	−9.5
100	−9.7
105	−9.9
110	−10.2
115	−10.4
120	−10.6
125	−10.8
130	−11.1
135	−11.3
140	−11.5
145	−11.7
150	−11.9
155	−12.1

App. Alt. = Apparent altitude = Sextant altitude corrected for index error and dip.

Figure 48

ALTITUDE CORRECTION TABLES 10°-90°—SUN, STARS, PLANETS

OCT.—MAR. SUN App. Alt.	Lower Limb	Upper Limb	APR.—SEPT. SUN App. Alt.	Lower Limb	Upper Limb
° ′	′	′	° ′	′	′
9 34	+10.8	−21.5	9 39	+10.6	−21.2
9 45	+10.9	−21.4	9 51	+10.7	−21.1
9 56	+11.0	−21.3	10 03	+10.8	−21.0
10 08	+11.1	−21.2	10 15	+10.9	−20.9
10 21	+11.2	−21.1	10 27	+11.0	−20.8
10 34	+11.3	−21.0	10 40	+11.1	−20.7
10 47	+11.4	−20.9	10 54	+11.2	−20.6
11 01	+11.5	−20.8	11 08	+11.3	−20.5
11 15	+11.6	−20.7	11 23	+11.4	−20.4
11 30	+11.7	−20.6	11 38	+11.5	−20.3
11 46	+11.8	−20.5	11 54	+11.6	−20.2
12 02	+11.9	−20.4	12 10	+11.7	−20.1
12 19	+12.0	−20.3	12 28	+11.8	−20.0
12 37	+12.1	−20.2	12 46	+11.9	−19.9
12 55	+12.2	−20.1	13 05	+12.0	−19.8
13 14	+12.3	−20.0	13 24	+12.1	−19.7
13 35	+12.4	−19.9	13 45	+12.2	−19.6
13 56	+12.5	−19.8	14 07	+12.3	−19.5
14 18	+12.6	−19.7	14 30	+12.4	−19.4
14 42	+12.7	−19.6	14 54	+12.5	−19.3
15 06	+12.8	−19.5	15 19	+12.6	−19.2
15 32	+12.9	−19.4	15 46	+12.7	−19.1
15 59	+13.0	−19.3	16 14	+12.8	−19.0
16 28	+13.1	−19.2	16 44	+12.9	−18.9
16 59	+13.2	−19.1	17 15	+13.0	−18.8
17 32	+13.3	−19.0	17 48	+13.1	−18.7
18 06	+13.4	−18.9	18 24	+13.2	−18.6
18 42	+13.5	−18.8	19 01	+13.3	−18.5
19 21	+13.6	−18.7	19 42	+13.4	−18.4
20 03	+13.7	−18.6	20 25	+13.5	−18.3
20 48	+13.8	−18.5	21 11	+13.6	−18.2
21 35	+13.9	−18.4	22 00	+13.7	−18.1
22 26	+14.0	−18.3	22 54	+13.8	−18.0
23 22	+14.1	−18.2	23 51	+13.9	−17.9
24 21	+14.2	−18.1	24 53	+14.0	−17.8
25 26	+14.3	−18.0	26 00	+14.1	−17.7
26 36	+14.4	−17.9	27 13	+14.2	−17.6
27 52	+14.5	−17.8	28 33	+14.3	−17.5
29 15	+14.6	−17.7	30 00	+14.4	−17.4
30 46	+14.7	−17.6	31 35	+14.5	−17.3
32 26	+14.8	−17.5	33 20	+14.6	−17.2
34 17	+14.9	−17.4	35 17	+14.7	−17.1
36 20	+15.0	−17.3	37 26	+14.8	−17.0
38 36	+15.1	−17.2	39 50	+14.9	−16.9
41 08	+15.2	−17.1	42 31	+15.0	−16.8
43 59	+15.3	−17.0	45 31	+15.1	−16.7
47 10	+15.4	−16.9	48 55	+15.2	−16.6
50 46	+15.5	−16.8	52 44	+15.3	−16.5
54 49	+15.6	−16.7	57 02	+15.4	−16.4
59 23	+15.7	−16.6	61 51	+15.5	−16.3
64 30	+15.8	−16.5	67 17	+15.6	−16.2
70 12	+15.9	−16.4	73 16	+15.7	−16.1
76 26	+16.0	−16.3	79 43	+15.8	−16.0
83 05	+16.1	−16.2	86 32	+15.9	−15.9
90 00			90 00		

STARS AND PLANETS App Alt.	Corrⁿ
° ′	′
9 56	−5.3
10 08	−5.2
10 20	−5.1
10 33	−5.0
10 46	−4.9
11 00	−4.8
11 14	−4.7
11 29	−4.6
11 45	−4.5
12 01	−4.4
12 18	−4.3
12 35	−4.2
12 54	−4.1
13 13	−4.0
13 33	−3.9
13 54	−3.8
14 16	−3.7
14 40	−3.6
15 04	−3.5
15 30	−3.4
15 57	−3.3
16 26	−3.2
16 56	−3.1
17 28	−3.0
18 02	−2.9
18 38	−2.8
19 17	−2.7
19 58	−2.6
20 42	−2.5
21 28	−2.4
22 19	−2.3
23 13	−2.2
24 11	−2.1
25 14	−2.0
26 22	−1.9
27 36	−1.8
28 56	−1.7
30 24	−1.6
32 00	−1.5
33 45	−1.4
35 40	−1.3
37 48	−1.2
40 08	−1.1
42 44	−1.0
45 36	−0.9
48 47	−0.8
52 18	−0.7
56 11	−0.6
60 28	−0.5
65 08	−0.4
70 11	−0.3
75 34	−0.2
81 13	−0.1
87 03	0.0
90 00	

App. Alt.	Additional Corrⁿ
2003	
VENUS	
Jan. 1–Feb. 20	
°	′
0	+0.2
41	+0.1
76	
Feb. 21–Dec. 31	
°	′
0	+0.1
60	
MARS	
Jan. 1–May 2, Dec. 17–Dec. 31	
°	′
0	+0.1
60	
May 3–June 26, Oct. 26–Dec. 16	
°	′
0	+0.2
41	+0.1
76	
June 27–Aug. 1, Sept. 23–Oct. 25	
°	′
0	+0.3
34	+0.2
60	+0.1
80	
Aug. 2–Sept. 22	
°	′
0	+0.4
29	+0.3
51	+0.2
68	+0.1
83	

DIP Ht. of Eye	Corrⁿ	Ht. of Eye
m	′	ft.
2.4	−2.8	8.0
2.6	−2.9	8.6
2.8	−3.0	9.2
3.0	−3.1	9.8
3.2	−3.2	10.5
3.4	−3.3	11.2
3.6	−3.4	11.9
3.8	−3.5	12.6
4.0	−3.6	13.3
4.3	−3.7	14.1
4.5	−3.8	14.9
4.7	−3.9	15.7
5.0	−4.0	16.5
5.2	−4.1	17.4
5.5	−4.2	18.3
5.8	−4.3	19.1
6.1	−4.4	20.1
6.3	−4.5	21.0
6.6	−4.6	22.0
6.9	−4.7	22.9
7.2	−4.8	23.9
7.5	−4.9	24.9
7.9	−5.0	26.0
8.2	−5.1	27.1
8.5	−5.2	28.1
8.8	−5.3	29.2
9.2	−5.4	30.4
9.5	−5.5	31.5
9.9	−5.6	32.7
10.3	−5.7	33.9
10.6	−5.8	35.1
11.0	−5.9	36.3
11.4	−6.0	37.6
11.8	−6.1	38.9
12.2	−6.2	40.1
12.6	−6.3	41.5
13.0	−6.4	42.8
13.4	−6.5	44.2
13.8	−6.6	45.5
14.2	−6.7	46.9
14.7	−6.8	48.4
15.1	−6.9	49.8
15.5	−7.0	51.3
16.0	−7.1	52.8
16.5	−7.2	54.3
16.9	−7.3	55.8
17.4	−7.4	57.4
17.9	−7.5	58.9
18.4	−7.6	60.5
18.8	−7.7	62.1
19.3	−7.8	63.8
19.8	−7.9	65.4
20.4	−8.0	67.1
20.9	−8.1	68.8
21.4		70.5

DIP Ht. of Eye	Corrⁿ
m	′
1.0	−1.8
1.5	−2.2
2.0	−2.5
2.5	−2.8
3.0	−3.0
See table ←	
m	′
20	−7.9
22	−8.3
24	−8.6
26	−9.0
28	−9.3
30	−9.6
32	−10.0
34	−10.3
36	−10.6
38	−10.8
40	−11.1
42	−11.4
44	−11.7
46	−11.9
48	−12.2
ft.	′
2	−1.4
4	−1.9
6	−2.4
8	−2.7
10	−3.1
See table ←	
ft.	′
70	−8.1
75	−8.4
80	−8.7
85	−8.9
90	−9.2
95	−9.5
100	−9.7
105	−9.9
110	−10.2
115	−10.4
120	−10.6
125	−10.8
130	−11.1
135	−11.3
140	−11.5
145	−11.7
150	−11.9
155	−12.1

App. Alt. = Apparent altitude = Sextant altitude corrected for index error and dip.

Figure 48a

Sextant corrections in the proforma

Step 1 (Figure 49) Input your sextant altitude (SA) and underline the circle to indicate that our sight was 'lower limb'.

Step 2 (Figure 50) Input your index error and undertake calculation (this would have been established when undertaking our sextant corrections).

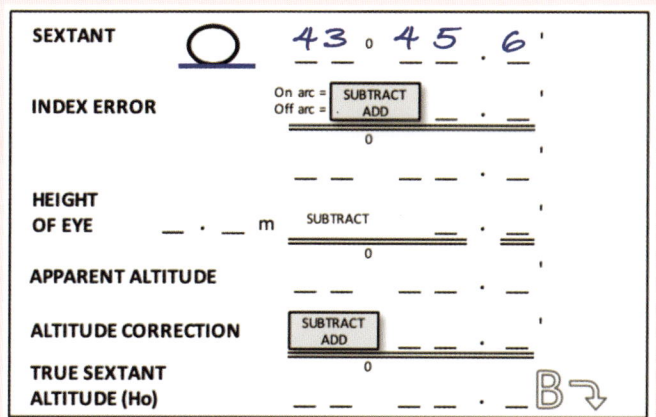

Figure 49

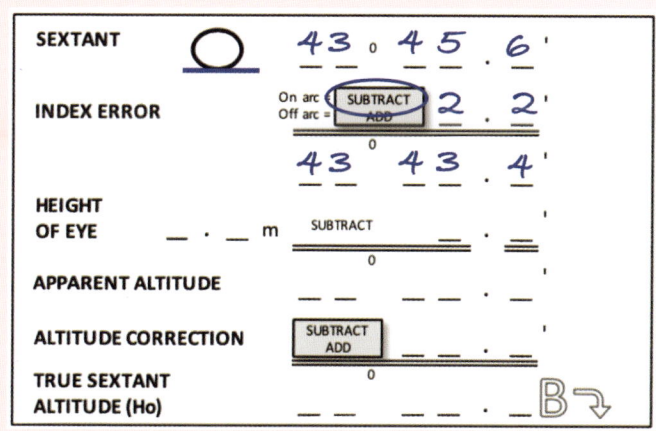

Figure 50

Step 3 (Figure 51) Input your height of eye above sea level into the proforma. Refer to the Alt' Corr' Table shown in Figure 48a. Looking at the orange box, look up your height and select the corresponding correction. This correction is in minutes of angle and is always subtracted. 4.3 sits between 3.6 or 3.7. It won't make much difference if you choose either. However, given this situation you should go for the figure diagonally upwards, eg 3.6.

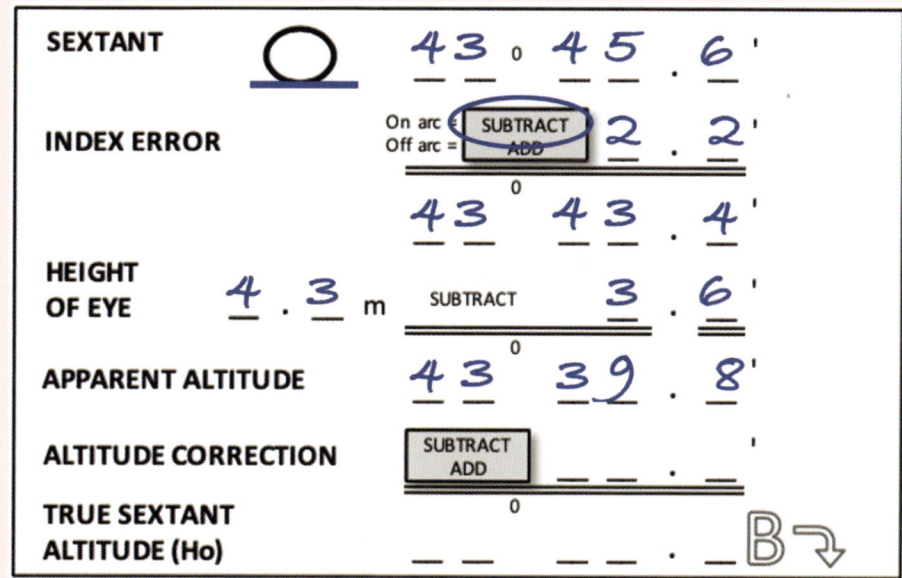

Figure 51

Step 4 (Figure 52) We now take our last result (Apparent Altitude) and refer to the blue box. This blue box looks at the altitude corrections discussed earlier. It is split into two halves, depending on the time of year. Because of our date, we require the right half. This right half now gives us the choice of Lower Limb or Upper Limb. Because our sight was lower limb we require the information contained within the red box. We find our value of 43° 39.8' sits between 42° 31.0' and 45° 31.0'. We therefore apply a correction of +15' to our proforma.

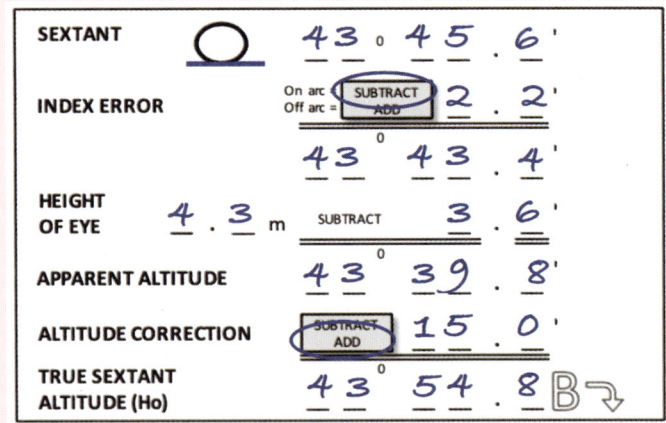

Figure 52

This result of 43° 54.8' is now referred to as our *true sextant altitude* or *Ho*.

Why is the *true sextant altitude* called *Ho*? The *H* stands for horizon. For the purpose of understanding this definition, instead of thinking that the sextant is used to measure the altitude (angle) of the sun *from the horizon*, think of it as measuring the altitude of the horizon *from the sun*. The angle is the same either way, it's just a matter of perception. '*o*' stands for observed because it's the altitude that we have actually taken.

We'll look at how this 'piece of the jigsaw' fits in due course.

CHAPTER FIVE

The PZX triangle

We're now going to continue from where we left off at the end of Chapter 2. We'd established that the great circle relationship means that the ZD (ZD = 90° – SA) is directly related to our distance from the GP. We said that we could plot this, but due to scale this wouldn't offer us accurate position fixing. Before we look at the process we use to improve our accuracy, let's look at some more background.

We can establish the length of ZX using our sextant relationship to ZD as shown in Figure 22 (reproduced again below). In other words, there is a relationship between our sextant altitude and our distance from the GP (or distance from Z to X).

Just to be sure we've completed the 'circle' in our understanding, Figure 22 represents a cut through of the (blue) great circle created in Figure 53. In other words, we've sliced the earth in half, along the blue great circle, removed the bottom half and Figure 22 is a view of the earth from the direction of the arrow in Figure 53.

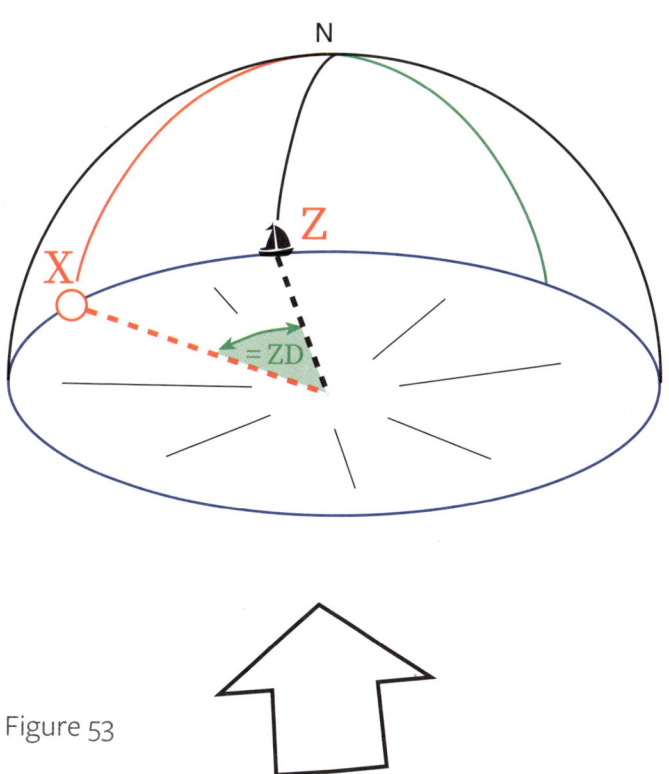

Figure 22

Figure 53

Let's look at the PZX triangle. Several mathematical relationships exist in this arrangement that use spherical trigonometry. The following isn't exactly how spherical trigonometry works, but it can help to think of it as follows:

We will be using tables, based on spherical trigonometry, that <u>calculate</u> the length of ZX – or, more accurately, they will give us a hypothetical sextant altitude based on this distance. The reasons for this will become clear in the next chapter.

A BIT OF BACKGROUND

Figure 54 illustrates a situation we might have at any given time. Imagine we have ourselves and the sun in a frozen moment of time. The sun's GP sits on a great circle because it is on a meridian and all meridians form part of a great circle. Our vessel also sits on a great circle for the same reason. We then have our third great circle, which is the extension of connecting the DR position and the sun's GP. (The terms dead reckoning, DR, and estimated position, EP, are often interchanged in celestial navigation. We'll be using DR, this being our position based on distance and direction travelled.) As part of our second definition of a great circle, we said that if we draw a line between any two points on the earth's surface and connect them with

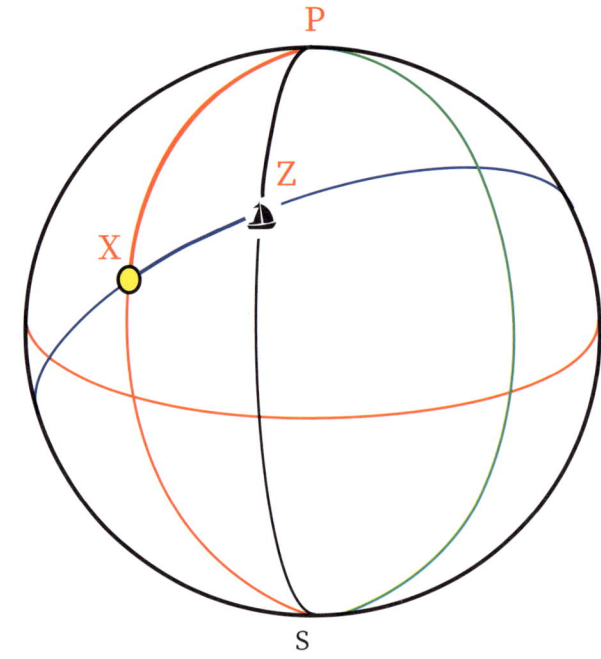

Figure 54

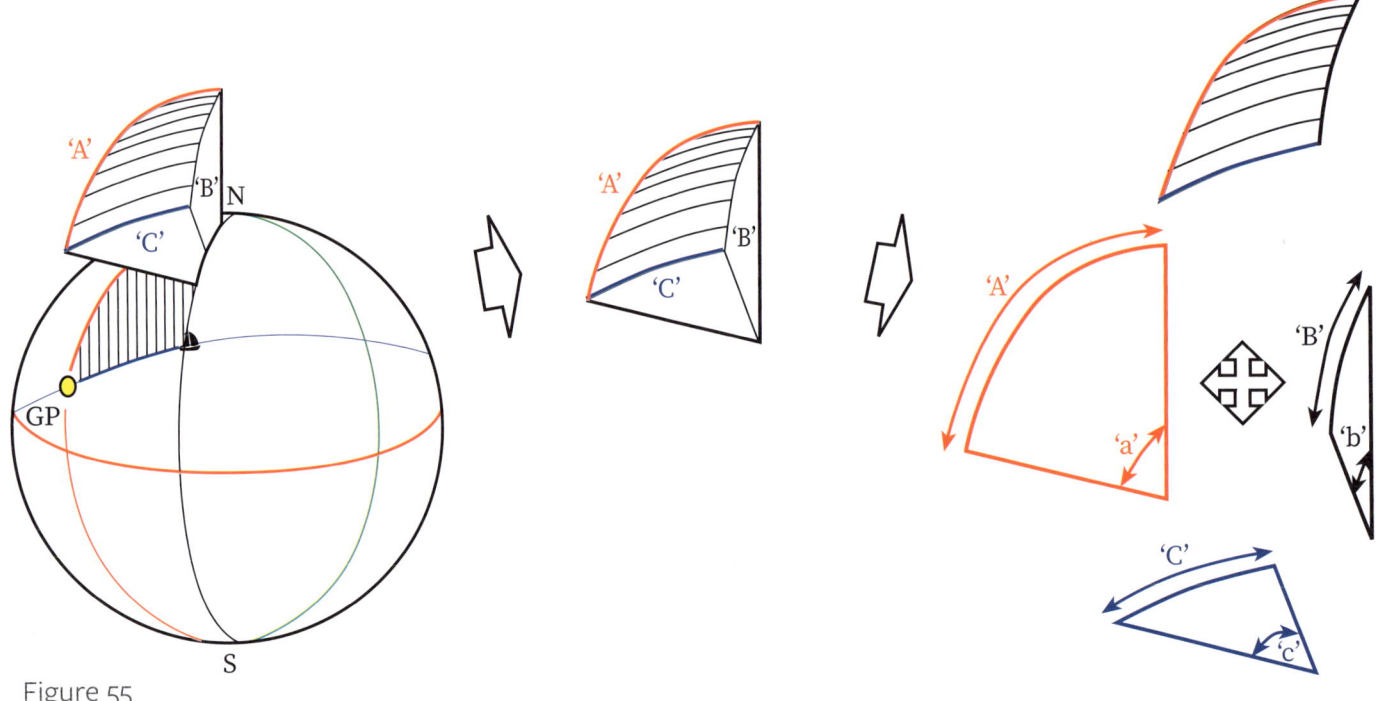

Figure 55

the shortest possible line, we would also form a great circle. In other words, we have created a triangle on the surface of the earth, one with all its sides being formed by great circles. This is significant.

Let's explore this important relationship in a bit more detail using Figure 55.

We've now removed the wedge-shaped triangle. Looking at the right-hand images, we have a very interesting relationship. Now, we've already said each side forms part of a great circle. We therefore have a situation where:

The length of side 'A' is related to angle 'a'
The length of side 'B' is related to angle 'b'
The length of side 'C' is related to angle 'c' (equals ZD)

– all due to the great circle relationship.

We're not going any further down this rabbit hole in this book, but the relationship becomes even more interesting because the angular relationship is extended to the *green* angles contained in Figure 56. Now you get the idea where the association between celestial navigation and spherical trigonometry comes from.

Remember that the length 'C' (blue) is of importance to us as this gives us our vessel's distance from the sun's GP.

Centuries ago, some very clever mathematicians used the remarkable relationship we've been discussing in Chapters 1, 2 and now again here, to come up with the solution to position fixing at sea, one that offered the degree of accuracy to 3 or 4nm quoted earlier.

In summary, we can establish the length of ZX using our sextant (relationship to ZD).

In Chapter 7 we'll be introducing some tables known as 'Sight Reduction Tables'. These tables *calculate* the length of ZX, using the PZX triangle and spherical trigonometry, and give us a hypothetical *calculated* sextant altitude based on this distance. The next chapter looks at the significance of this.

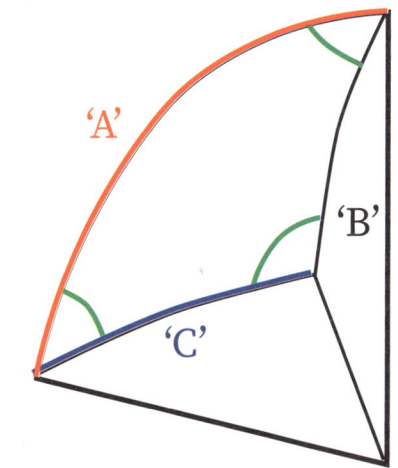

Figure 56

CHAPTER SIX

The intercept method

Before continuing, let's take stock of where our understanding should be up to.

We should understand:

- the great circle relationship (angles versus distance around circumference)

- the terms geographical position (GP), dead reckoning (DR) position, zenith and zenith distance (ZD)

- the great circle relationships whereby, given a sextant altitude (SA), we can obtain our distance from the GP and we can 'reverse engineer' the process and obtain a sextant altitude from a given distance

- the terms declination (Dec.) and Greenwich Hour Angle (GHA)

- how to obtain the GP (made up of Dec. and GHA)

- that the sextant is used to measure the angle between the horizon and the sun in order to obtain the SA

- the terms *index error, dip, semi-diameter, parallax* and *refraction* and how to apply these corrections to our sextant altitude using the Altitude Correction Tables which will give us our *true sextant altitude (Ho)*

- the 'PZX' triangle.

So, with all of those under our hats, get yourself a cup of tea and here goes....

We've said, using our sextant, we *could* establish our distance from the GP but due to scale this wouldn't give us an accurate result. So what do we do instead? Let's break this down step by step.

Opposite: French skipper Jean-Luc van den Heede sails his boat off Les Sables D'Olonne before winning the Golden Globe race on 29 January 2019. This round-the-world race only allows celestial navigation.

Intercept method

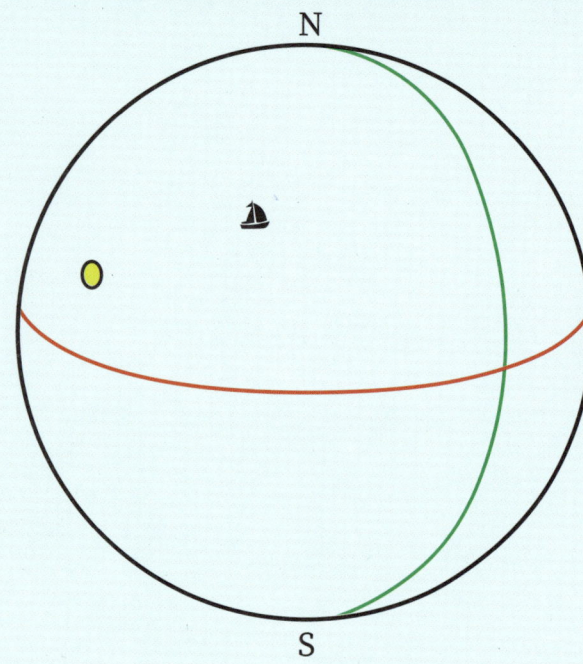

Figure 57

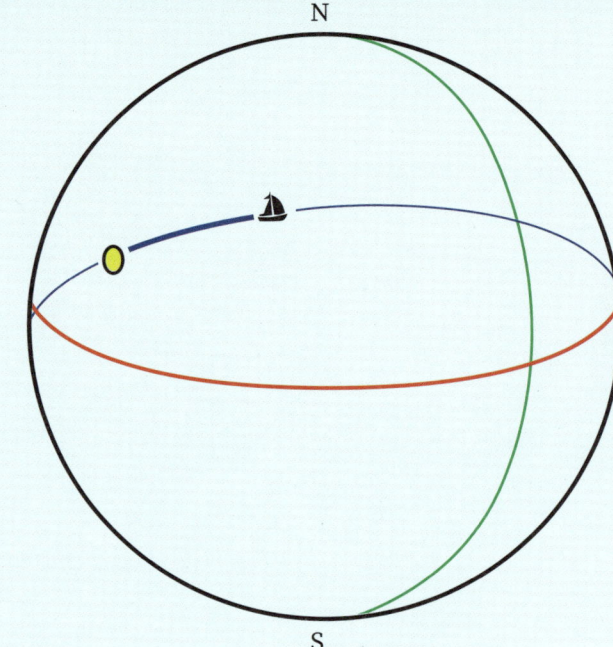

Figure 58

In any given moment, we will know an approximate position of our vessel based on dead reckoning. Dead reckoning gives a position based on our last fix plus the application of how far we have travelled since and in which direction we have been travelling. Now this DR position, shown in Figure 57, may not be very accurate, but that's not too important.

We could then develop this picture, as shown in Figures 58 and 59.

In Figure 58 we have taken the situation into a frozen moment of time and connected the DR position to the GP with the shortest line. In doing so, we have formed part of a great circle (in blue). Figure 59 takes this blue great circle and shows it in cross-section..

Right, here's the clever bit! Remembering the relationship we have in Figure 60, what if we could input certain information regarding our current DR position and the position of the Sun (GP) into specifically prepared tables (based on the mathematical relationship we saw in Chapter 5)? And what if these tables were able to calculate a hypothetical ZD based on this information?

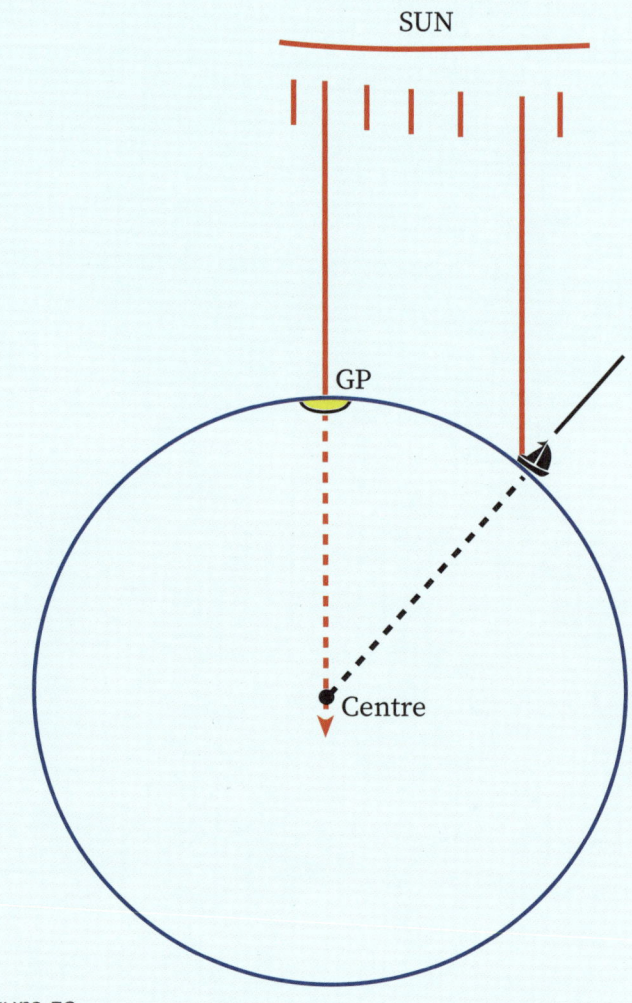

Figure 59

Of course, if they could do this, they could also *calculate* a hypothetical sextant altitude **Hc** (SA = 90° – ZD).

In other words, these tables can *calculate* (hence the 'c' Hc) a hypothetical SA from our DR position. One that *if* we are on our DR position, we should be able to observe ourselves from our vessel.

Let's say that this hypothetical or calculated sextant altitude **Hc** is 70° 00.0'

Now, if we were actually at our DR position, which is highly unlikely given its nature, we would observe the same true sextant altitude (Ho) of 70° 00.0', as shown in Figure 61. Although slightly irrelevant, 70° 00.0' would also be observed from anywhere on the red position circle.

What if in this moment we actually took a sight of the sun, and after corrections, we found we had an *actual* true sextant altitude **Ho** of **70° 10.0'**, as shown in Figure 62? That means we can't be at our DR position (because if we were, we would have an angle of 70° 00.0'). Instead, we are a distance of 10nm from our DR position.

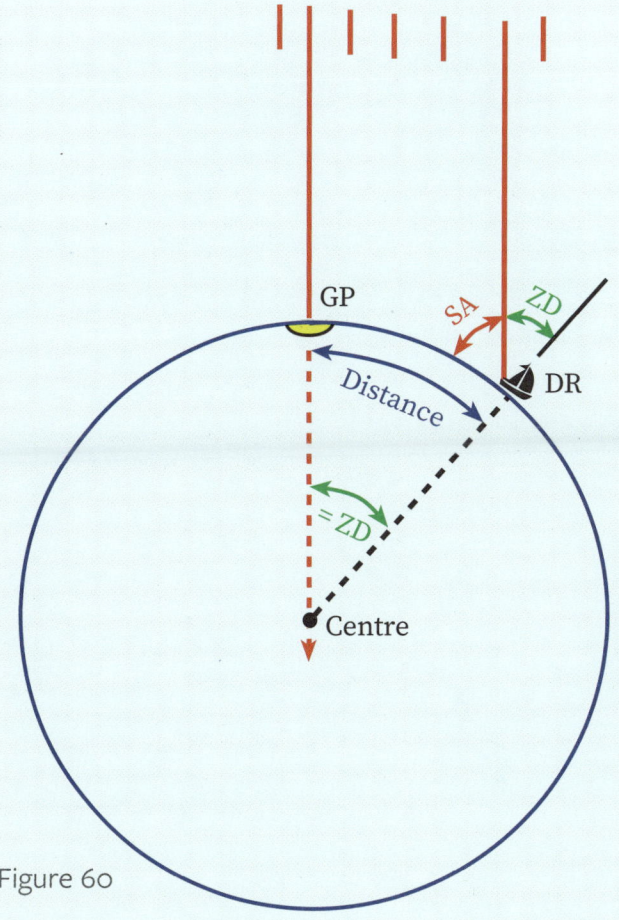

Figure 60

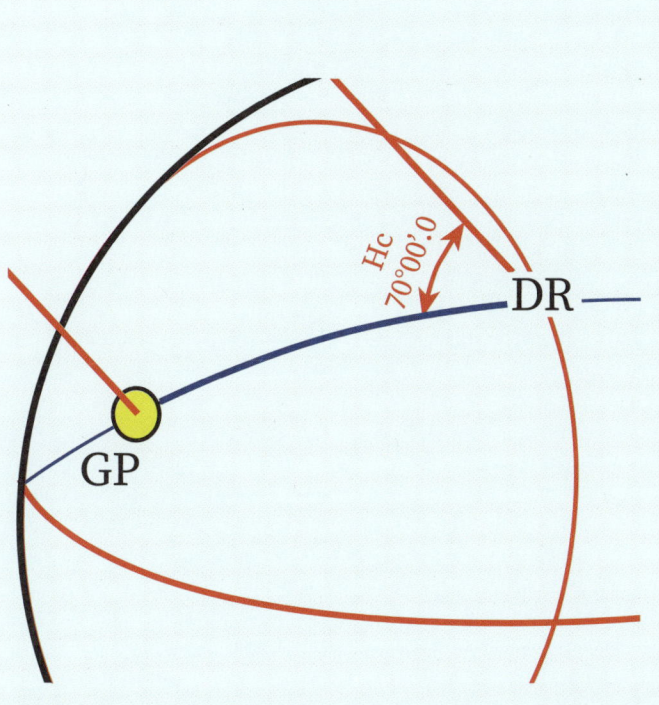

Figure 61

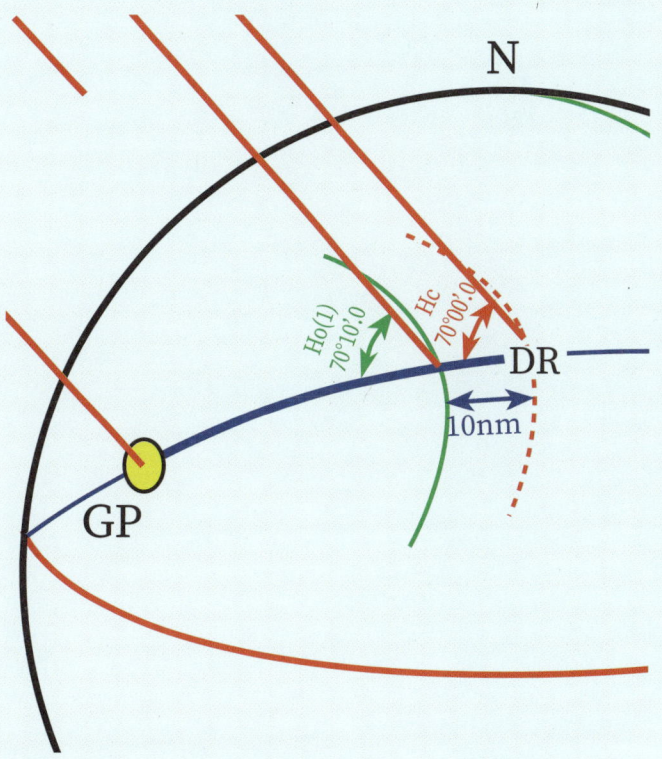

Figure 62

Why? Because the difference between 70° 00.0' and 70° 10.0' = 10' and 10' = 10nm.

We've established we are a distance of 10nm from the DR position, but are we 10nm *away* from the sun's GP or 10nm *towards* the sun's GP from the DR position?

As mentioned previously, if we move *away* from the sun, our SA *decreases* and if we move *towards* the sun the SA *increases*.

Therefore, in this scenario, we are not at our DR position, we are 10nm *towards* the sun from our DR position. We are *definitely* somewhere on the 'green' LOP.

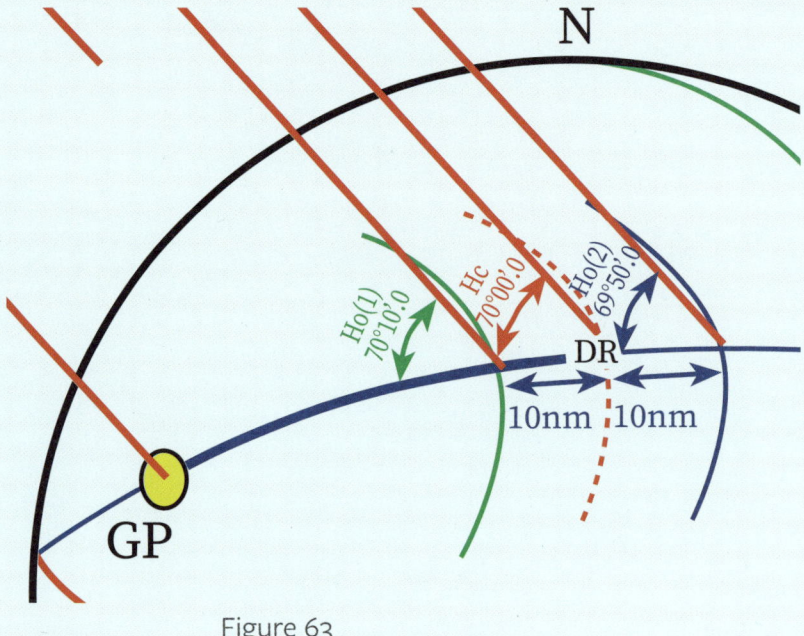

Figure 63

Instead of using the sextant to work out how far away we are from the GP (which doesn't work because of the scale), we use tables to **calculate** a hypothetical sextant altitude from our DR position. We then take the **calculated** sextant altitude and our **observed** sextant altitude and **compare** the difference. Then, using this difference, we measure from the DR position either in a direction **towards** or **away** from the sun.

So, instead of measuring potentially thousands of miles from the GP, we are now only measuring small distances from our DR position. Instead of requiring a small-scale chart (large area) we could do this on a large-scale chart. We'll talk about plotting later. In actual fact we don't use a chart at all, as there are no features that would be pointless. Instead we make our own plotting sheets.

The difference between **calculated** and **observed** sextant altitudes (10nm) is known as the **intercept**. And the method we are using here to obtain our green Line of Position (LOP) is known as the **intercept method**.

It is also known as the **Marcq St Hilaire Method**, named after the captain (later admiral) who proposed the approach. Among all others, it is the most popular method for celestial navigation, and it's the one we are learning here.

As in Figure 63, what if our actual observed true sextant altitude (Ho) had instead been 69° 50.0'? The intercept would have still been 10nm. But this time, because our Ho is smaller, we would be 10nm away from the sun and therefore we would be somewhere on the blue LOP.

Referring back to the scenario in Figure 62, we've calculated that we are *definitely* somewhere on the green line, but where? At the moment we only have half of the picture. We need a second LOP, one that will tell us *where* on the green line we are. Just as we did when looking at the radar scenario in Figure 17 on page 16, a second LOP will tell us where. In order to get that, we need the Sun to move (two or three hours is usually sufficient). We can then take a second sun sight, one that after reduction will give us a second LOP. During this time interval, our vessel will have moved, and we'll also need to factor this movement in. This is what we call a **Sun Run Sun**. The picture will become clearer when we look at plotting.

CHAPTER SEVEN

Sight Reduction Tables

If you've understood everything so far, great, but if not don't worry. It takes time to reread and absorb things.

You'll probably be pleased to hear we're on the slide down to the finish now. There are some hurdles to overcome regarding how the tables are used, and we need to know how to plot and establish our fix, but we are over the summit.

Let's have a look at the tables we use to establish the **calculated sextant altitude (Hc)**, what other information they give us, and what information they require from us.

The tables we use are called **Sight Reduction Tables**. Figure 64 shows the Admiralty ones, produced by the UK Hydrographic Office. Here we have Volumes 2 and 3.

Figure 64

Figure 64a shows alternatives originally designed for air navigation. These offer space and weight saving and are also a very popular choice for sailors (if you think celestial navigation is tricky as you work your way through, imagine doing it while flying an aeroplane).

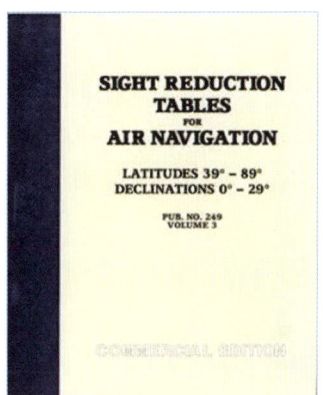
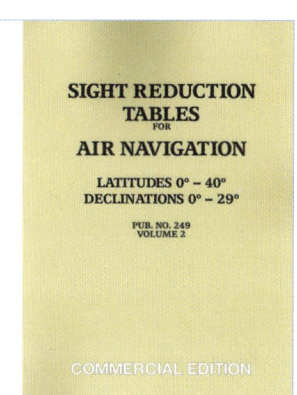

Figure 64a

In essence, these books are very similar. NP 303 (AP 3270) is produced in the UK, whereas No. 249 is produced in the USA.

> For downloadable alternatives go to www.philsomerville.com. Although it should be pointed out that using electronic alternatives does slightly go against the ethos of celestial navigation, where really the use of electronics is not to be relied upon.

THE FOUR KEYS

These tables require from us: latitude, declination, something called Local Hour Angle (LHA) and a condition that needs answering with *same* or *contrary*. Think of these as four *keys* we need to gather through the proforma completion process.

LATITUDE

What the tables actually require is the angle 'b', shown in Figure 65, which is the *Co-lat*. This is a term we haven't mentioned yet. Angle 'a' is often referred to as Co-dec or the Polar Distance. Equally, 'b' is often referred to as the Co-lat. These are used behind the scenes within the tables we will be looking at. 'Co' meaning compliment. However, if we give the tables our DR latitude, the tables can obtain the Co-lat because: Co-lat = 90° – Latitude.

DECLINATION

Again, the tables actually require angle 'a', which we refer to as the *Co-dec* or *Polar Distance*.

If we give the tables the declination, they establish the Co-dec by:

Co-dec = 90° – Declination.

LOCAL HOUR ANGLE (LHA)

The third piece of information required by the tables is called the Local Hour Angle (LHA). True, it has a strange name like GHA, but as we're now aware, when talking about longitude, there is a direct link between angles of longitude and time (see Table 1 on page 7).

Figure 66 introduces this new angle. It is the angle shown in green and it's the angle between the meridian of our vessel's DR position and the meridian of the sun. In other words, it's the difference in longitude between ourselves and the sun's GP.

How do we determine what that is? That depends on whether we are west of the Greenwich Meridian or east of it. So far, all of our illustrations have seen our longitude as west.

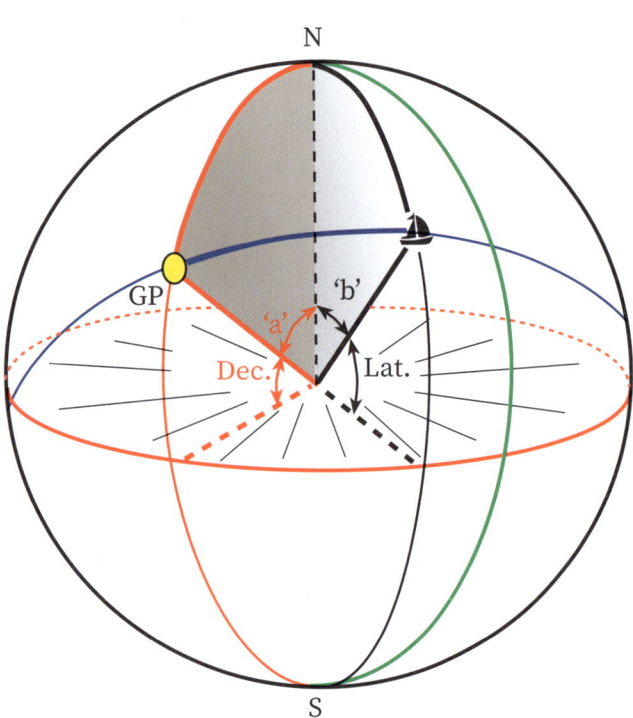

Figure 65

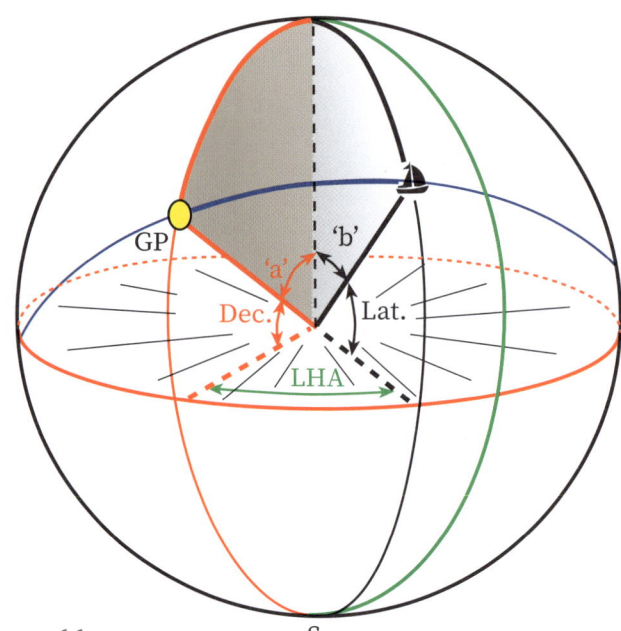

Figure 66

LONGITUDE WEST

Figure 67 develops the picture we've been using. As you can see our longitude is west. So, in this instance:

LHA = GHA – Long.

LONGITUDE EAST

If we are east, we have a slightly different picture, shown in Figure 68.

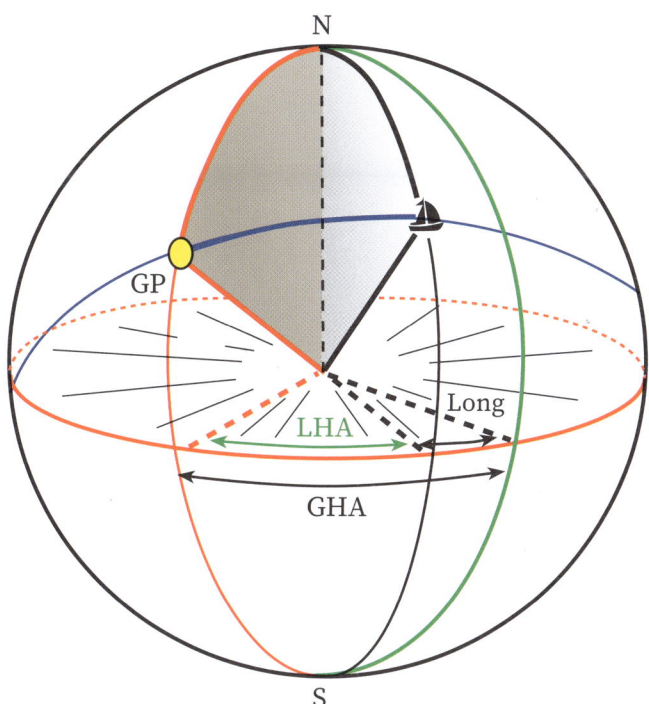

Figure 67

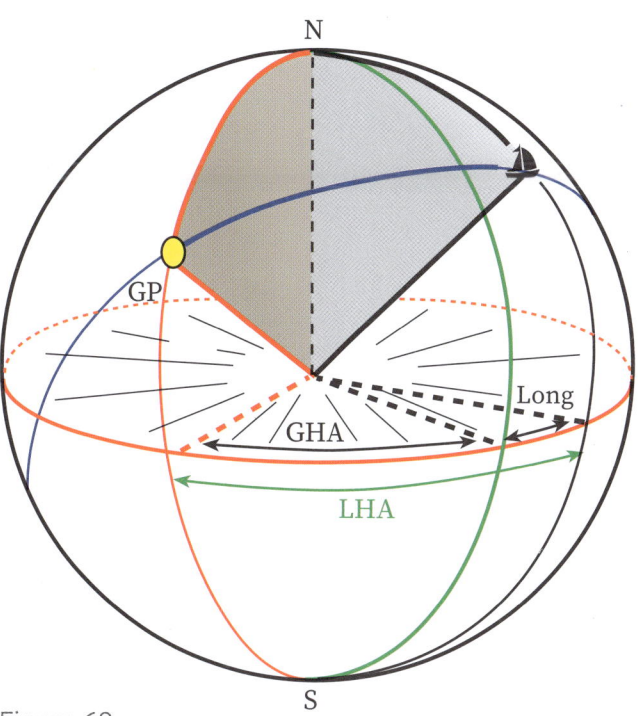

Figure 68

This looks similar to our previous picture. However, this time the PZX triangle is spanning across the Greenwich Meridian.

In this scenario:

LHA = GHA + Long.

DETERMINING IF WE HAVE 'SAME' OR 'CONTRARY'

In the next chapter we'll be undertaking an example of a full sight reduction, so we'll look at these terms as we go through the process.

CHAPTER EIGHT

Undertaking a full sight reduction

OK, we've still got some ground to cover, but the easiest way to cover the remaining hurdles is to undertake a full sun sight reduction. This will take some time and it's better to do this all in one go, so make sure you've got some time free. This will allow for the recap that we'll do at the end and an opportunity to reflect on the process.

We'll look at the following sight:

- 17 April 2020
- DR 50° 47.3' North 015° 47.8' West
- Observed sextant altitude 40° 40.0' taken at 10hr 43min 24sec UT
- Index error 2.0' on the arc
- Height of eye 2.8m
- Sight taken of lower limb.

Extracts from the following will be included as we go through the reduction. However, it will be much better if you obtain the following resources. Being able to navigate through these publications is an important part of the learning process and having them available will help you start this process.

In order to undertake the sight reduction, we need a number of publications.

> ### RESOURCES
>
> - A **nautical almanac**. (I have used a 2020 nautical almanac throughout this book.) Older nautical almanacs are often easy to obtain. Coded vessels are required to carry these and have to update them every year, leaving the old one usually in pristine condition. Included within will be:
> - Altitude Correction Tables 10° to 90° Sun, Stars and Planets
> - Increments and Corrections
> - **Sight Reduction Tables Vol. 3** (39° to 89°)
>   Included within will be:
>   o Table 5
>
> For advice regarding online resources visit www.philsomerville.com.

Armed with all of these, let's go to the proforma.

Sight reduction

Step 1 (Figure 69) Input date and DR position (DR and EP tend to be interchangeable in the world of celestial navigation.)

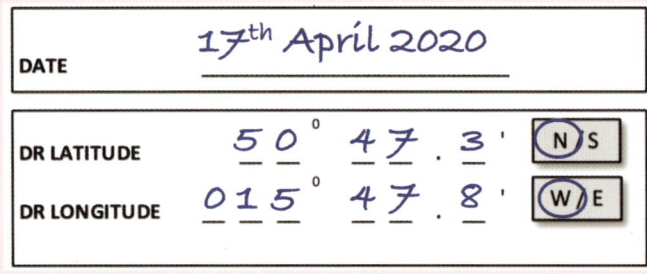

Figure 69

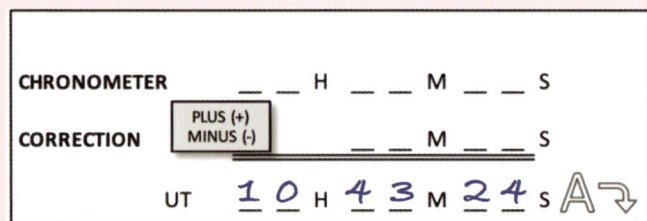

Figure 70

Step 2 (Figure 70) Input the UT time as per illustration (see Chapter 14 for how the rest of the time box is used. In practice this is used to obtain the UT time and date, which on most vessels will be available with a dedicated clock or watch set to UT).

Earlier in the book we likened the sight reduction process to a platform game. We said we collect *key* pieces of information that we need further on in the process. The proforma transfers these *keys* using a lettering system. You will see in Figure 70, there is a capital 'A' with an outward moving arrow. Figure 71 has an inward 'A' indicating that the information, in this case the time, needs transferring.

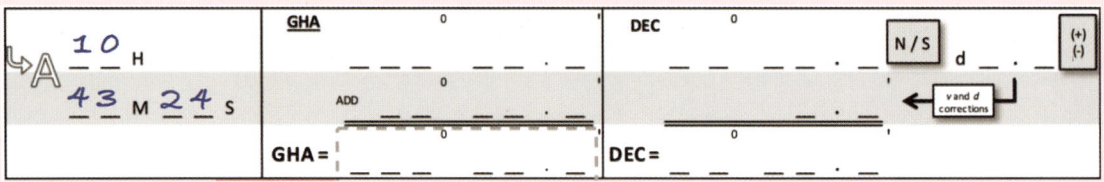

Figure 71

Step 3 (Figure 72) Transfer time and obtain GHA and declination. Have a go at doing this yourself (go back to Chapter 3 if you need a reminder of how to do this).

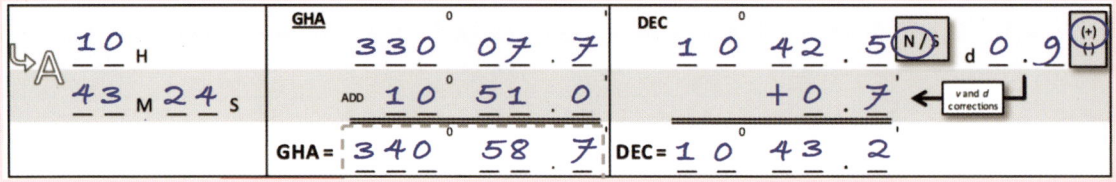

Figure 72

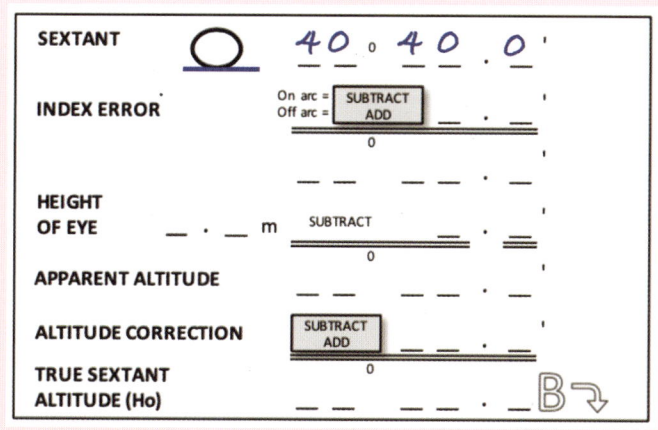

Figure 73

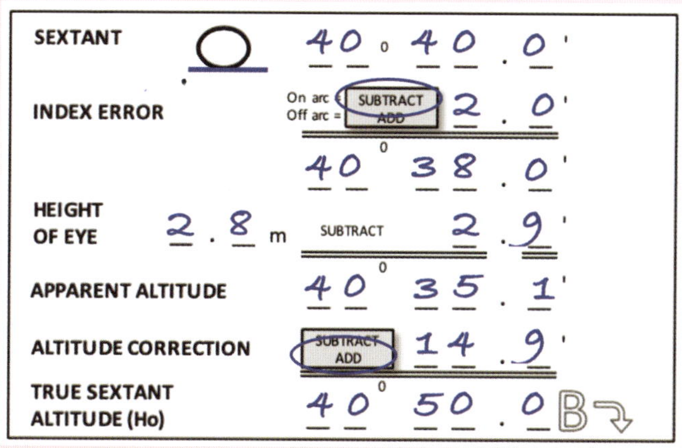

Figure 74

Step 4 (Figure 73) Input sextant altitude, underline lower limb and undertake corrections. Again, try this for yourself, referring to Chapter 4 if needed, before checking your work in Figure 75.

OK, so far, we should have a proforma looking like Figure 75:

Before we continue completing the proforma, we have a concept to get our heads around. But first have a look at Figure 76.

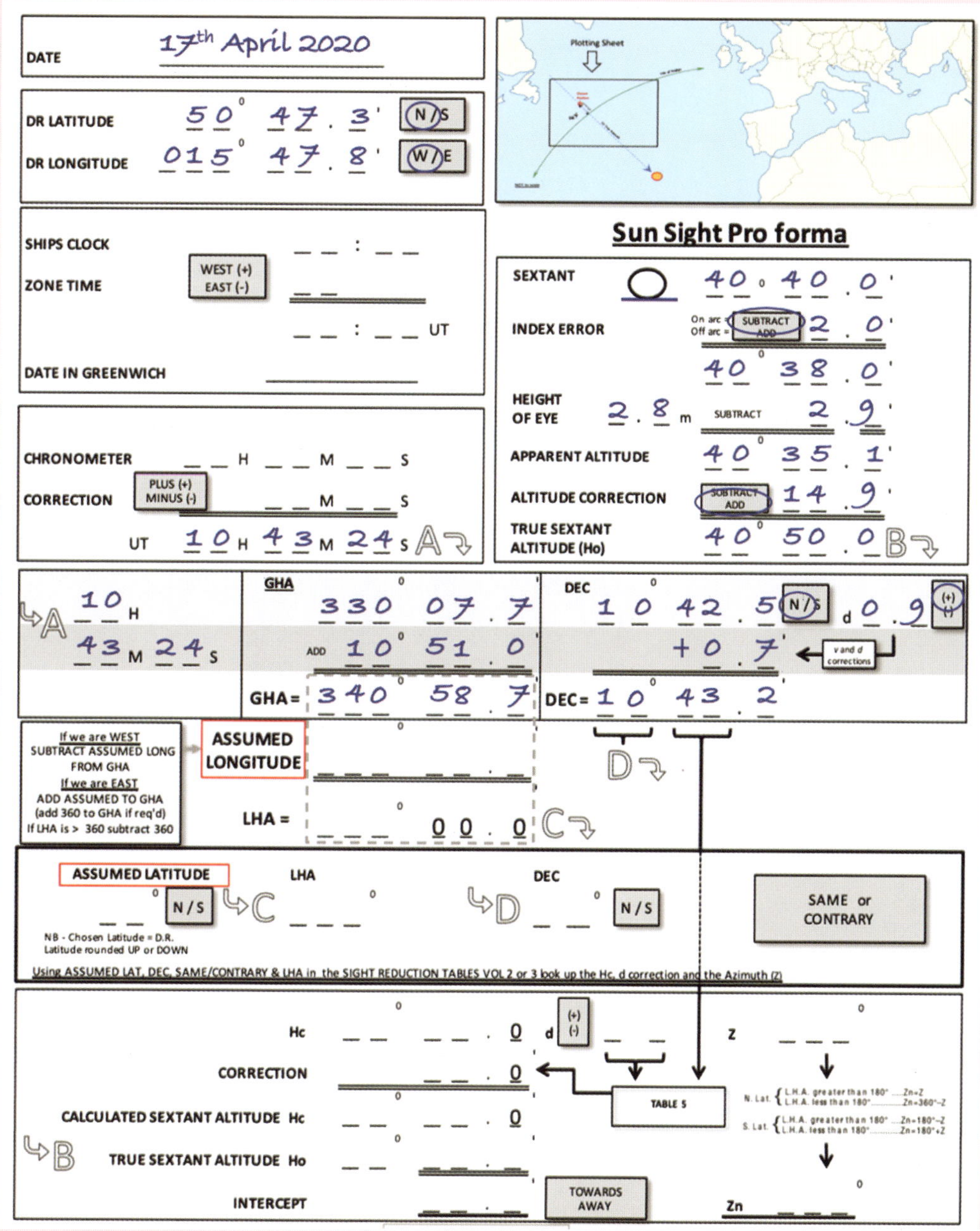

Figure 75

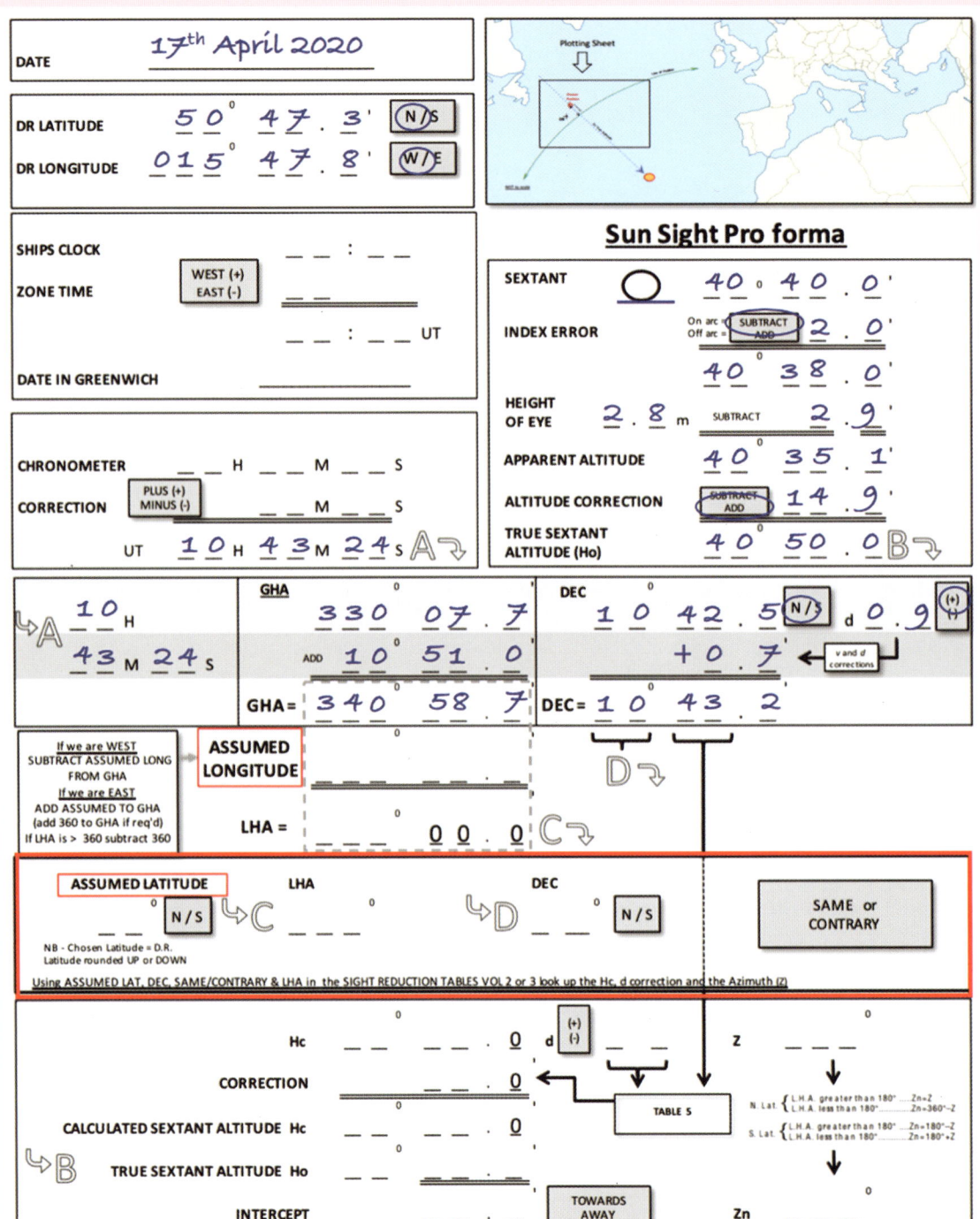

Figure 76

The red box contains the four pieces of information (keys) we need to unlock the Sight Reduction Tables, as discussed in Chapter 6. They are latitude, LHA, declination and same/contrary. Of these, we actually have three of the four, but for now we need to obtain LHA.

Before we continue, it might well be worth revisiting the end of Chapter 7 (in particular Figures 67 and 68) to make sure the information regarding the LHA is fresh in our minds.

In order to obtain the LHA, we either subtract our longitude from the GHA (if west) OR add our longitude to the GHA (if east).

The grey dotted rectangle looks after this calculation on the proforma – as shown in Figure 77. A reminder of how we obtain the LHA is also contained in the proforma – see red box in Figure 78.

Step 5 (Figure 77)

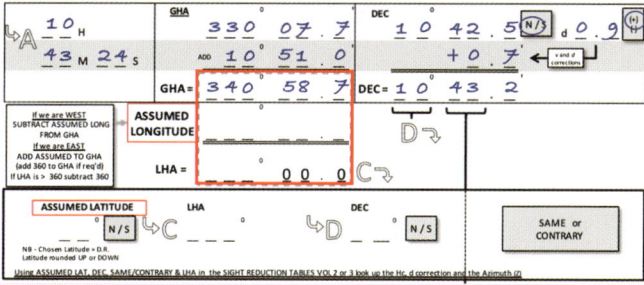

Figure 77

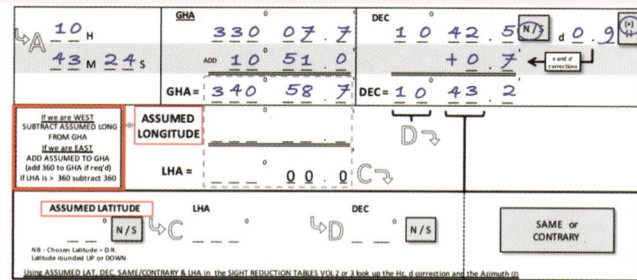

Figure 78

Right, we are west, so we will be subtracting our longitude from the GHA (as per Figure 67).
If we were to input our DR Longitude, we would have the result shown in Figure 79.

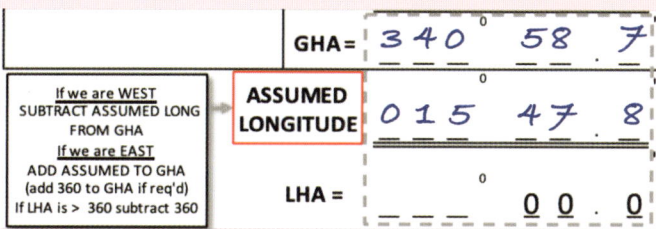

Figure 79

But we have a problem! The tables will only accept an LHA with *whole* degrees, ie there <u>cannot</u> be minutes!

So we have to go back a step, but before we do, let's ask ourselves something. How accurate do we think our DR position is? Several years ago, when crossing the Southern Atlantic, after two days of dead reckoning in stormy weather our DR position was compared with a GPS fix. The DR position was found to be nearly 100nm away. However, inaccuracies in the DR position aren't of vital importance because the intercept compensates for this error (see also Moitessier's quote at the beginning of this book). Our DR position will be the result of a fix (probably 24 hours ago but maybe longer) and then the application of our course and distance steered. Assuming our fix was accurate in the first place, there are a number of variables that will degrade our DR position, ie compass inaccuracy, leeway, log errors, ocean currents etc. In other words, our DR position will not be super accurate.

Therefore, on the basis that it's not that accurate, does it matter if we modify it slightly? The answer is no. We need a reference point near our location, but whether it's our DR position or another location close by, doesn't matter.

So that's what we do. We have to modify both our DR latitude and DR longitude (by as little as possible), to allow the tables to be much smaller than they otherwise would be if they included minutes of LHA instead of just whole degrees.

This new position, which will be near to our DR position, becomes known as an *assumed position* (sometimes known as a chosen position) and is made up of *assumed latitude* and *assumed longitude*.

OK, back to our grey dotted box.

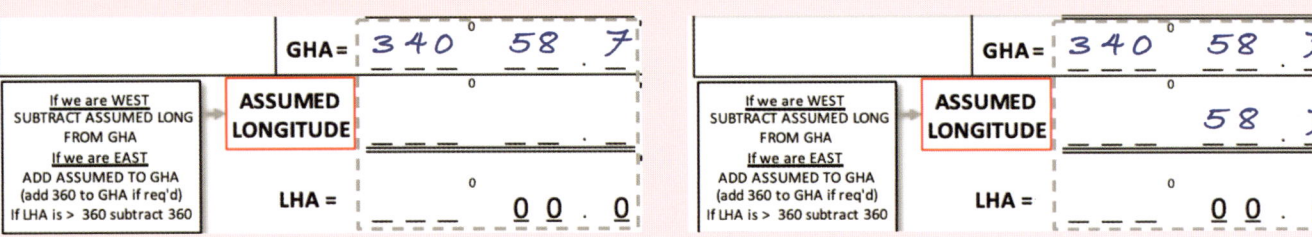

Figure 80

Figure 81

Looking at the minutes, what is the only number that when subtracted (because we are west), would leave 00.0'? The answer is 58.7'.

But really we wanted to input our DR longitude of 015° 47.8' in Figure 81.

So now we must modify our DR longitude, but the question is, what is the closest option?

Should we: move *down* to 014° 58.7'

or

move *up* to 015° 58.7'?

It may help at this point to see our situation on a longitude scale, as shown in Figure 82.

Clearly, 015° 58.7' is closer to our DR longitude, and this is the one we should pick.

Assumed Longitude is a hurdle that can present issues. Sometimes, this is trickier and often needs a bit more thought. (Appendix 9 looks at this aspect in more detail.)

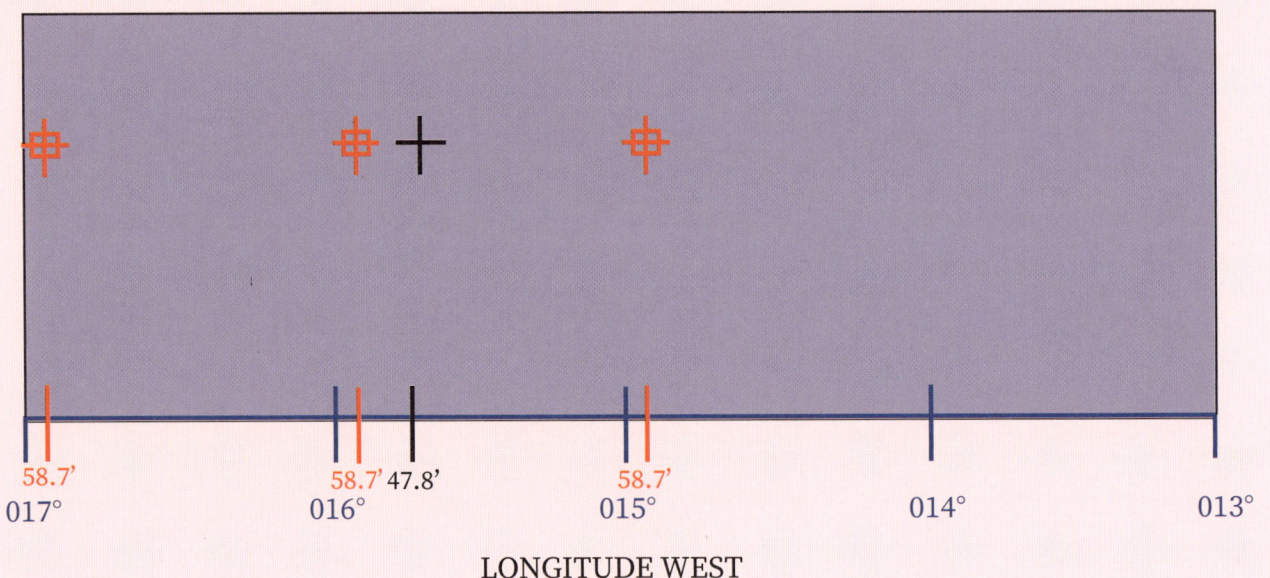

Figure 82

Having decided on 015° 58.7' we can complete our calculation, as shown in Figure 83.

We can now input some of the *keys* we'll need for the Sight Reduction Tables, as shown in Figure 84.

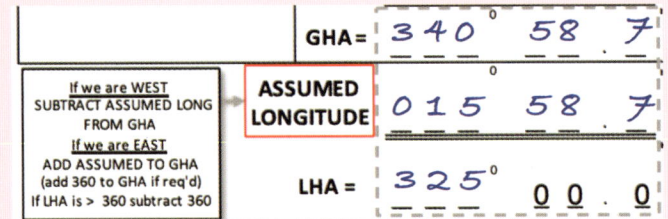

Figure 83

Step 6 (Figure 84)

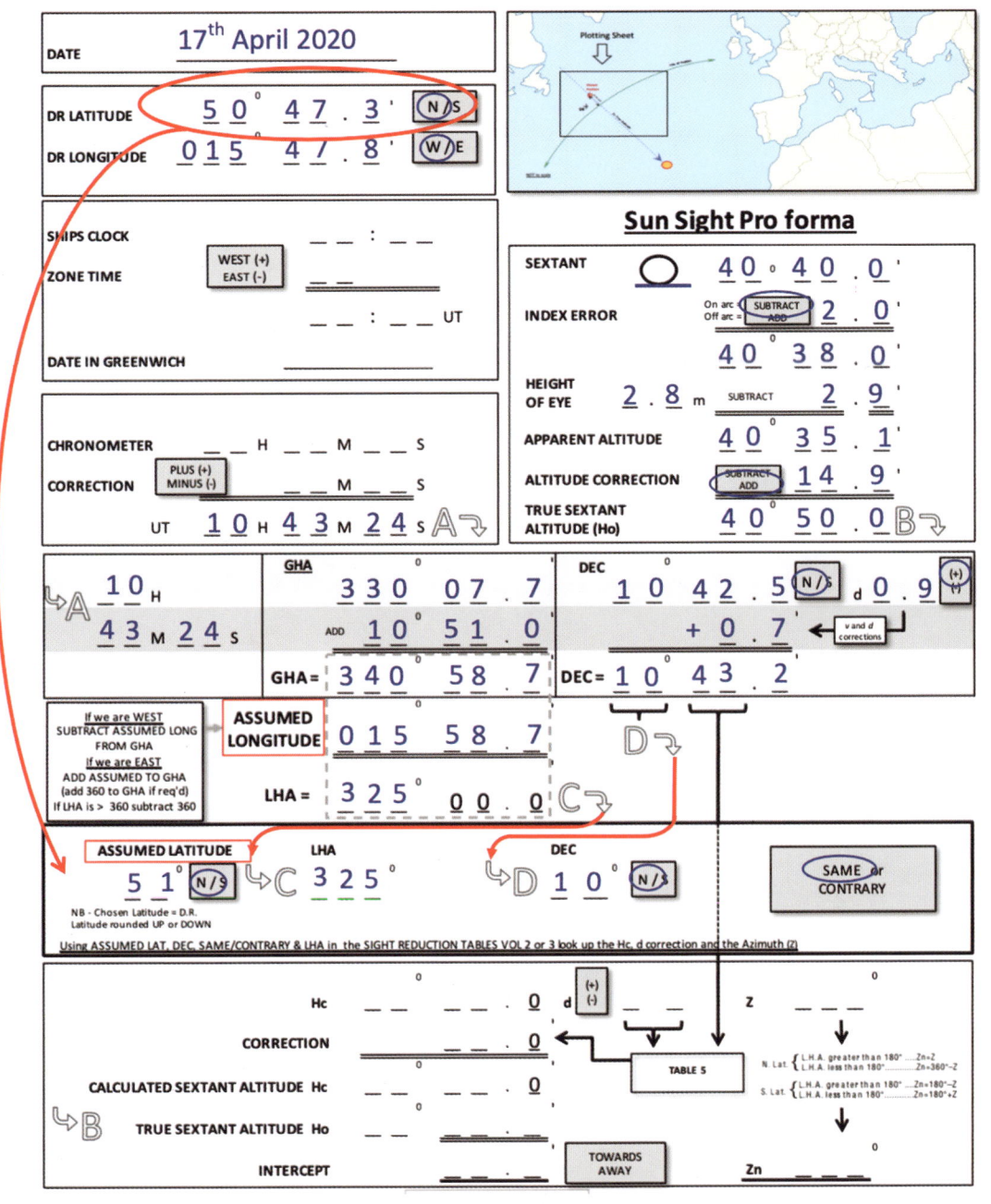

Figure 84

Assumed latitude is our DR latitude rounded <u>up</u> or <u>down</u> to the nearest full degree (in this case our DR position, 50° 47.3' is nearer to 51° than 50°).

LHA follows our system, capital C *out* moved to C *in*.

Declination: Here we take only the *degrees* of declination – we take care of the minutes later. (D *out* moved to D *in*.)

Same or *Contrary* is a condition we need to solve. We need to compare our position and the sun's position and see if we are in the same hemisphere (Same) or opposite hemispheres (Contrary).

Here we can see we are 51° North and the sun is 10° North. Therefore, both are in the northern hemisphere and therefore we circle 'Same'.

SAME OR CONTRARY?

If we are north and the sun's declination north = Same

If we are in the north and the sun in the south = Contrary

If we are in the south and the sun in the south = Same

If we are in the south and the sun in the north = Contrary

We now have the four keys (pieces of information) needed for the Sight Reduction Tables.

Step 7

The sight reduction tables need some familiarisation. We'll be looking at the Sight Reduction Table 40° to 89° because our latitude is 51°. Flicking through the tables you will see they progress through the degrees, one degree at a time.

Let's look at an example. We'll be needing the table for 51°, so let's use that in Figure 85.

This is the first page for 51°.

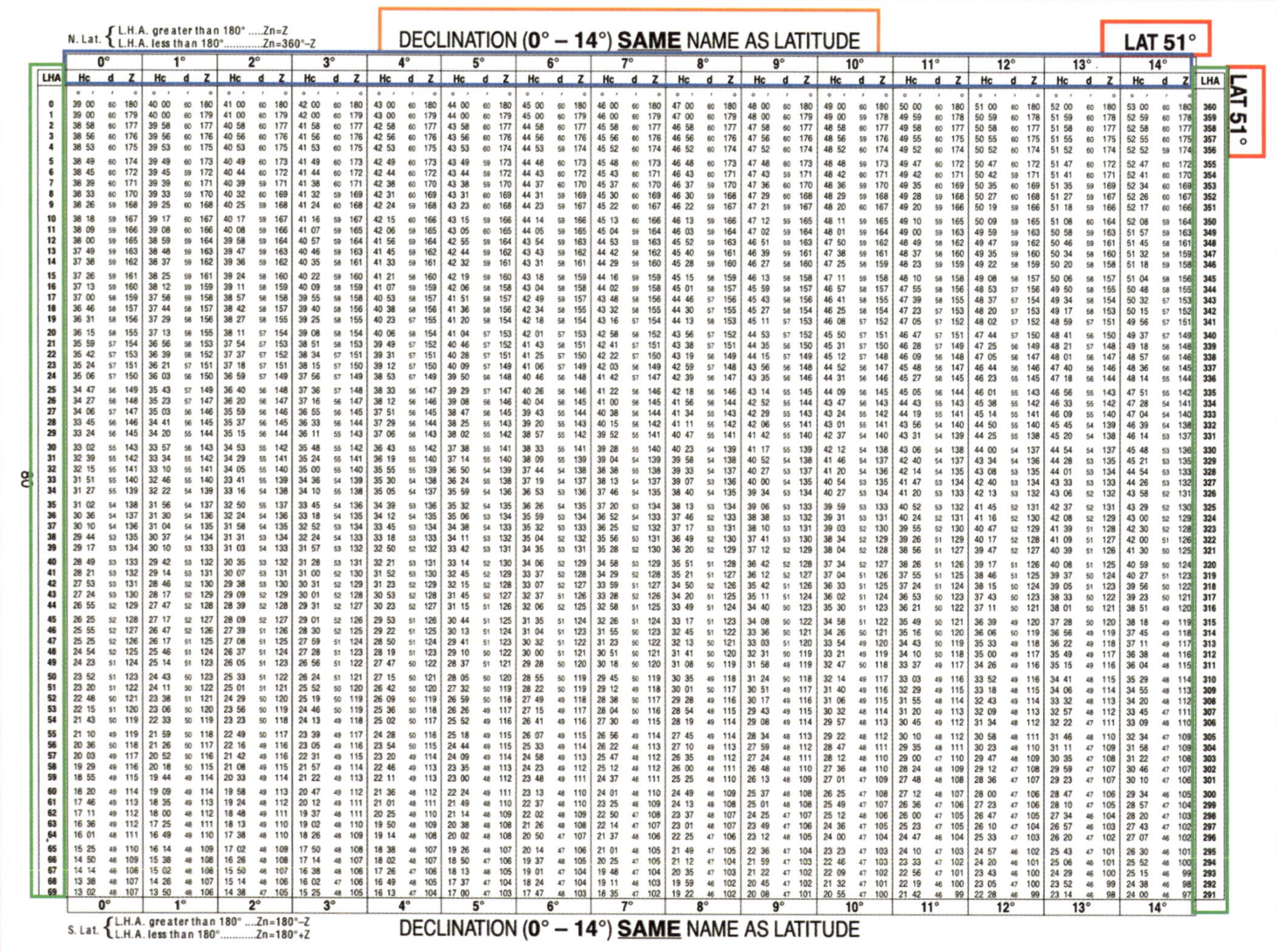

Figure 85

The **red box area** - tells us the latitude page we're on.

The **orange box area** - tells us we're on the page for 0° to 14° declination and Same.

The **blue box area** - details the declinations of 0° to 14° and the information contained in the main body, ie Hc (calculated sextant altitude), d and Z.

The **green box area** - details the LHA. Note that they run down both sides of the page. In fact, on any particular line, if you were to add the left- and right-hand columns together, it would equal 360°. This helps reduce the size of the tables.

Figure 85 happens to be the table we want, but before we move on, let's look at the progression through the pages in the tables (see Figures 86 to 92).

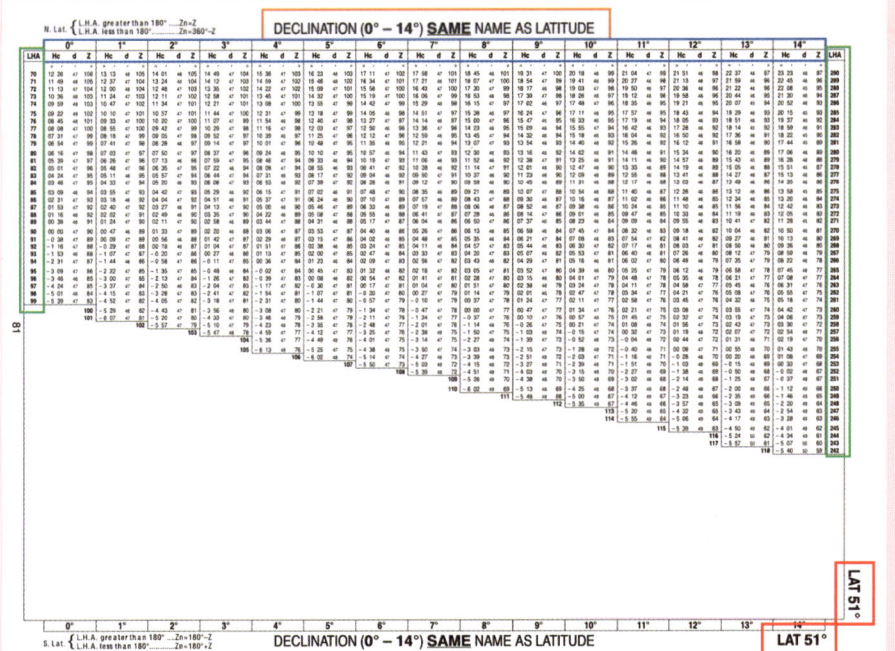

← Pages continue as per Figure 85, but with different LHA values.

Figure 86

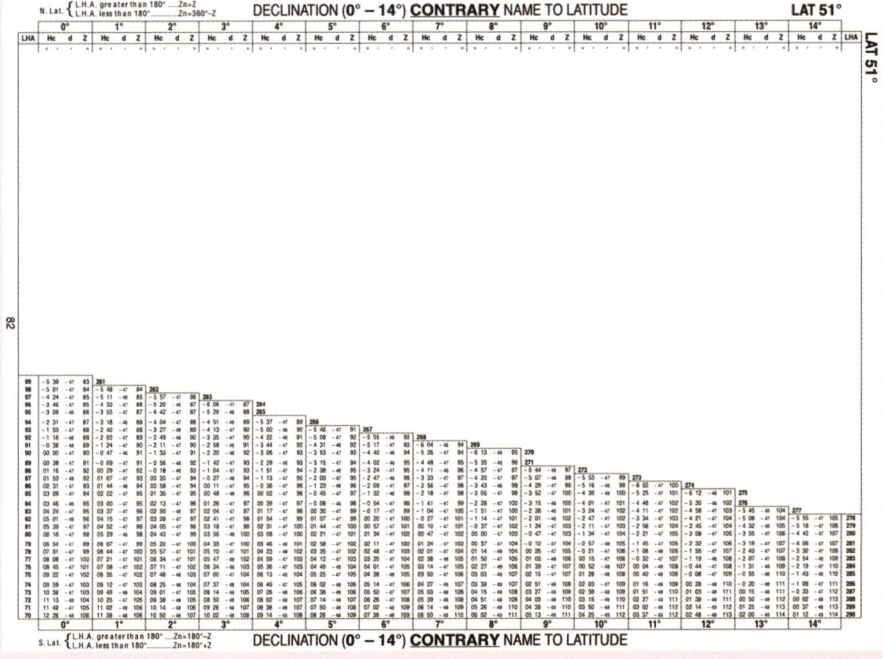

← Then pages stay with declination 0° to 14° but move on to Contrary.

Figure 87

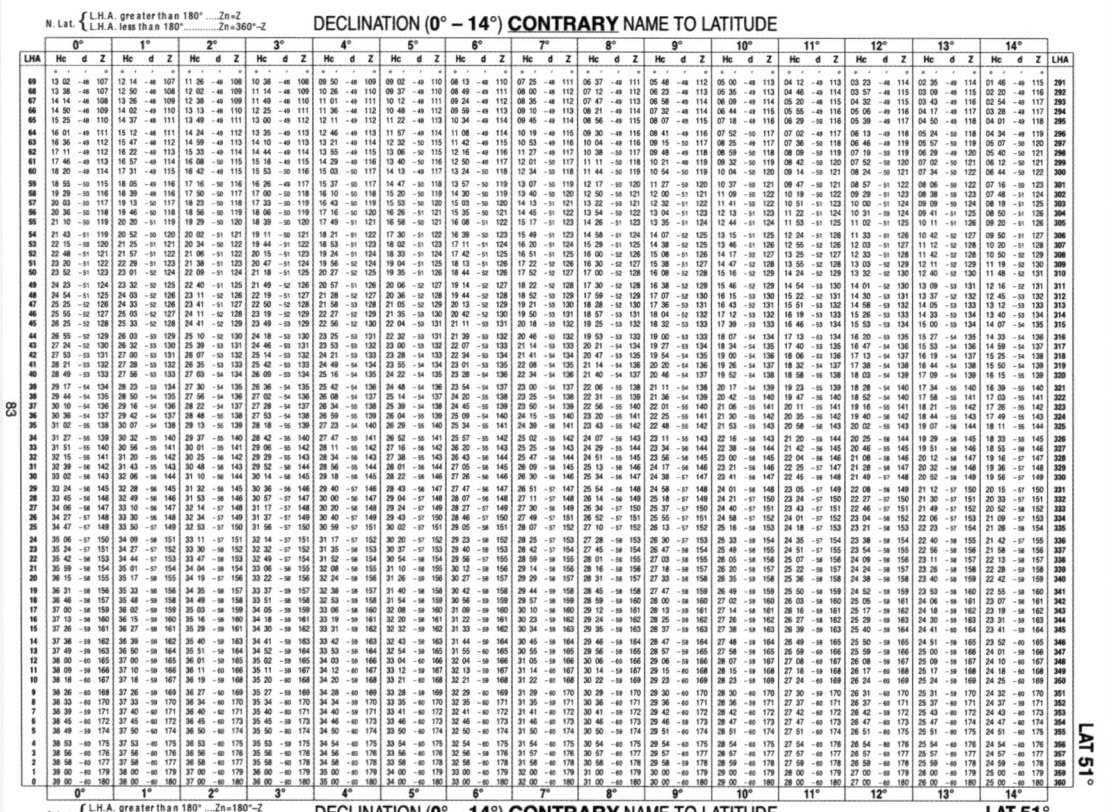

Figure 88

← Pages continue as per Figure 87, but with different LHA values.

Figure 89

← Then they move on to declinations 15° to 29° Same (these are detailed along the top of the table).

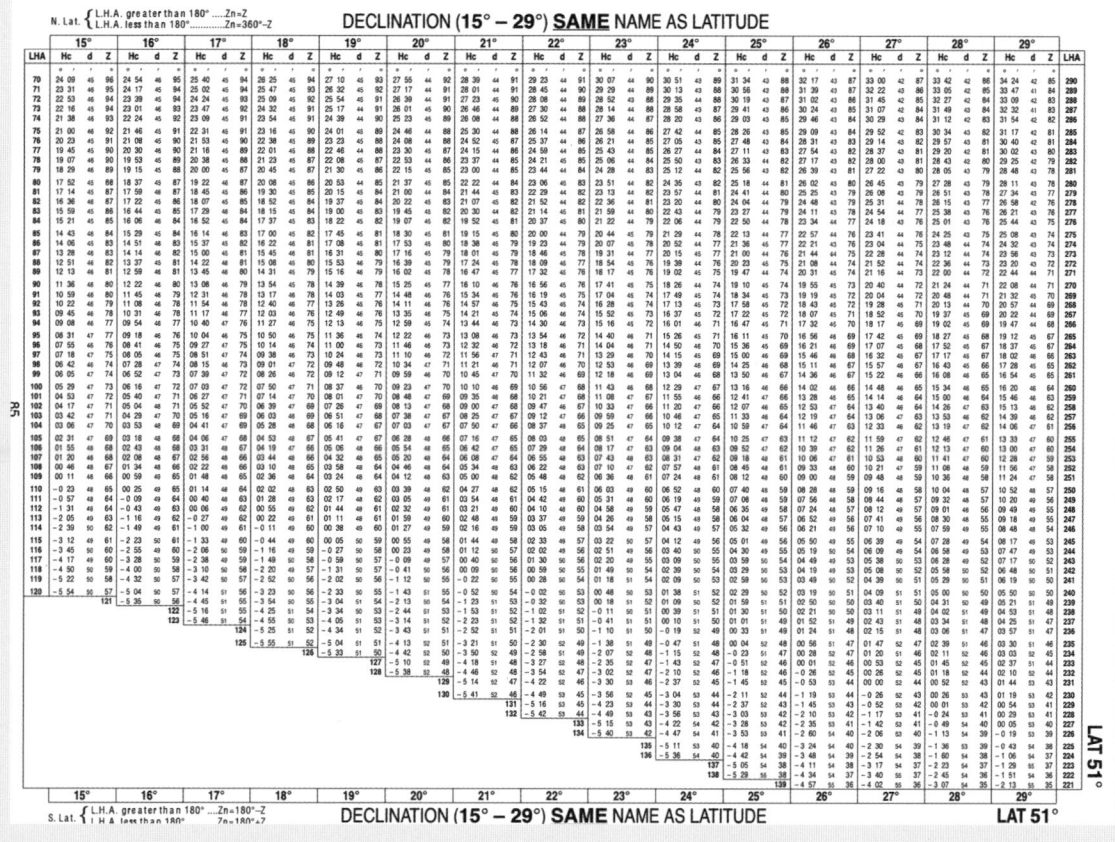

Figure 90

← Pages continue as per Figure 89, but with different LHA values.

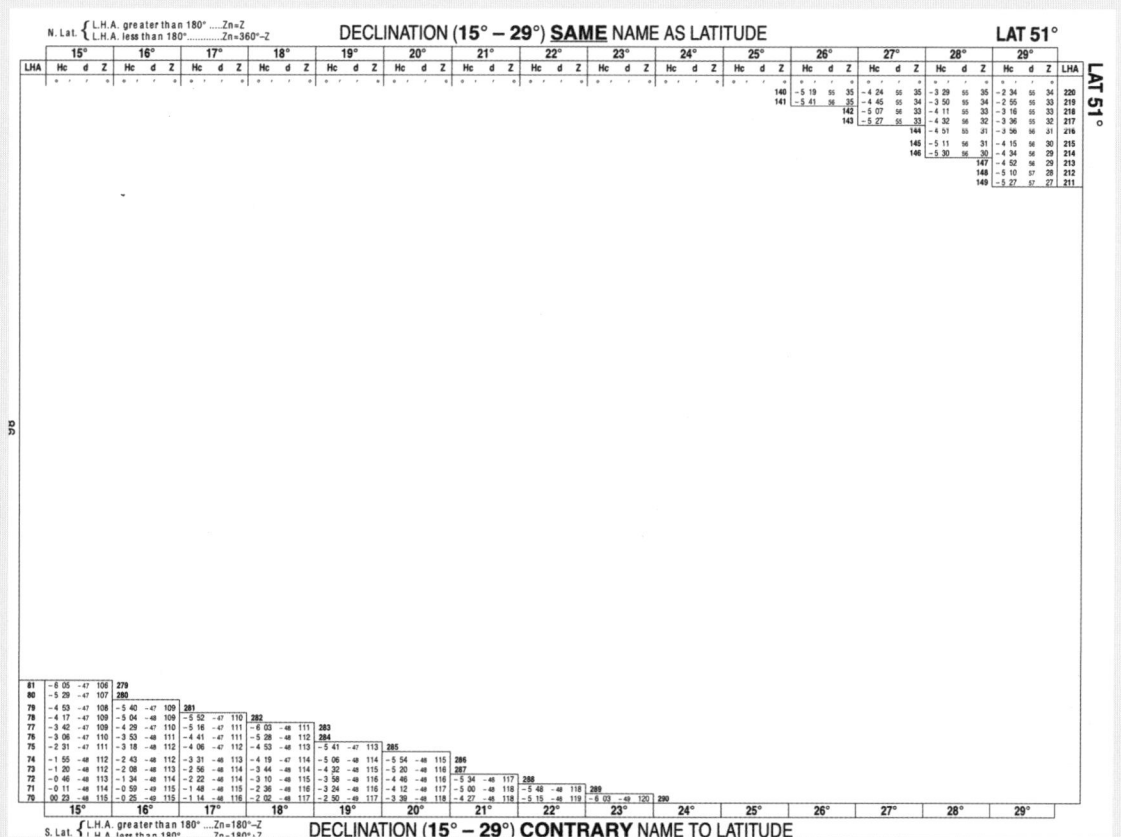

Figure 91

← Before moving on to 15° to 29° Contrary.

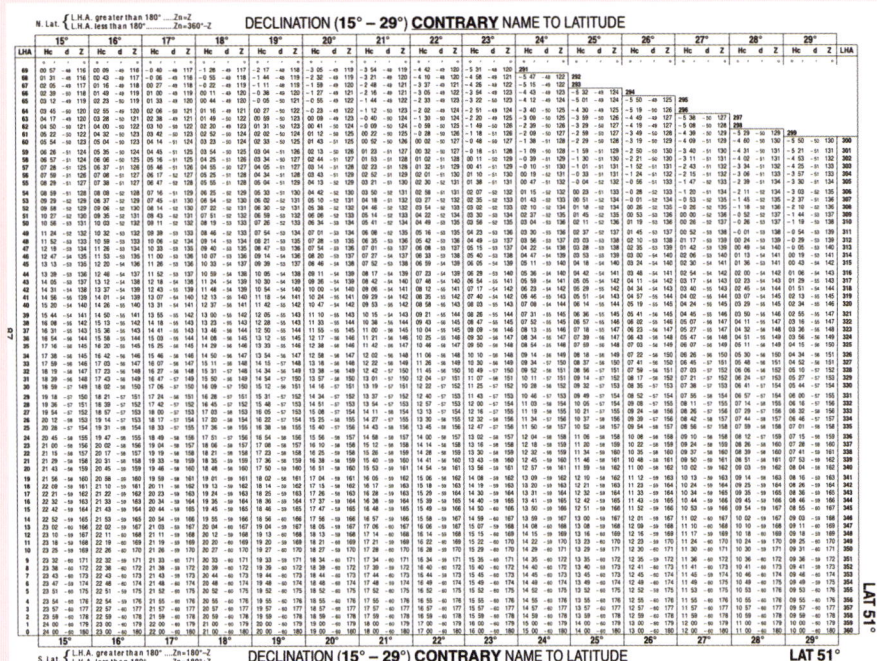

Figure 92

← And finally, this is a continuation of Figure 91 before moving on to 52°.

From what we've just seen, with all the pages together, the tables are one continuous stream of data. Patience and time are needed to select the correct page that meets all of the four *key* criteria we have from our proforma.

Now it's Figure 85 that we require for our example.

Figure 93 is a reminder of what we're looking for.

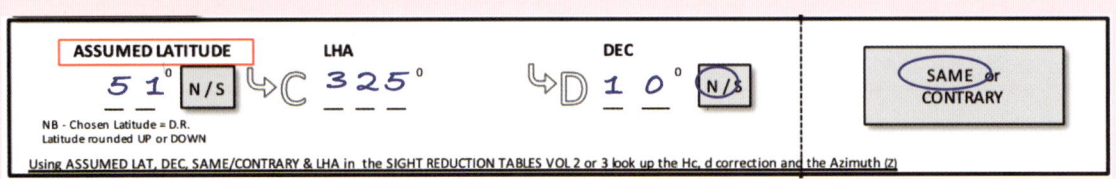

Figure 93

Looking at Figure 94 we already have 51° and Same, and we're looking for the 10° declination column and an LHA of 325°. We want to obtain the Hc, d and Z.

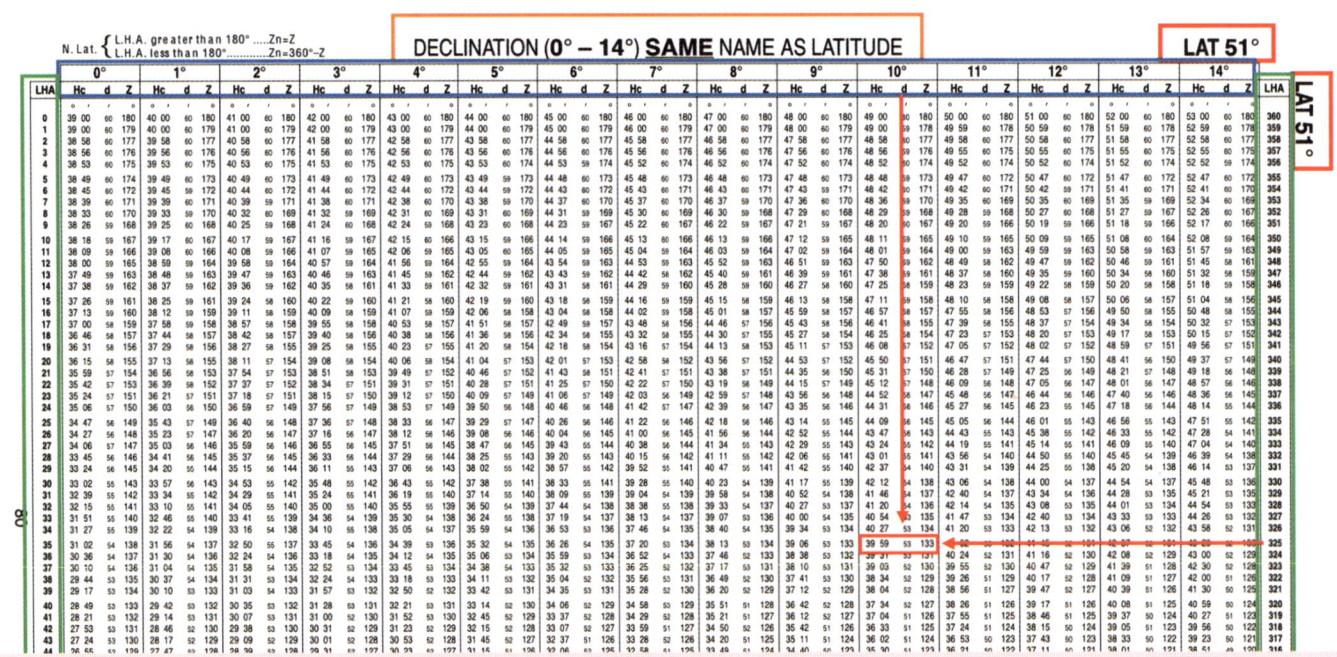

Figure 94

Now, you're probably losing sight of what we're doing at this point, but despair not. We're nearly through the sight reduction process and we'll do a recap at the end, so just stick with it.

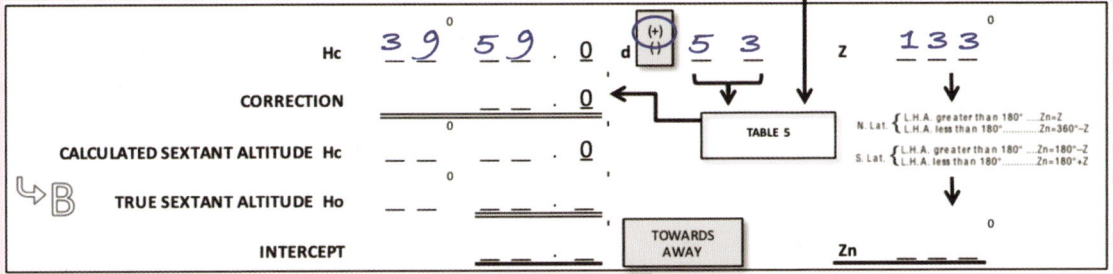

Figure 95

We've now obtained three values: Hc (calculated sextant altitude), a 'd' value and Z. We'll look at these individually, but let's first put them on to the proforma as shown in Figure 95.

Hc, 'd' AND Z

So what are these values?

Hc is the calculated sextant altitude we require. This will shortly enable us to compare it against our actual observed sextant altitude.

'd' If you look at the declination in Figure 84, we took the value of 10° into the tables, but we left behind the 43.2'. The 'd' value will address this shortly. You'll note in Figure 95 that the + has been circled. The tables omit the positive next to the 'd' value if it's positive but show a '–' sign if it's minus. In other words, if there is no sign then the 'd' value is positive.

Z We'll have a look at this in more detail in Appendix 8 (for those who want a more thorough explanation), but essentially it represents an angle of the sun.

Let's continue with the proforma and explore these in more detail.

Focusing on the Z value:

Z = Azimuth angle
Zn = Azimuth bearing

Z is an angle, but it isn't yet a compass bearing (something we'll need when plotting later on). To convert Z to a compass bearing Zn, we need to refer back to our sight reduction tables.

We need to look at the top left and bottom left of the page, select the appropriate one of the two scenarios given and then identify the relevant statement.

Figure 96 shows the two scenarios.

We select one or the other according to whether our DR latitude is north or south, ie whether our vessel is currently in the northern or southern hemisphere.

Figure 96

In our example, we are in the northern hemisphere, so we want to be referring to the top scenario.

Now, referring to our LHA, we ask ourselves: Is it greater than 180° or less than 180°? Be careful here, it's a common mistake to look at the Z value instead of the LHA.

In our example, our LHA is 325° and therefore the statement tells us that Zn = Z. Therefore, our Zn (Azimuth or true compass bearing) is also 133°. We'll talk about this more when plotting, but what this is now telling us is that the true compass bearing from our position to the sun is 133°. We can input this on to our proforma.

Step 8 (Figure 97)

When we went to the sight reduction tables before, we used a declination value of 10° and didn't consider the minutes of declination. Looking at Figure 97, the red outline looks at how we address these minutes. Using a new table called 'Table 5' found at the back of the Sight Reduction Tables, we take our 43.2' of declination and the new 'd' value of 53' and Table 5 gives us a correction we use to apply to our

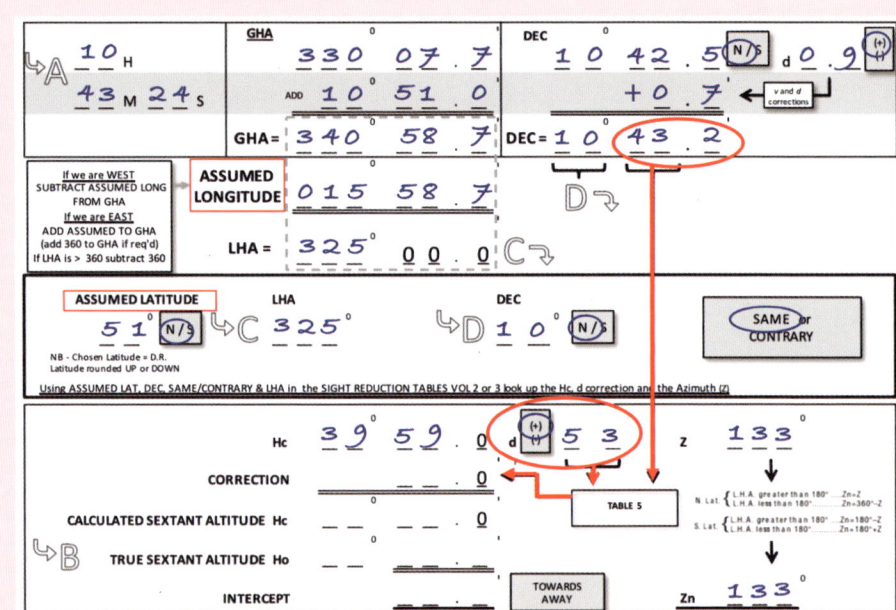

Figure 97

Figure 98

calculated sextant altitude (Hc) (currently 39° 59.0'). The 'd' value of 53' is telling us that for every degree the declination changes by, the Hc will change by 53'. We don't need a whole degree though; we need 43.2 minutes' worth. In effect, Table 5 is doing this calculation for us, ie 53/60 x 43.

As shown in Figure 98, we take our two values of 53' and 43' (43.2' rounded to nearest full minute) and look at Table 5. It doesn't matter which way around the numbers are looked up, because the value will be the same either way. The correction (38') can be put into the proforma – here it will be positive because the 'd' value was positive (see Figure 99).

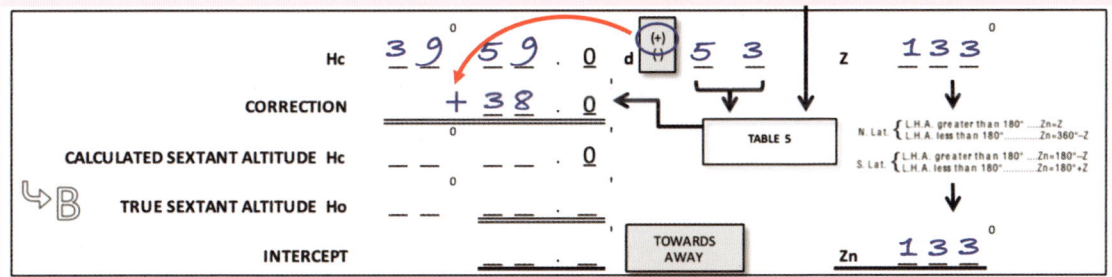

Figure 99

Step 9 (Figure 100)

We can now add this correction to our Hc.

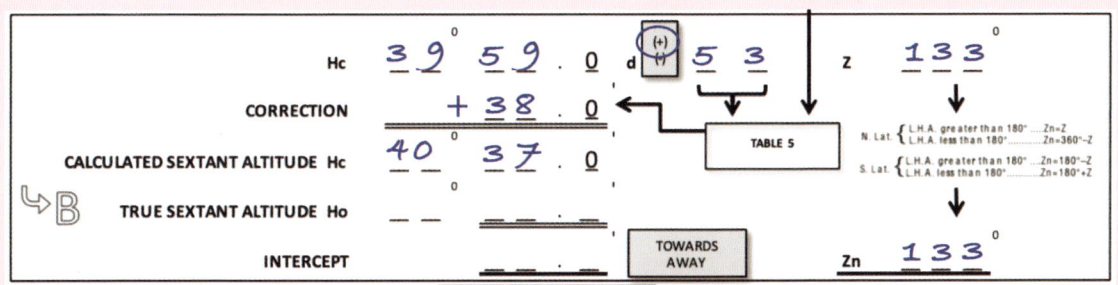

Figure 100

Step 10 (Figure 101) We then bring in our true sextant altitude (Ho). B *out* to B *in*.

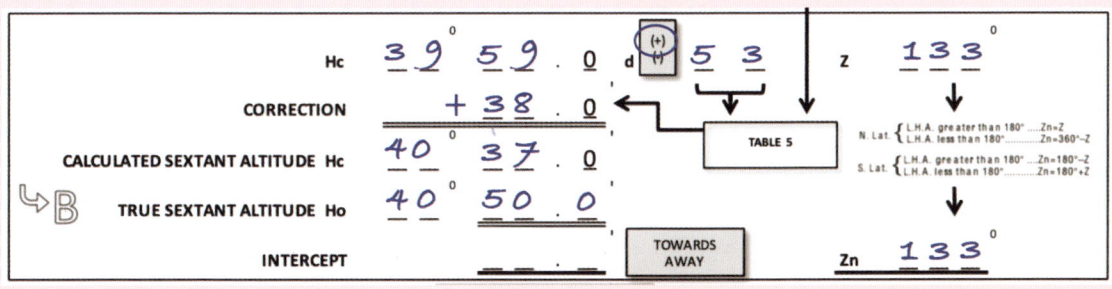

Figure 101

We then *compare* them, as shown in Figure 102. We simply take whichever is the smaller value from whichever is the larger. In this case, we have a difference or *intercept* of 13' (which equals 13nm).

The final decision to make is: Are we 13nm *towards* the sun or 13nm *away*?

Now you may have lost sight of what we're trying to do here and that's quite normal so don't fret, it will take some absorption time to take it all in. We'll be doing a full recap shortly.

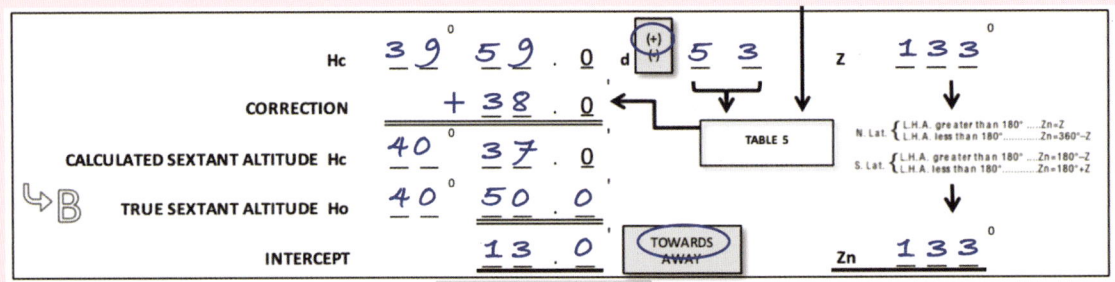

Figure 102

Before we do, let's just cover why, in this scenario, we have *towards*. The calculated sextant altitude (Hc) we have obtained has been calculated from the tables from our assumed position. This is a made-up position (our DR latitude of 50° 47.3'N became an assumed latitude of 51°N and our DR longitude of 015° 47.8' became an assumed Longitude of 015° 58.7'), so it is highly unlikely that we are actually there in that position. However, *if* we were on that spot, we would observe a sextant altitude of 40° 37.0'. But we haven't, we have observed a sextant altitude of 40° 50.0'. Therefore, because our angle is bigger, we must be towards the sun (the angle gets larger, the closer we move towards the sun).

TOWARDS OR AWAY?

There are a couple of mnemonics that might help here to check our assessment of whether it should be towards or away. It's better not to rely on them too much though as it's much better to understand the concept:

GOAT:

GREATER **O**BSERVED **A**LTITUDE equals **T**OWARDS

(If the observed altitude is greater then it's towards)

HoMoTo:

Ho (Observed sextant altitude)
Mo (more or greater) **To** (towards)

That's it! We have completed a full sight reduction (Figure 103). It won't perhaps have much clarity yet, but we've done it. We now have the components we need to do some plotting and obtain a Line of Position (LOP).

Before we do that, let's do the step-by-step recap of what we've done.

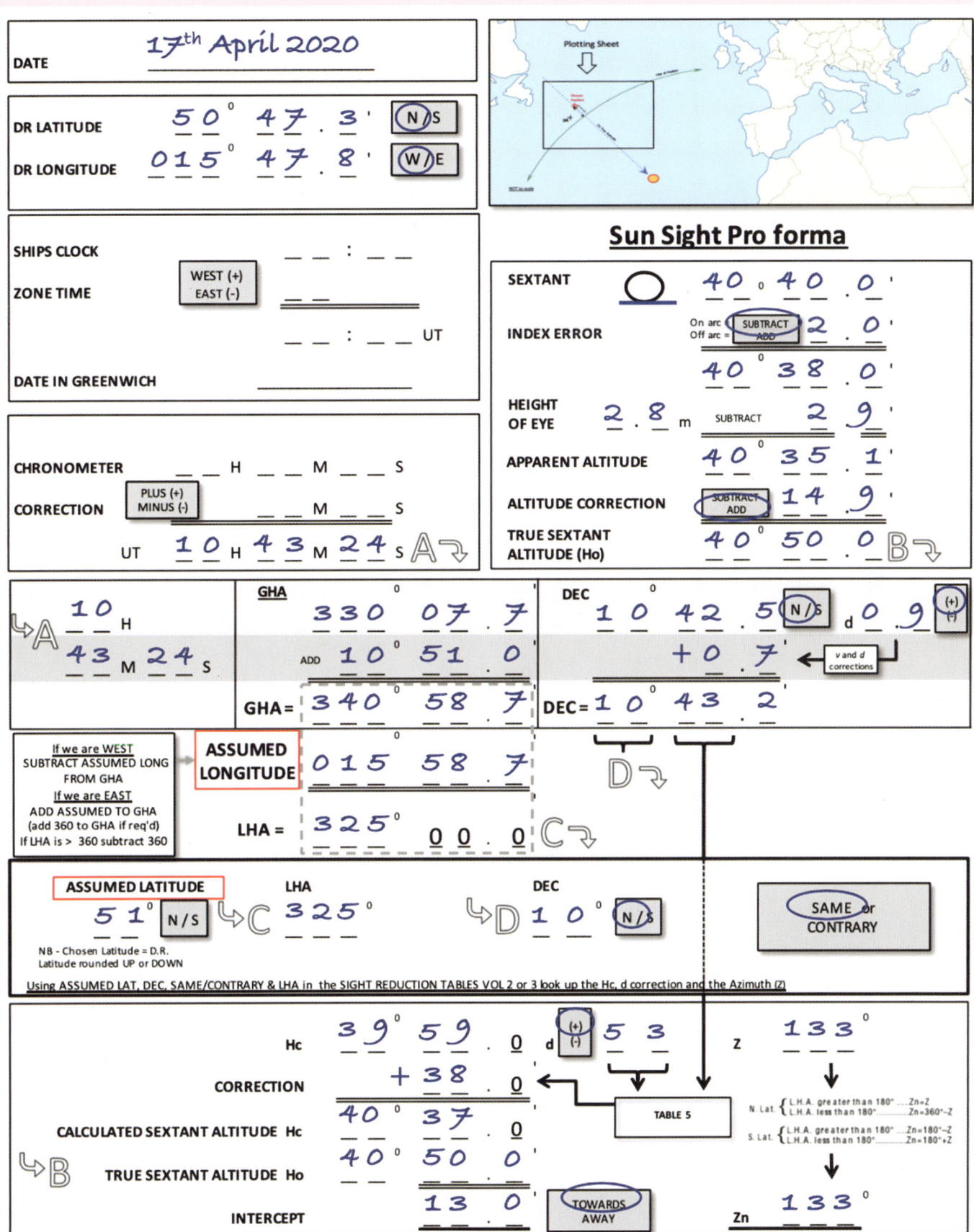

Figure 103

CHAPTER NINE

Sun sight reduction
Quick Start and recap

> If using this for a *Quick Start*, please also refer to Appendix 2.

Earlier we said we can use the sextant as a range finder to establish our distance from the sun's GP.

Then, in Chapter 6, we adapted our approach, as shown in Figure 104, and said that, instead of measuring our distance from the GP (which is impractical), we could do things in a different way. Instead, we use tables to calculate a hypothetical sextant altitude from our DR position. We then compare this with an actual observed sextant altitude. This difference in angles gives us a distance (intercept) that we can measure from our DR position to establish an LOP, a position line that our vessel is definitely on.

Instead of using our DR position (which by its nature is unlikely to be very accurate), we must modify our DR latitude and DR longitude slightly, to create an assumed latitude and assumed longitude, in order to use the tables.

RESOURCES

- A **nautical almanac**
  Included within will be:
  o Altitude correction tables 10° to 90° Sun, Stars and Planets
  o Increments and corrections

- **Sight Reduction Tables Vol. 2 or 3.**
  (depending on latitude)
  Included within will be:
  o Table 5

For advice regarding online resources visit www.philsomerville.com

- An accurate watch set to UT
- Sextant (checked for errors)
- Plotting sheets
- Pen, pencil and paper
- Plotting instruments – parallel rule/plotter

Figure 104

Completing a sun sight reduction

In the first instance we'll take a sight of the sun, during which we should note the following information:

- Sextant altitude observed
- Index error
- Our height of eye
- Lower or upper limb
- UT time, exact to the second
- A quick assessment of the bearing of the Sun using hand-bearing compass
- The vessel's DR position
- The vessel's log reading and heading

We will use the proforma shown in Figure 105.

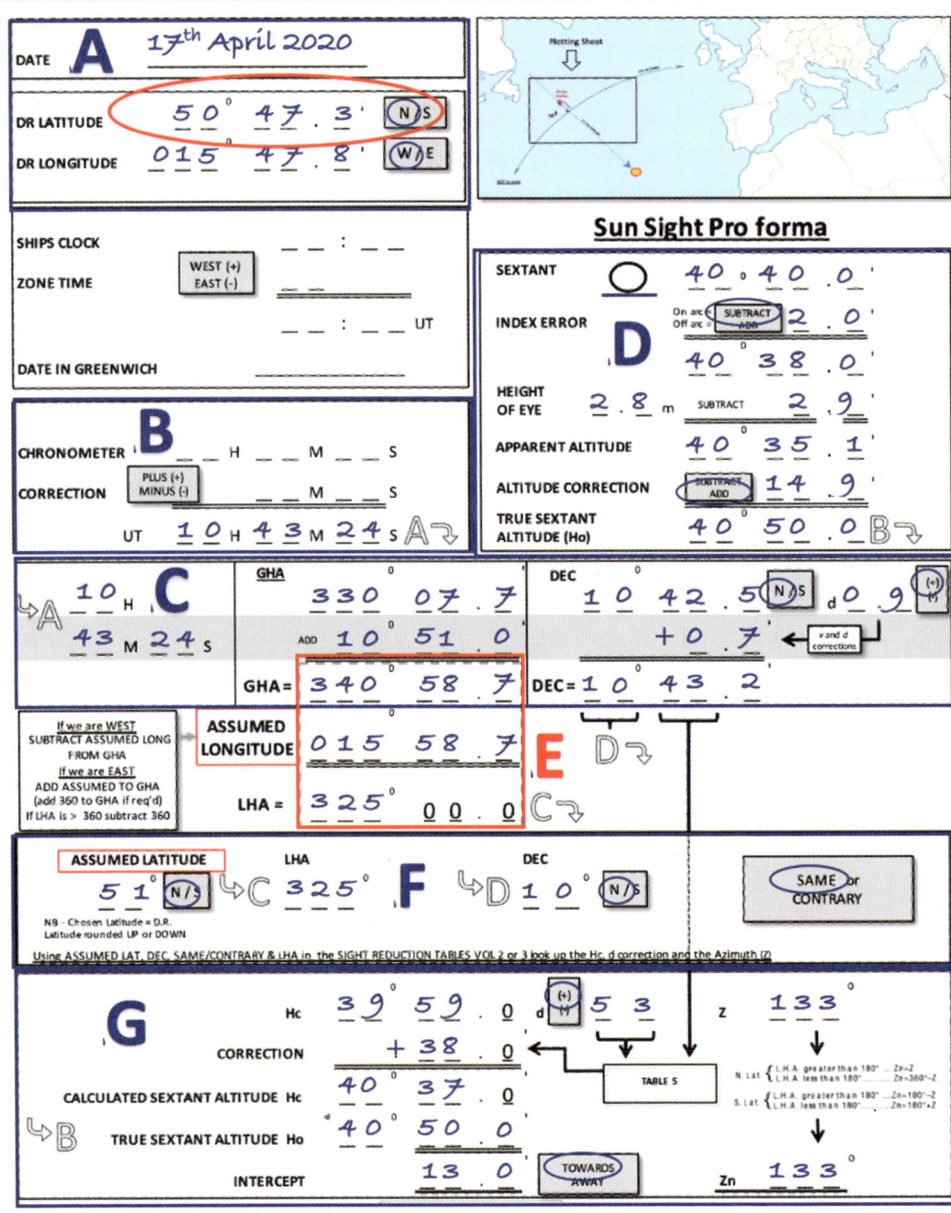

Figure 105

Step 1
Box 'A': Input the Greenwich date and the vessel's DR position (Note: this will be DR2 from our first plot if this is the second sight of the day).

Step 2
Box 'B': Input the UT time that sight was taken.

Step 3
Box 'C': Obtain the geographical position of the sun (GHA and declination) using the 'Daily Pages' and 'Increments and Corrections' in the nautical almanac.

Step 4
Box 'D': Undertake the corrections required to obtain the true sextant altitude (Ho) using the 'Altitude Correction Tables – Sun, Stars, Planets', which is usually a loose sheet within the nautical almanac.

Step 5
Box 'E': Calculate the LHA. In order to do this, we need to modify our DR longitude to come up with an 'assumed' longitude that suits the tables. (Appendix 9 helps here if you get stuck.)

Step 6
Box 'F': Identify the four keys required for the tables.

Step 7 to Step 10
Box 'G': Look up the four keys in the sight reduction tables.

These will give us:
- 'Hc', a calculated sextant altitude.
- 'd', used in Table 5 to correct the Hc, taking account for the minutes of declination.
- 'Z' is turned into a compass bearing 'Zn' using the arguments from the same page in the tables.
- We then compare the Hc against the Ho and the difference between the two gives us an intercept.
- Determine if our intercept is towards or away – GOAT or HoMoTo.

IN SUMMARY

The tables have calculated a sextant altitude (Hc) from the assumed position. In the highly unlikely event that we happen to be in that same position, we would actually observe this sextant altitude from our vessel. In reality, we will observe a different sextant angle, and it's the difference between the two sextant readings – the intercept (because angle = distance on a great circle) that tells us how far away we are from the assumed position. Now, if someone told you you were 13nm from a certain position, the first question you are likely to ask is 'in which direction?'. And that's where the bearing of the sun comes in. We'll look at this in more detail in the plotting.

CHAPTER TEN

Meridian passage

Now, before we move on to plotting, there's something else we should know. We've said that in order to get a fix we need two position lines (or LOPs as we've been calling them), and this chapter looks at another way of obtaining one. Don't worry, this is much simpler than a full sight reduction.

It was mentioned earlier that mariners of old could obtain their latitude, it was longitude that was the tricky part. This is one the techniques they used.

The process is known as the *meridian passage*, often referred to as *mer pass* or the *noon sight*.

Now, first we must forget that we often refer to noon as 12 o'clock local time. In fact our noon, wherever we are, is actually the point in time when the sun is at the highest point in the sky, and this will depend on where we are, ie our longitude.

At this point, when the sun is overhead, we have an interesting situation which we can take advantage of.

Figure 106 shows this interesting new situation: At the moment of the mer pass, we have a situation where our vessel and the sun are sitting on the same meridian (hence the name).

We've said all along that all meridians of longitude are great circles, so here we are back to our familiar friend once again.

In this moment of the meridian passage, as we share the same meridian as the sun, the LHA momentarily becomes zero. And this gives us a simple calculation in order to obtain our latitude. To get our Latitude we simply add the declination to the ZD:

Latitude = Dec + ZD.

Declination comes from the Daily Pages in the nautical almanac, as before.

ZD comes from deducting our true observed sextant altitude (Ho from 90°, ie ZD = 90° – Ho).

Figure 107 is a visual reminder of how we obtain ZD.

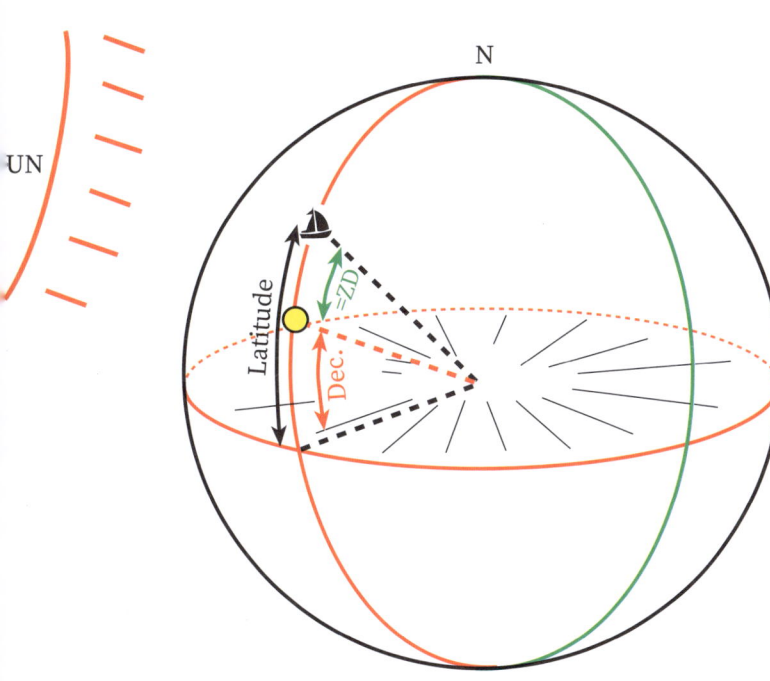

Figure 106

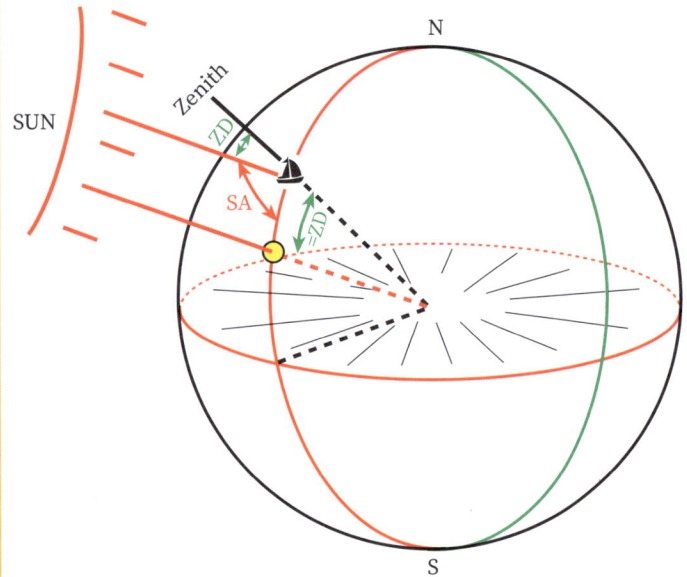

Figure 107

So, to recap, the fact that the LHA is zero means we have a fairly easy and quick way of establishing our latitude. And latitude gives us a position line, a horizontal one.

There are actually three scenarios we might be faced with and Figure 107, that we have just been looking at, is one of the three.

Referring to Figure 108 which details these three scenarios:

Top: We are in the same hemisphere as the sun, and our DR latitude is greater than the sun's declination (although our vessel and the sun are in the northern hemisphere in this example, it would be the same formula if our vessel and the sun were both in the southern hemisphere, ie a mirror image).

Middle: Here, we are in the same hemisphere, but this time our DR latitude is smaller than the sun's declination. In reality, this would only occur if we were sailing in the tropics (between 23°.5 N and 23°.5 S). Again, this could be a mirror image if our vessel and the sun were both in the southern hemisphere.

Bottom: In this scenario we are in opposite hemispheres (or mirror image).

You can see that each scenario has its own equation. The good news is that it's hard to get the mer pass wrong. Because if you do, your calculation is likely to put your position thousands of miles away from where you thought you were. You'll have an interesting time telling your thermal wearing crew that you've calculated that you're actually just north of the equator.

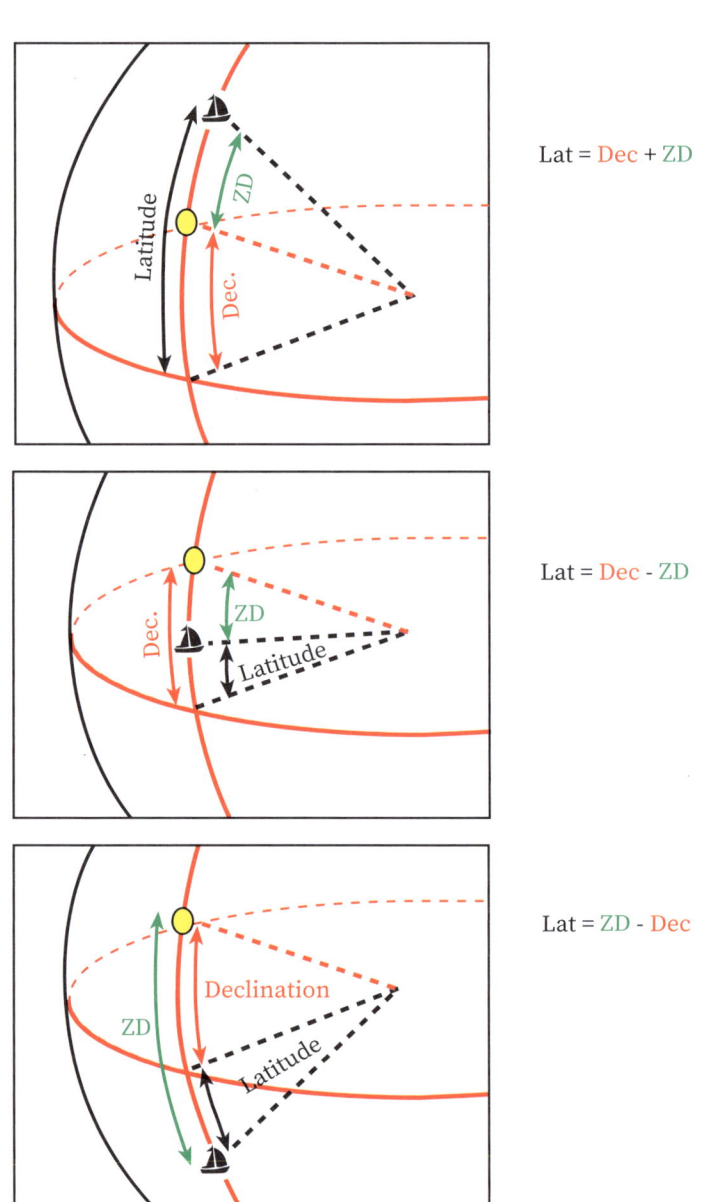

Lat = Dec + ZD

Lat = Dec - ZD

Lat = ZD - Dec

Figure 108

HOW WE TAKE THE SIGHT

Before we look at the calculation of the mer pass in more detail, we need to look at the mechanics of the sight taking process.

The first thing we need to do is find out at what time the mer pass will occur on the Greenwich Meridian, on the day in question. Secondly, we need to establish the time it will occur in our position. Unless we're already somewhere on the Greenwich Meridian, which is highly unlikely, this will be earlier or later.

Having established the time it will occur in our position, we go on deck 20 minutes or so before that time with our sextant, sight the sun and bring it down to the horizon. We then wait for 30 seconds. When we view the sun through the sextant again, we will find the sun has risen above the horizon, this is because the sun is still rising in the sky. We bring the sun back down to the horizon using the micrometre drum and wait a further 30 seconds and keep repeating the process. Each time we repeat, we will notice the sun rises less, this is because the Sun is reaching our meridian and the highest point in the sky.

At some point during the above repetitions, the sun will appear to stand still – at that moment, we have captured the sun on the meridian. If we keep observing through the sextant, the sun will appear to start dropping below the horizon – <u>do nothing</u> with the sextant.

The sextant reading we have captured will enable us to obtain the ZD (ZD = 90° – Ho), as shown in Figure 107 above.

In order to help us with the mer pass, both now and in the future, we have a dedicated proforma (see Appendix 3). It follows a very similar layout to the one we've been using but with changes where required. Appendix 4 is a mer pass proforma guide for future reference.

WORKED EXAMPLE

In order to work our way through the process, let's undertake an example. We'll use the same day as per our previous example to enable us to plot a *Sun Run Sun* later. The DR position here is the same as the one used earlier for our sun sight reduction. In reality this wouldn't be our position at the time of actually taking the mer pass sight, but, as we'll see, we need a position from which to estimate the time of the mer pass. The difference between the morning sight position and that of the mer pass might introduce a slight error in our declination value, but this will not be large enough to concern us.

- 17 April 2020
- DR 50° 44'.3 North 015° 47.8' West
- Observed sextant altitude 49° 11.0'
- Index error 2.0' on the arc
- Height of eye 2.6m
- Sight taken of lower limb

RESOURCES

In order to undertake the mer pass reduction, we need similar publications once again:

- A **nautical almanac**

  Included within will be:

  o Altitude Correction Tables 10° to 90° Sun, Stars, Planets

  o Increments and Corrections

  o Conversion of Arc to Time table

Looking at a printed copy of the mer pass proforma or referring to Appendix 3, let's go.

First of all, let's fill in the date and our DR position as shown in Figure 109.

Now, we said in order to have observed the mer pass in the first instance, we would have to know when it was occurring on the Greenwich Meridian and then calculate when it would occur in our position (DR longitude).

In order to find this out we use the area of the proforma shown in Figures 110 and 111.

We'll look at where we obtain the mer pass in Greenwich shortly. Before we do, we are going to need the time difference between ourselves and Greenwich. We looked at the rotation of the earth in Table 1 on page 7, ie one hour equals

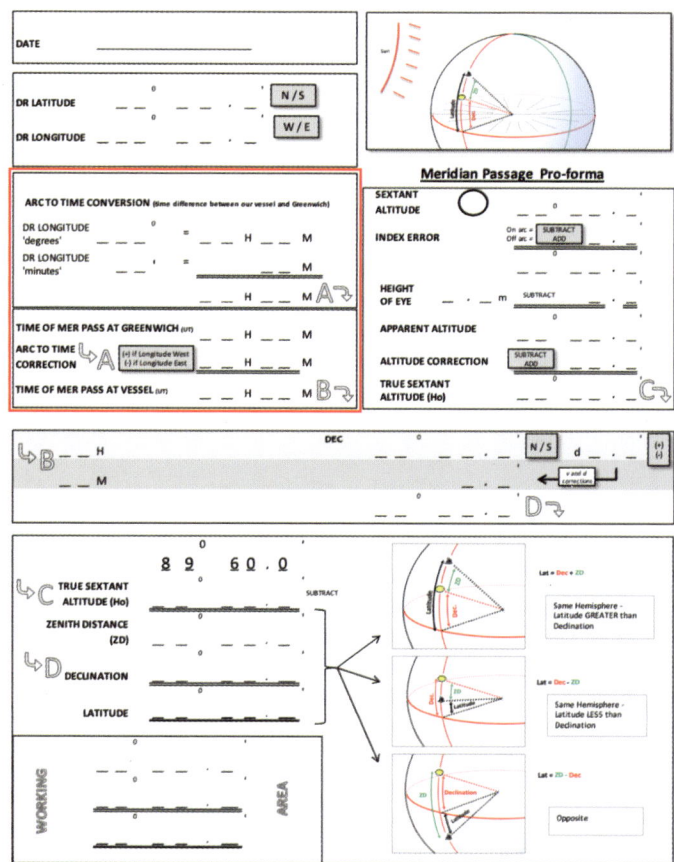

Figure 110

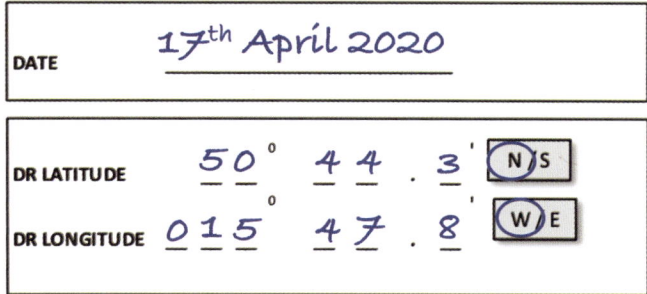

Figure 109

Figure 111

15°, two hours equal 30° etc. In other words, if our longitude was 15° West, any event happening at Greenwich will happen to us one hour later (later rather than earlier because of the earth's rotation).

So, on any particular day, if we found that the mer pass was going to happen at 12 o'clock in Greenwich, if we were 15° West, our mer pass would happen at 1300UT. Our local time at 15° West would be 1200hr. However, we're interested in the UT time because that's what the nautical almanac uses.

Likewise, if we were 30° West it would be two hours later and so on. Here the maths is easy, but what if we were 23° 45'.0 West? Now the maths gets a bit more difficult. Luckily, there is a table we can refer to, one that enables us to work out increments of longitude versus time of rotation. This table is known as *Conversion of Arc to Time*. Think of ***arc*** as meaning angle, or even better, angle of longitude.

Conversion of Arc to Time

0° - 59°			60° - 119°			120° - 179°			180° - 239°			240° - 299°			300° - 360°			0' - 59'			0" - 59"	
°	h	m	°	h	m	°	h	m	°	h	m	°	h	m	°	h	m	'	m	s	"	s
0	0	00	60	4	00	120	8	00	180	12	00	240	16	00	300	20	00	0	0	00	0	0.00
1	0	04	61	4	04	121	8	04	181	12	04	241	16	04	301	20	04	1	0	04	1	0.07
2	0	08	62	4	08	122	8	08	182	12	08	242	16	08	302	20	08	2	0	08	2	0.13
3	0	12	63	4	12	123	8	12	183	12	12	243	16	12	303	20	12	3	0	12	3	0.20
4	0	16	64	4	16	124	8	16	184	12	16	244	16	16	304	20	16	4	0	16	4	0.27
5	0	20	65	4	20	125	8	20	185	12	20	245	16	20	305	20	20	5	0	20	5	0.33
6	0	24	66	4	24	126	8	24	186	12	24	246	16	24	306	20	24	6	0	24	6	0.40
7	0	28	67	4	28	127	8	28	187	12	28	247	16	28	307	20	28	7	0	28	7	0.47
8	0	32	68	4	32	128	8	32	188	12	32	248	16	32	308	20	32	8	0	32	8	0.53
9	0	36	69	4	36	129	8	36	189	12	36	249	16	36	309	20	36	9	0	36	9	0.60
10	0	40	70	4	40	130	8	40	190	12	40	250	16	40	310	20	40	10	0	40	10	0.67
11	0	44	71	4	44	131	8	44	191	12	44	251	16	44	311	20	44	11	0	44	11	0.73
12	0	48	72	4	48	132	8	48	192	12	48	252	16	48	312	20	48	12	0	48	12	0.80
13	0	52	73	4	52	133	8	52	193	12	52	253	16	52	313	20	52	13	0	52	13	0.87
14	0	56	74	4	56	134	8	56	194	12	56	254	16	56	314	20	56	14	0	56	14	0.93
15	1	00	75	5	00	135	9	00	195	13	00	255	17	00	315	21	00	15	1	00	15	1.00
16	1	04	76	5	04	136	9	04	196	13	04	256	17	04	316	21	04	16	1	04	16	1.07
17	1	08	77	5	08	137	9	08	197	13	08	257	17	08	317	21	08	17	1	08	17	1.13
18	1	12	78	5	12	138	9	12	198	13	12	258	17	12	318	21	12	18	1	12	18	1.20
19	1	16	79	5	16	139	9	16	199	13	16	259	17	16	319	21	16	19	1	16	19	1.27
20	1	20	80	5	20	140	9	20	200	13	20	260	17	20	320	21	20	20	1	20	20	1.33
21	1	24	81	5	24	141	9	24	201	13	24	261	17	24	321	21	24	21	1	24	21	1.40
22	1	28	82	5	28	142	9	28	202	13	28	262	17	28	322	21	28	22	1	28	22	1.47
23	1	32	83	5	32	143	9	32	203	13	32	263	17	32	323	21	32	23	1	32	23	1.53
24	1	36	84	5	36	144	9	36	204	13	36	264	17	36	324	21	36	24	1	36	24	1.60
25	1	40	85	5	40	145	9	40	205	13	40	265	17	40	325	21	40	25	1	40	25	1.67
26	1	44	86	5	44	146	9	44	206	13	44	266	17	44	326	21	44	26	1	44	26	1.73
27	1	48	87	5	48	147	9	48	207	13	48	267	17	48	327	21	48	27	1	48	27	1.80
28	1	52	88	5	52	148	9	52	208	13	52	268	17	52	328	21	52	28	1	52	28	1.87
29	1	56	89	5	56	149	9	56	209	13	56	269	17	56	329	21	56	29	1	56	29	1.93
30	2	00	90	6	00	150	10	00	210	14	00	270	18	00	330	22	00	30	2	00	30	2.00
31	2	04	91	6	04	151	10	04	211	14	04	271	18	04	331	22	04	31	2	04	31	2.07
32	2	08	92	6	08	152	10	08	212	14	08	272	18	08	332	22	08	32	2	08	32	2.13
33	2	12	93	6	12	153	10	12	213	14	12	273	18	12	333	22	12	33	2	12	33	2.20
34	2	16	94	6	16	154	10	16	214	14	16	274	18	16	334	22	16	34	2	16	34	2.27
35	2	20	95	6	20	155	10	20	215	14	20	275	18	20	335	22	20	35	2	20	35	2.33
36	2	24	96	6	24	156	10	24	216	14	24	276	18	24	336	22	24	36	2	24	36	2.40
37	2	28	97	6	28	157	10	28	217	14	28	277	18	28	337	22	28	37	2	28	37	2.47
38	2	32	98	6	32	158	10	32	218	14	32	278	18	32	338	22	32	38	2	32	38	2.53
39	2	36	99	6	36	159	10	36	219	14	36	279	18	36	339	22	36	39	2	36	39	2.60
40	2	40	100	6	40	160	10	40	220	14	40	280	18	40	340	22	40	40	2	40	40	2.67
41	2	44	101	6	44	161	10	44	221	14	44	281	18	44	341	22	44	41	2	44	41	2.73
42	2	48	102	6	48	162	10	48	222	14	48	282	18	48	342	22	48	42	2	48	42	2.80
43	2	52	103	6	52	163	10	52	223	14	52	283	18	52	343	22	52	43	2	52	43	2.87
44	2	56	104	6	56	164	10	56	224	14	56	284	18	56	344	22	56	44	2	56	44	2.93
45	3	00	105	7	00	165	11	00	225	15	00	285	19	00	345	23	00	45	3	00	45	3.00
46	3	04	106	7	04	166	11	04	226	15	04	286	19	04	346	23	04	46	3	04	46	3.07
47	3	08	107	7	08	167	11	08	227	15	08	287	19	08	347	23	08	47	3	08	47	3.13
48	3	12	108	7	12	168	11	12	228	15	12	288	19	12	348	23	12	48	3	12	48	3.20
49	3	16	109	7	16	169	11	16	229	15	16	289	19	16	349	23	16	49	3	16	49	3.27
50	3	20	110	7	20	170	11	20	230	15	20	290	19	20	350	23	20	50	3	20	50	3.33
51	3	24	111	7	24	171	11	24	231	15	24	291	19	24	351	23	24	51	3	24	51	3.40
52	3	28	112	7	28	172	11	28	232	15	28	292	19	28	352	23	28	52	3	28	52	3.47
53	3	32	113	7	32	173	11	32	233	15	32	293	19	32	353	23	32	53	3	32	53	3.53
54	3	36	114	7	36	174	11	36	234	15	36	294	19	36	354	23	36	54	3	36	54	3.60
55	3	40	115	7	40	175	11	40	235	15	40	295	19	40	355	23	40	55	3	40	55	3.67
56	3	44	116	7	44	176	11	44	236	15	44	296	19	44	356	23	44	56	3	44	56	3.73
57	3	48	117	7	48	177	11	48	237	15	48	297	19	48	357	23	48	57	3	48	57	3.80
58	3	52	118	7	52	178	11	52	238	15	52	298	19	52	358	23	52	58	3	52	58	3.87
59	3	56	119	7	56	179	11	56	239	15	56	299	19	56	359	23	56	59	3	56	59	3.93
60	4	00	120	8	00	180	12	00	240	16	00	300	20	00	360	24	00	60	4	00	60	4.00

h= hours of time **m**= minutes of time **s** = seconds of time **'** = minutes of arc **"** = seconds of arc

Figure 112

This one-page table can be found in the nautical almanac and is shown in Figure 112.

The area in the large red box covers degrees, the area in the green box covers minutes (we don't use the seconds column). You'll see that the table mirrors what we have been saying: 15° = 1hr, 30° = 2 hr etc.

But what if we wanted to know the time difference between ourselves and Greenwich given a longitude of 165° 44.0'? Looking at the blue boxes, we see that 165° gives a time difference of 11hr, and 44.0' a time difference of 2 min 56 sec. We need to add these together to get a total. However, we're not interested in too much accuracy here, so we round up or down to the nearest full minute. Therefore, 2min 56sec becomes 3min, giving a total time difference of 11hr 3min.

So, continuing with our proforma, we are 015° 47.8' West. Referring to Figure 113, we input this longitude and then, using the table in Figure

112, we establish the time difference that this longitude represents, in this case 1 hour and 3 minutes.

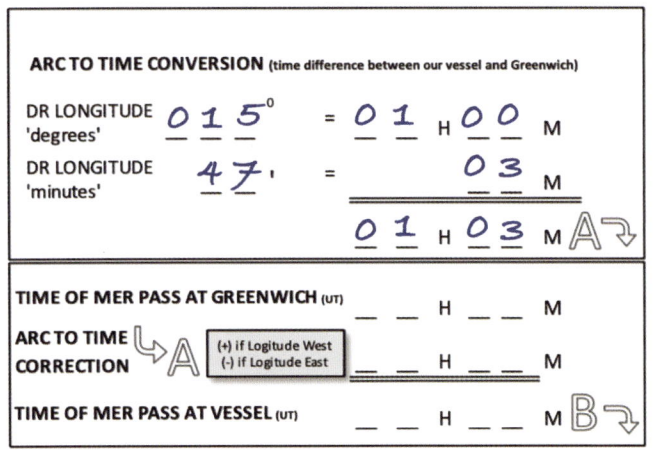

Figure 113

In essence what Figure 113 is telling us so far is that we have a time difference of 1hr 03min due to our longitude.

We now need to go to our Daily Pages within the nautical almanac to find the time of Mer Pass at Greenwich. Figure 114 shows the extract from the right-hand page we used earlier.

Within the red box we see three times for mer pass over the three days covered by this page. The time on the 17th is 1159 UT. This time goes on to the proforma.

In Figure 115, you'll see our mer pass time of 1159 UT has been entered. Then our time difference comes in (A out = A in).

We've circled the relevant condition, ie are we east or west? If we are east our noon or mer pass will happen earlier than in Greenwich. If we are west, then it will be later. In this case we are west and need to add our time difference. So we have worked out that the mer pass in our position will occur at 1302 UT.

So, we've been out on deck and caught the sun on its meridian. Now we can continue with our proforma. We need to undertake the sextant corrections at some point, so we might as well get them out of the way. Perhaps try having an attempt yourself using the Altitude Correction Tables (it's unlikely the index error will have changed, and unless you've taken the sight from a different part of the vessel, the height of eye will also remain the same). See Figure 116 for the result.

We now need to establish the declination, as shown in Figure 117.

Figure 114

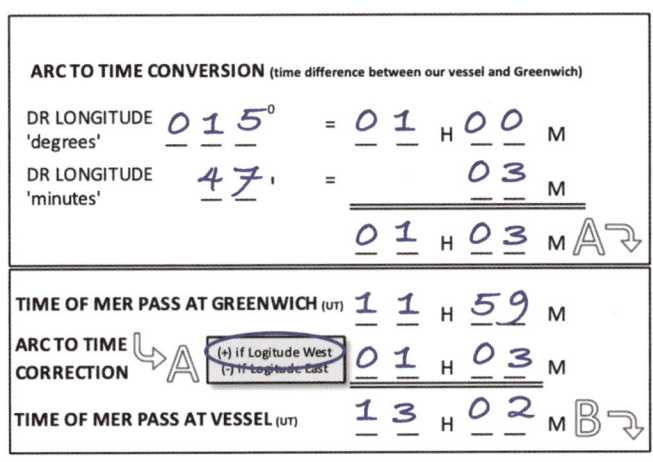

Figure 115

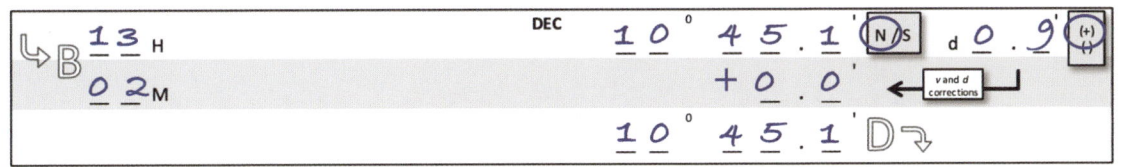

Figure 116

Figure 117

This, again, is obtained from the Daily Pages. Be careful here, we get used to obtaining both the GHA and the declination for sight reductions. Here, we only need the declination, but because the degrees of declination are omitted on many of the lines (remember, to save on unnecessary printing), it can lead to confusion. We will also need the Increments and Corrections tables once again but only for the 'd' value.

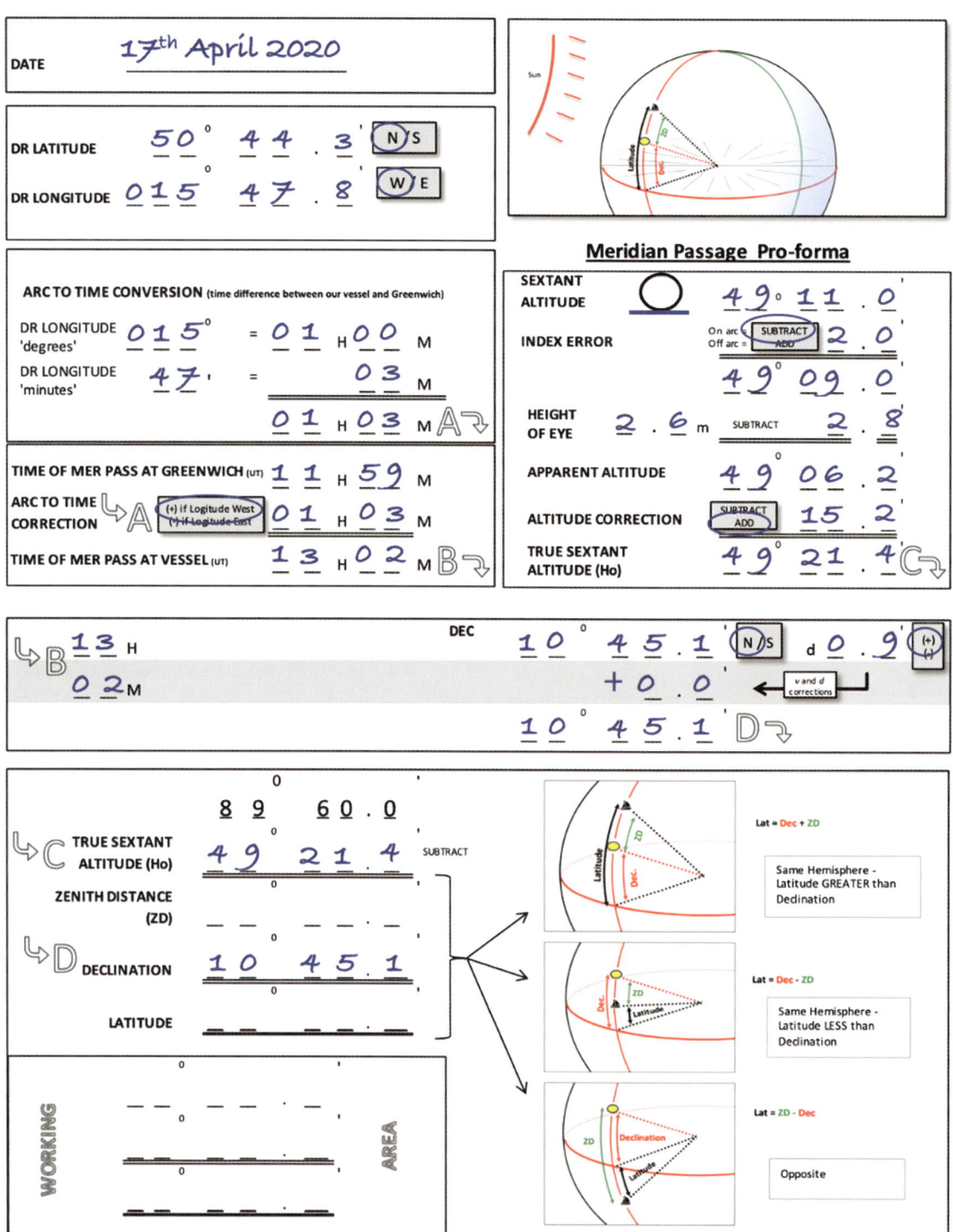

Figure 118

Figure 118 shows us our proforma so far. We've transferred the true sextant altitude (Ho) (C out = C in) and the Declination (D out = D in).

Now, we've said that ZD = 90° – Ho. So we need to subtract our Ho from 90°. We could do a subtraction that looks like this:

90° 00.0'
Minus 49° 21.4'

However, the maths here is tricky because we can't subtract 21.4' from zero. So, instead of 90° 00.0' we could call this 89° 60.0'. We've essentially borrowed a degree and turned it into 60 minutes, thus it simplifies the maths.

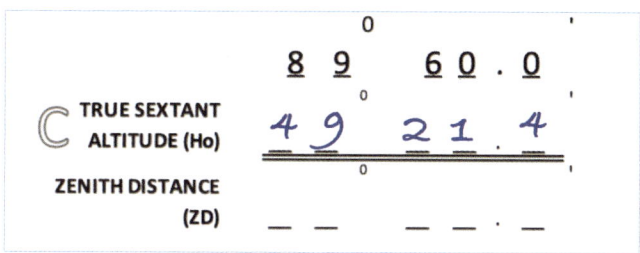

Figure 119

Figure 120

Using a calculator, we can now do a simple subtraction, as shown in Figure 119. This gives us our ZD as per Figure 120.

Figure 121 is where we're now up to, nearly there!

We now have the declination and ZD that we need. It's at this point we need to decide which of the three pictures we use. (The three options help with the trickier pictures. But if we remember here that we are trying to get somewhere close to our DR latitude of 50° N, there's only one way we can do this with a Dec. of 10° and a ZD of 40°, and that's by adding them together. It's a good way to check your choice of the three options.) To do this we compare the declination and our DR latitude. It's just a process of elimination. In this example we can see the top option (in Figure 108) is the correct one: both in the same hemisphere with our latitude greater than the Dec. This leads to:

Latitude = ZD + Dec.

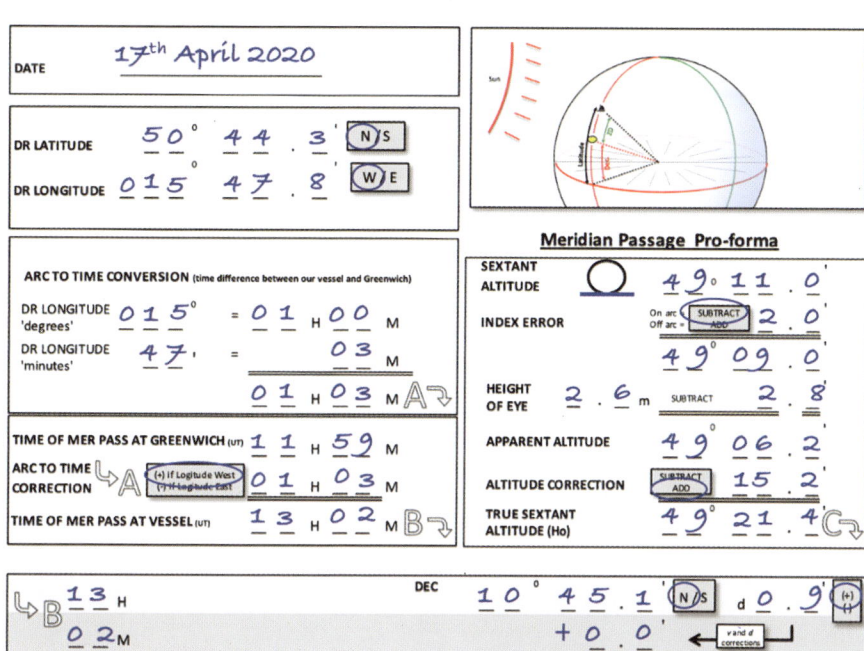

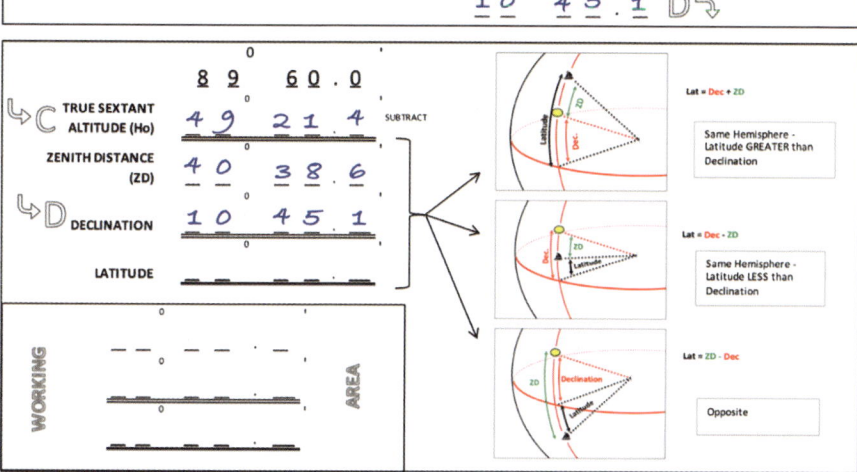

Figure 121

Figure 122 shows the finished meridian passage sight: our latitude is 51° 23.7' North. We've done it!

This example was a straightforward case of adding together the ZD and Dec. Sometimes it will be necessary to transfer the ZD and Dec. into the *working area* in order to undertake subtractions, ie possibly with options 2 and 3, which give different formulae.

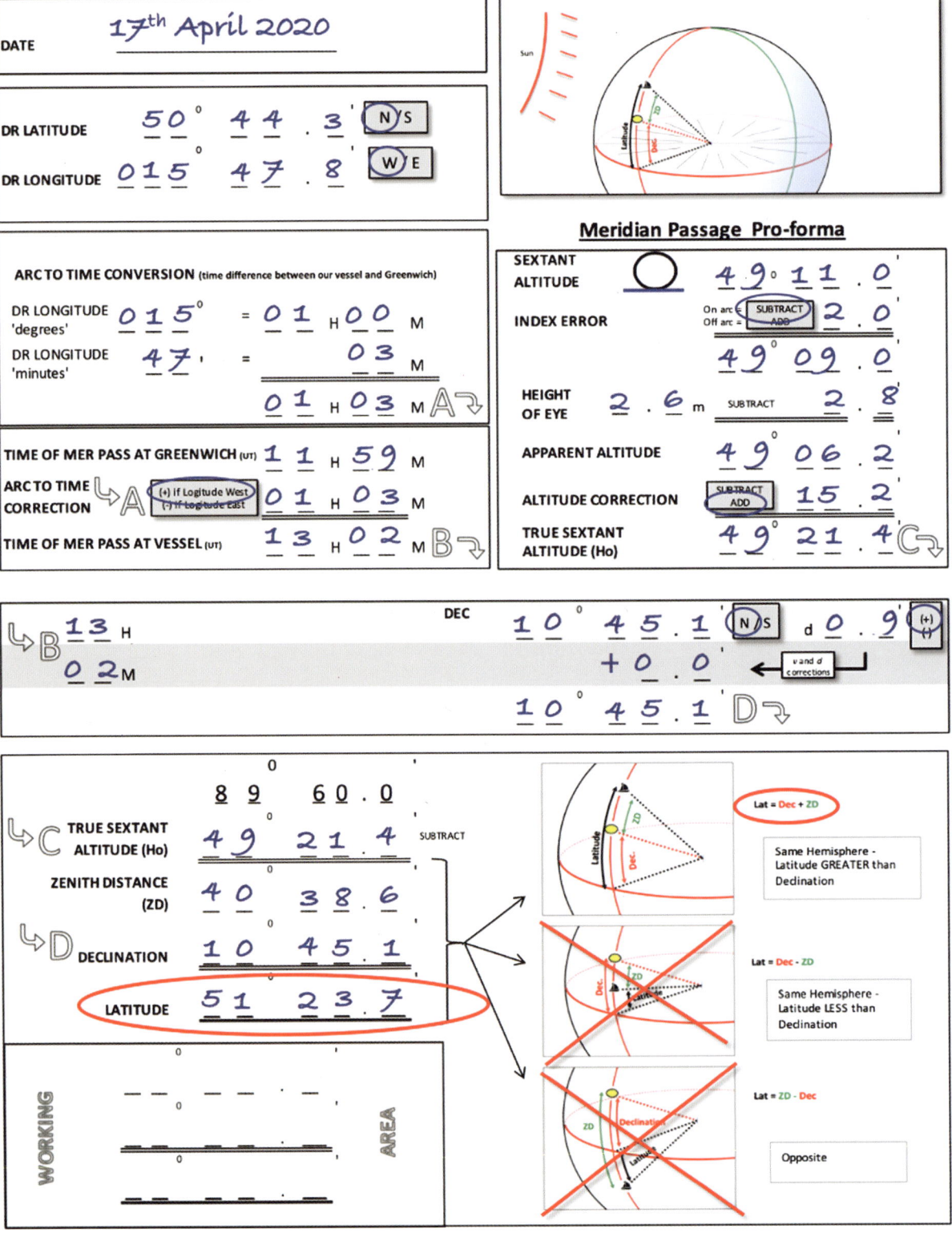

Figure 122

CHAPTER ELEVEN
Meridian passage
Quick Start and recap

If using this for a *Quick Start*, please also refer to Appendix 4

RESOURCES

- A **nautical almanac**

  Included within will be:
  - Altitude correction tables 10° to 90° Sun, Stars and Planets
  - Increments and Corrections
  - Conversion of Arc to Time table

  For advice regarding online resources visit www.philsomerville.com

- Accurate watch set to UT
- Sextant (checked for errors)

We've seen that undertaking a meridian passage sight offers us the chance of obtaining a position line without the need to undertake a full sun sight reduction. We obtain our latitude, and this gives us a horizontal position line. Regarding this horizontal position line, an interesting point to note is that at the time of the meridian passage, the sun will be exactly north or exactly south of you. There is one exception, and that is if you happen to be in the tropics and your latitude just so happens to be the same as the sun's declination, then the sun would be directly overhead.

Now, we have a short window of opportunity in which to observe the noon sight, and if it happens to be cloudy for this critical period, we will have to resort to a second full sun sight reduction.

We'll look at where knowing our latitude comes in when we look at plotting.

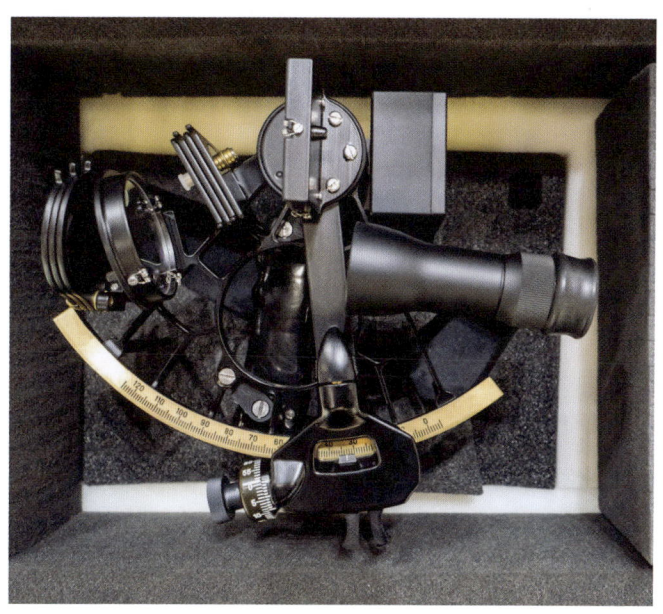

Completing a meridian passage sight

We will use the mer pass proforma shown in Figure 123.

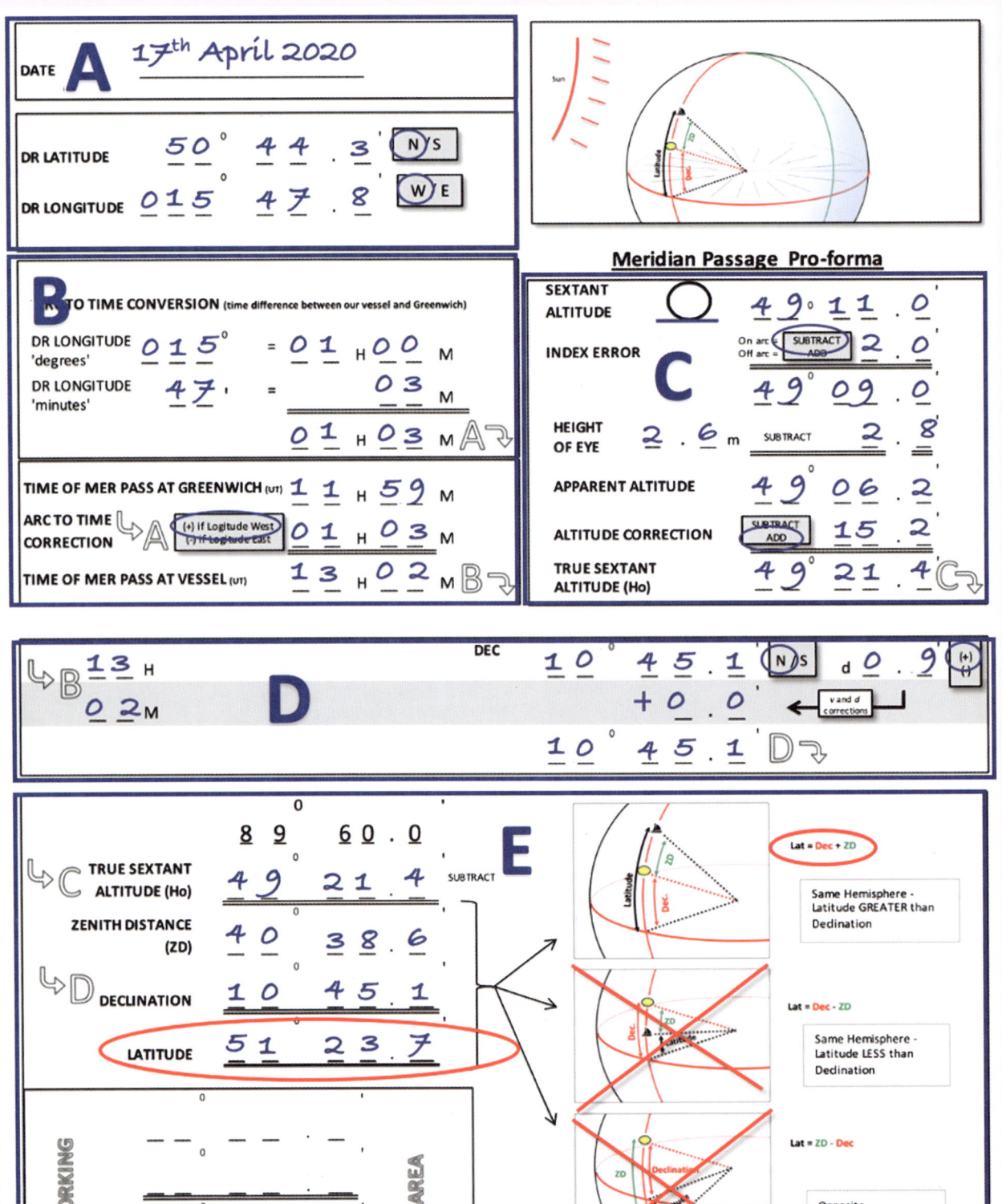

Figure 123

Step 1

Box 'A': Input the Greenwich date and the vessel's DR position.

Step 2

Box 'B': Calculate the time difference between ourselves and Greenwich in the Conversion of Arc to Time tables. Obtain the time of the mer pass for our given date from the Daily Pages in the nautical almanac. Next, apply our time difference (if our DR longitude is east, it will occur sooner, if west, later).

Step 3

20 minutes before the mer pass we go on deck and repeatedly bring the sun down to the horizon until the sun appears stationary or hovers on the horizon. Unlike when undertaking a full sight reduction (which is timing critical), the exact time of the mer pass is not so important, ie not down to an accuracy of seconds.

Step 4

Box 'C': Undertake the corrections required to obtain the true sextant altitude (Ho).

Step 5

Box 'D': Obtain the declination from the nautical almanac. Because the declination changes slowly, the exact timings here aren't critical.

Step 6

Box 'E': Input the Ho and the declination. Then obtain the ZD by deducting the Ho from 90° (89° 60.0').

We now have the keys we require. Next, we look at the three scenarios and choose the one that matches our situation. We then undertake the calculation as per the formula attached to the relevant scenario, using the working area if the ZD and Dec. are presented in the wrong order.

Step 7

Compare our answer (which should now be our latitude) with our original DR latitude and make a judgement call. Our judgement depends on how accurate we thought our DR position was in the first place. If we are degrees out (remember each degree is 60nm), then check working and scenario chosen.

CHAPTER TWELVE

Plotting

Now we're about to see the result of all our hard work and start finding out where we are!

Before we can do any plotting though, we need something to plot on. Ideally, we need a chart, one with a suitable scale to reflect the accuracy we're looking for. Now, we could take hundreds of pre-purchased charts, each one with a relevant latitude and longitude scale for our location, and apart from containing the right scale, we'd have lots of blank blue charts. Clearly, this would be expensive and pointless. So instead we make our own.

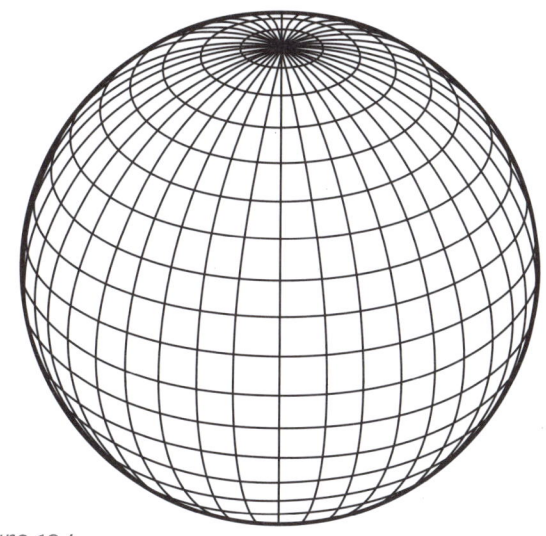

Figure 124

Opposite: Living up to an age of 50 years, these wonderful birds with their wingspans of up to 3.5m, live on the world's oceans, only returning to land for breeding.

In making our own, we need to first remember that once we leave the equator (on the equator, the distance on the surface of the earth represented by one degree of longitude equals that of latitude, ie 60nm), a degree of longitude, in terms of distance on the surface of the earth, becomes less than that of latitude, ie it becomes less than 60nm. The further we move from the equator, the smaller this distance becomes, as shown in Figure 124. So we need to reflect this latitude vs longitude relationship on our plotting sheet.

Figure 125 is our plotting sheet. This is a commonly used plotting sheet and can be purchased, usually in A3 format, in books. Plotting sheets are also widely available in PDF format online, for example at www.philsomerville.com. You'll notice the sheet has a latitude scale (covering two full degrees, ie 120nm), but it has no longitude scale. The area circled in red enables us to produce the longitude scale.

SUN RUN SUN: MORNING SUN SIGHT AND MERIDIAN PASSAGE

OK, we'll use the most common scenario for starters: a morning sight followed by a mer pass. As we've seen, the mer pass is desirable because it's a quicker alternative to a second full sight reduction.

We're going to run through a full plot, and in order to do so, we'll use the sight reduction undertaken in Chapter 8. The finished proforma was shown in Figure 103 and is reproduced opposite.

Appendix 6 contains a plotting guide for future *Quick Starts*.

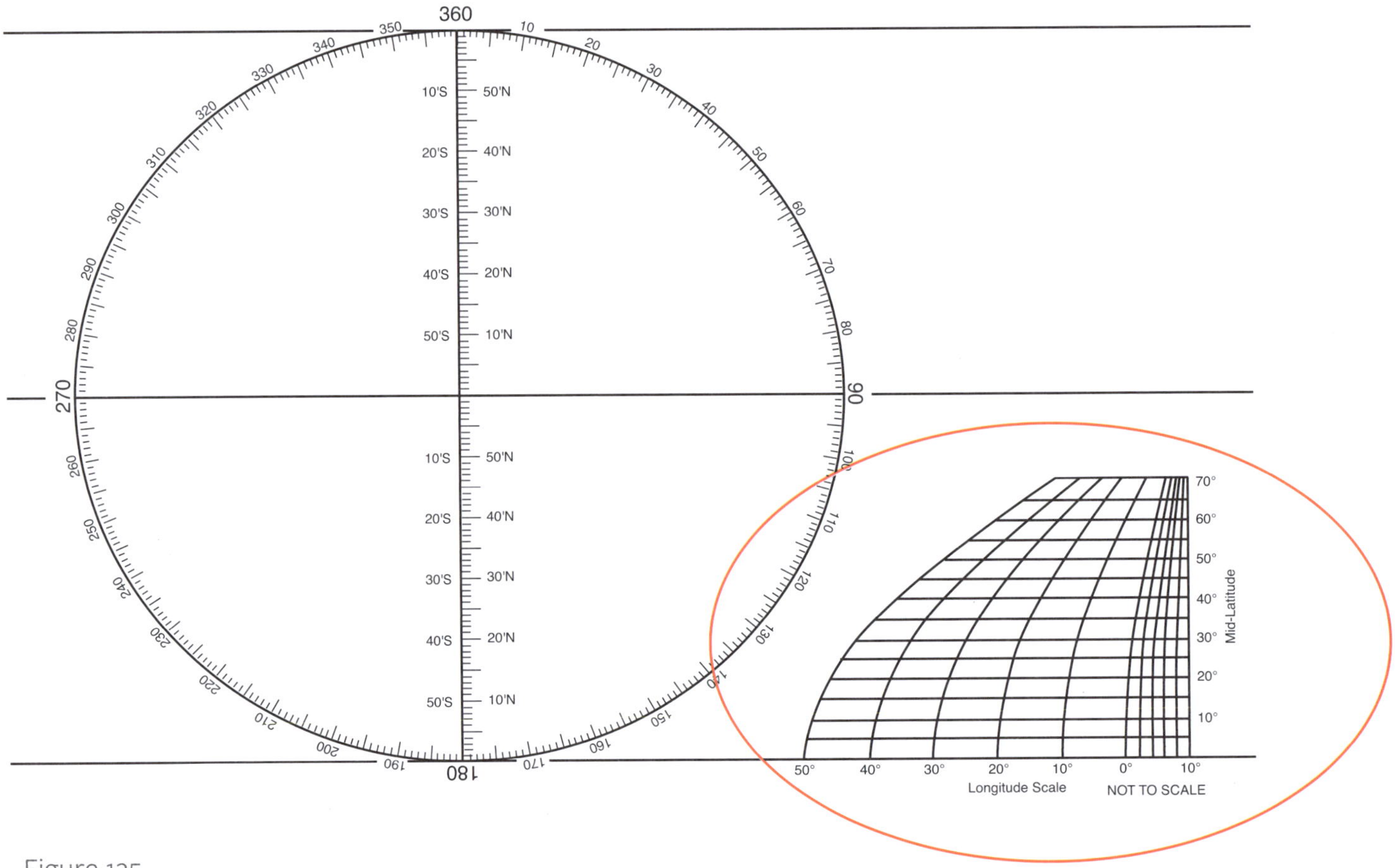

Figure 125

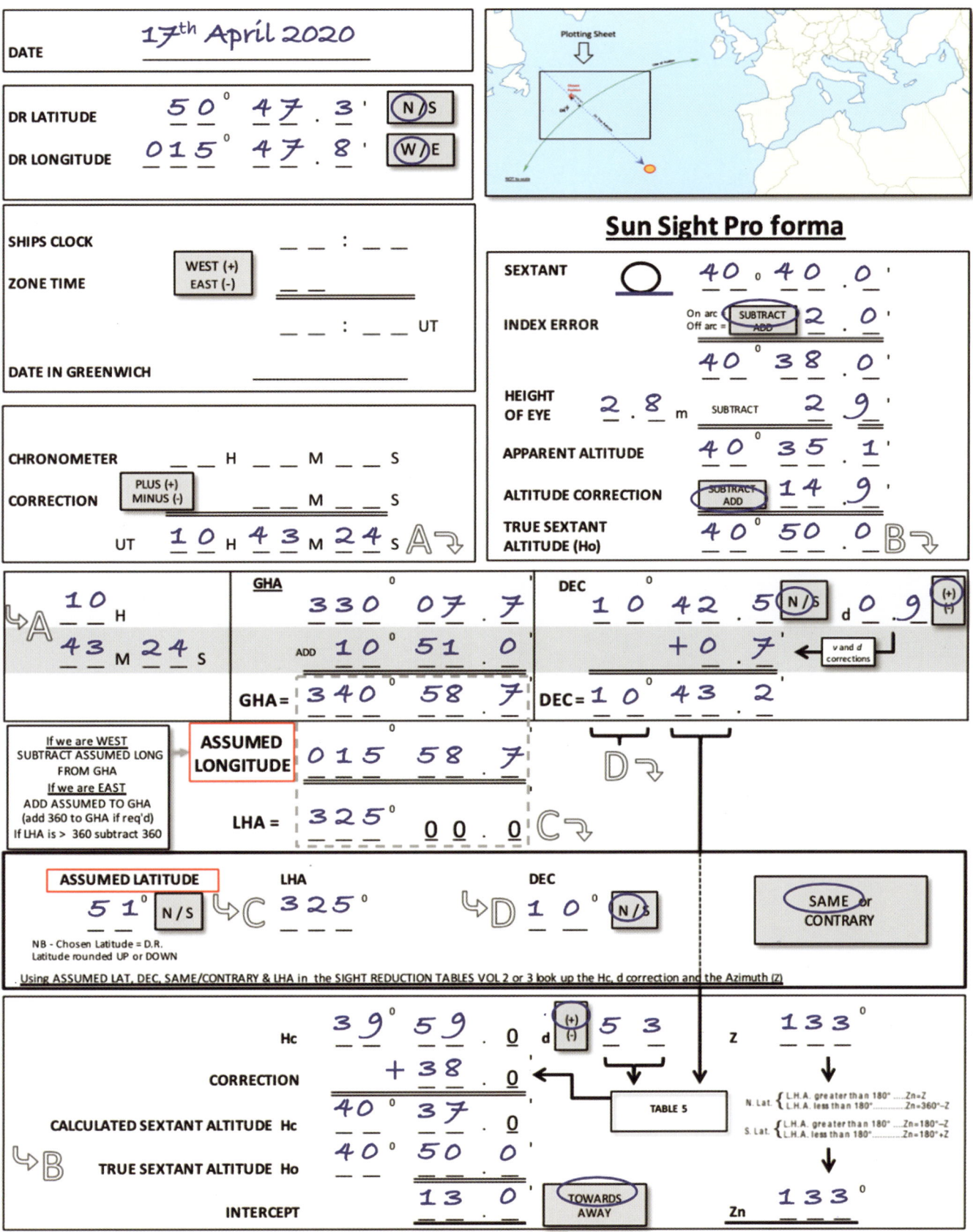

Figure 103

Plotting a Sun Run Sun

Step 1 of plotting is where we create the longitude scale. We usually plot in pencil. In our worked example we're using colour to help add clarity.

(1) - Mark Longitude scale according to present latitude.
(2) - Mark assumed position (AP) (Made up of assumed latitude & assumed longitude.)
(3) - Draw on Azimuth (Zn) (direction of Sun indicated with arrows).
(4) - Mark intercept - reference to the AP - either towards the sun from AP or away.
(5) - Extend the intercept perpendicular to the azimuth (Zn) forming a 'line of position' (which if extended would form a position circle). You are *definitely* somewhere on this line.
(6) - Mark on original DR (Lat and Long) and transfer onto LOP to DR1.
(7) - Draw on RUN from line of position (preferably from your 'probable position').
(8) - Transfer the 'line of position' (becomes 'transferred position line'). Marked with two arrow heads.
(9) - Point 9 becomes DR2. Used for a 2nd Sun Sight if a mer pass wasn't possible
(10) - Draw on Meridian Passage.
(11) - Now, we are *definitely* on the transferred line of position and *definitely* on the mer pass. Therefore the only place we can be is at their intersection - our Fix.

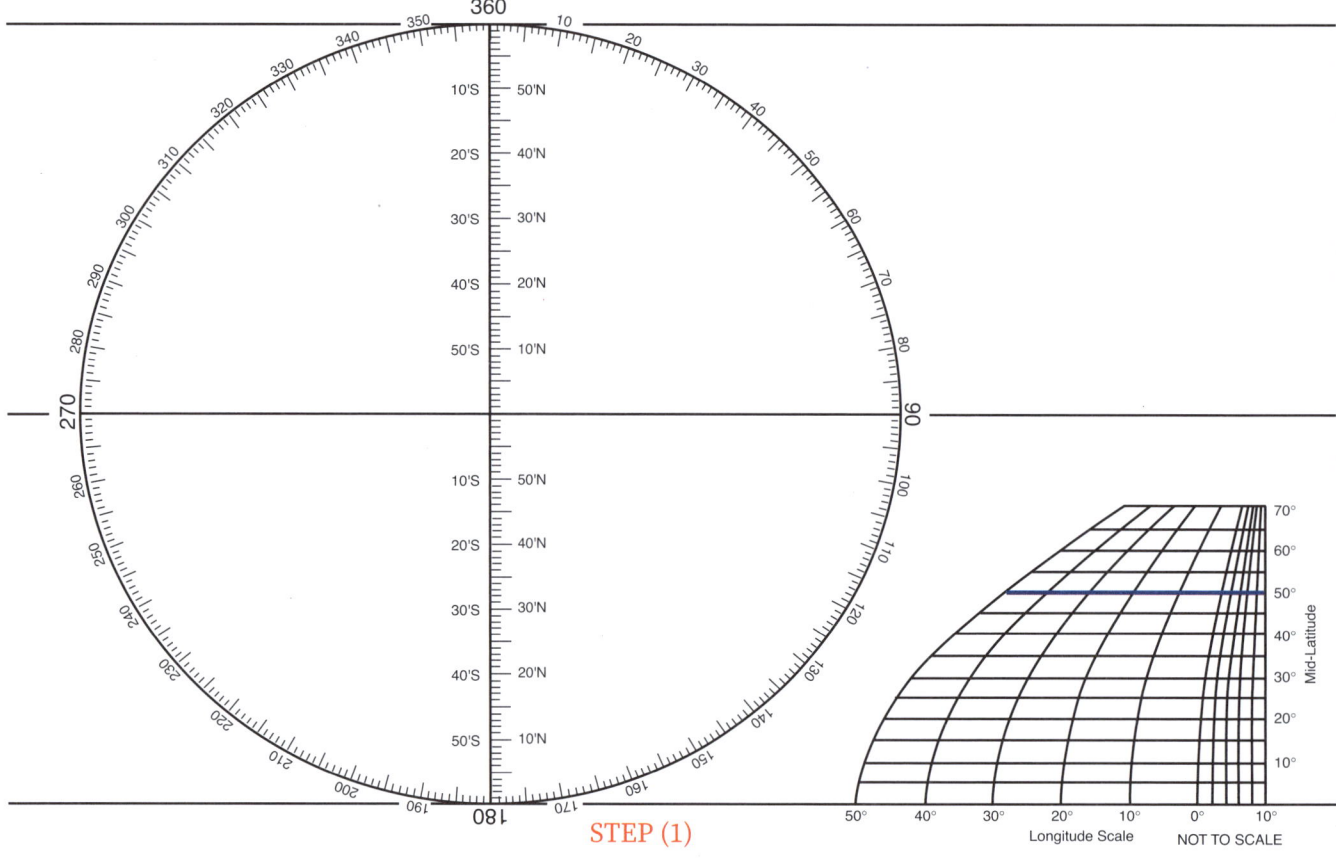

Figure 126

Step 1 Creating the longitude scale

We identify our **assumed latitude** from our proforma and mark this on the scale as shown in Figure 126 (*blue line*). The length of this blue line represents one degree of longitude at our latitude of 51°. You'll find details of how to use this odd-looking scale in Appendix 7.

(1) - Mark Longitude scale according to present latitude.
(2) - Mark assumed position (AP) (Made up of assumed latitude & assumed longitude.)
(3) - Draw on Azimuth (Zn) (direction of Sun indicated with arrows).
(4) - Mark intercept - reference to the AP - either towards the sun from AP or away.
(5) - Extend the intercept perpendicular to the azimuth (Zn) forming a 'line of position' (which if extended would form a position circle). You are *definitely* somewhere on this line.
(6) - Mark on original DR (Lat and Long) and transfer onto LOP to DR1.
(7) - Draw on RUN from line of position (preferably from your 'probable position').
(8) - Transfer the 'line of position' (becomes 'transferred position line'). Marked with two arrow heads.
(9) - Point 9 becomes DR2. Used for a 2nd Sun Sight if a mer pass wasn't possible
(10) - Draw on Meridian Passage.
(11) - Now, we are *definitely* on the transferred line of position and *definitely* on the mer pass. Therefore the only place we can be is at their intersection - our Fix.

CHAPTER TWELVE: PLOTTING

91

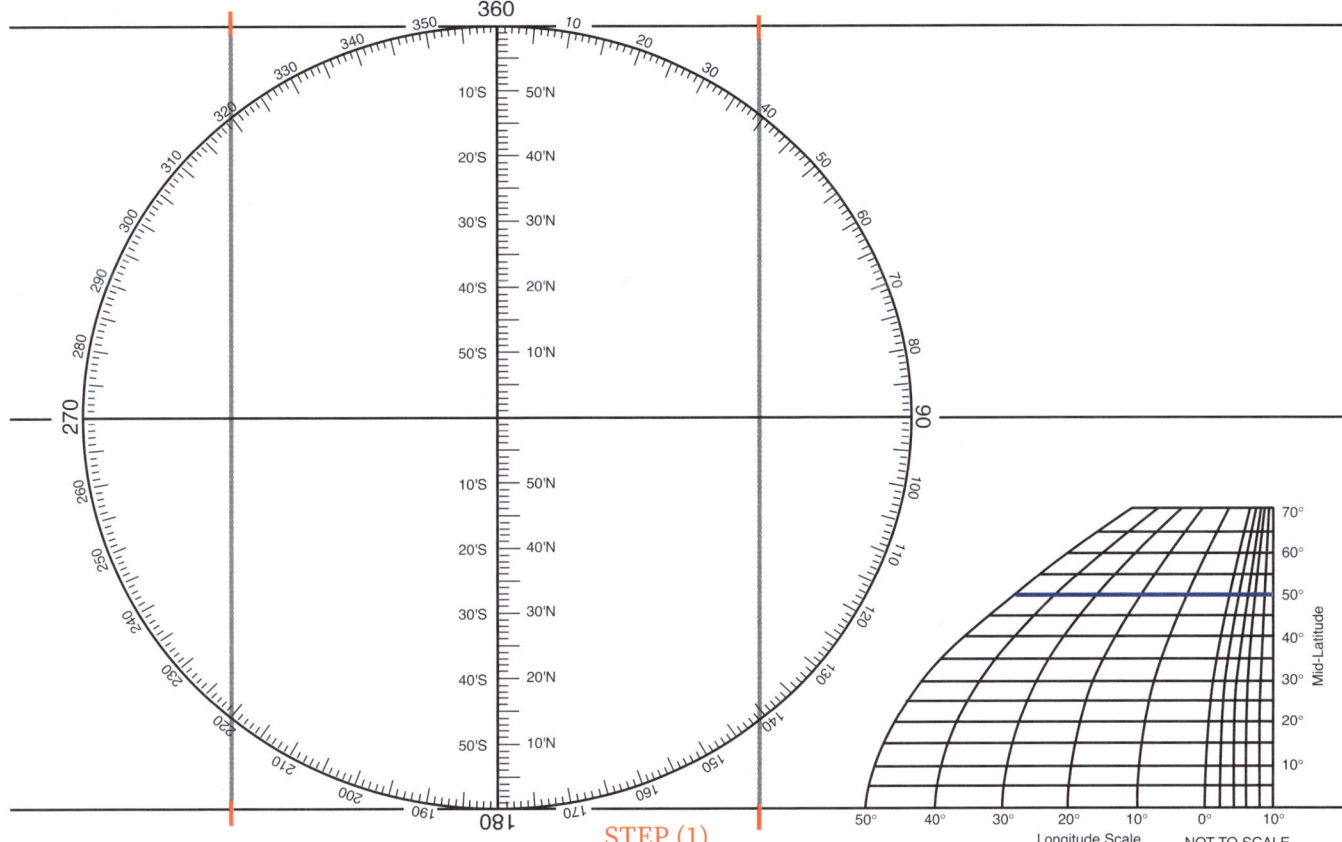

Figure 127

Then, using dividers and starting from the centre, we mark off degrees (top and bottom of plotting sheet) and join them up as shown in Figure 127. We now have a plotting sheet with the latitude and longitude appropriately proportioned for our latitude.

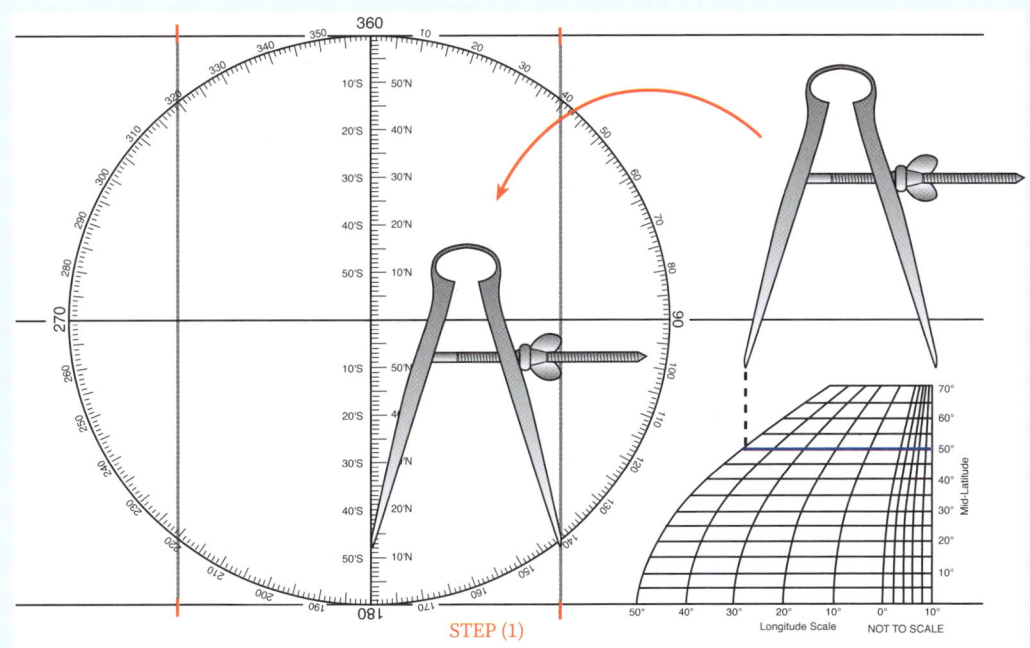

Figure 127a

Next, we need a scale (see Figure 128). The latitude is simple, the centre graticule (line) is our assumed latitude, in this scenario it's 51°.

Longitude is slightly trickier. The risk we face is running off the sheet during the plot. A good idea is to look at current vessel direction. If we're heading east, start on the left, and if heading west, start on the right.

Inevitably, on some occasions, a wrong judgement is made, and you may have to start again. Big intercepts, particularly when the intercept is in the same direction as that of the vessel's travel, can cause challenges. The best thing to do is not to get too hung up on pre-empting a problem, just get plotting and accept that occasionally you'll need to backtrack. The more plotting you undertake, the better the feel you get for this. In the scenario we're plotting we are north and west. Pay close attention to which direction the increments increase in, ie if we were in the southern hemisphere the latitude scale would increase as we moved from top to bottom. The same with longitude. If we were east, the scale would increase in the opposite direction. It may seem obvious, but this is a common error to make.

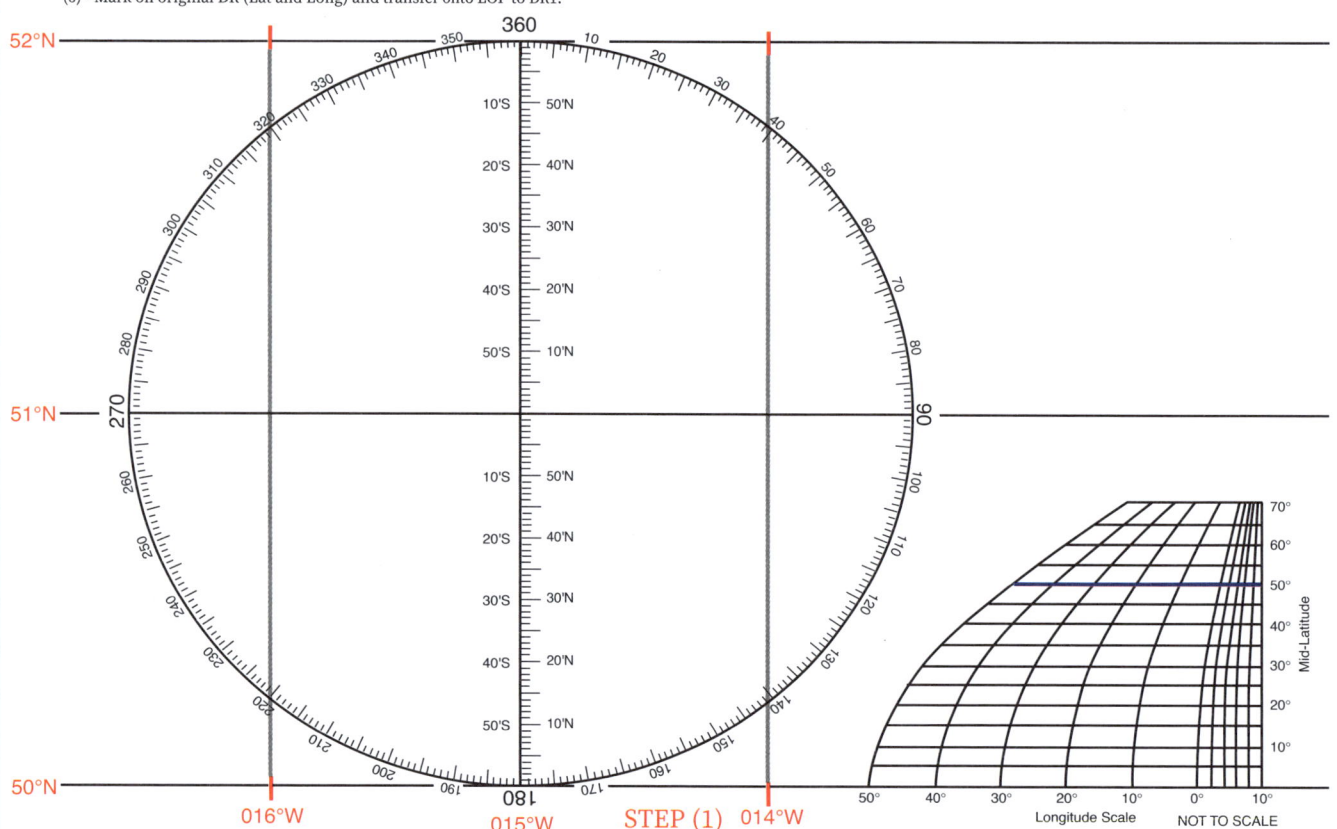

Figure 128

(1) - Mark Longitude scale according to present latitude.
(2) - Mark assumed position (AP) (Made up of assumed latitude & assumed longitude.)
(3) - Draw on Azimuth (Zn) (direction of Sun indicated with arrows).
(4) - Mark intercept - reference to the AP - either towards the sun from AP or away.
(5) - Extend the intercept perpendicular to the azimuth (Zn) forming a 'line of position' (which if extended would form a position circle). You are *definitely* somewhere on this line.
(6) - Mark on original DR (Lat and Long) and transfer onto LOP to DR1.
(7) - Draw on RUN from line of position (preferably from your 'probable position').
(8) - Transfer the 'line of position' (becomes 'transferred position line'). Marked with two arrow heads.
(9) - Point 9 becomes DR2. Used for a 2nd Sun Sight if a mer pass wasn't possible
(10) - Draw on Meridian Passage.
(11) - Now, we are *definitely* on the transferred line of position and *definitely* on the mer pass. Therefore the only place we can be is at their intersection - our Fix.

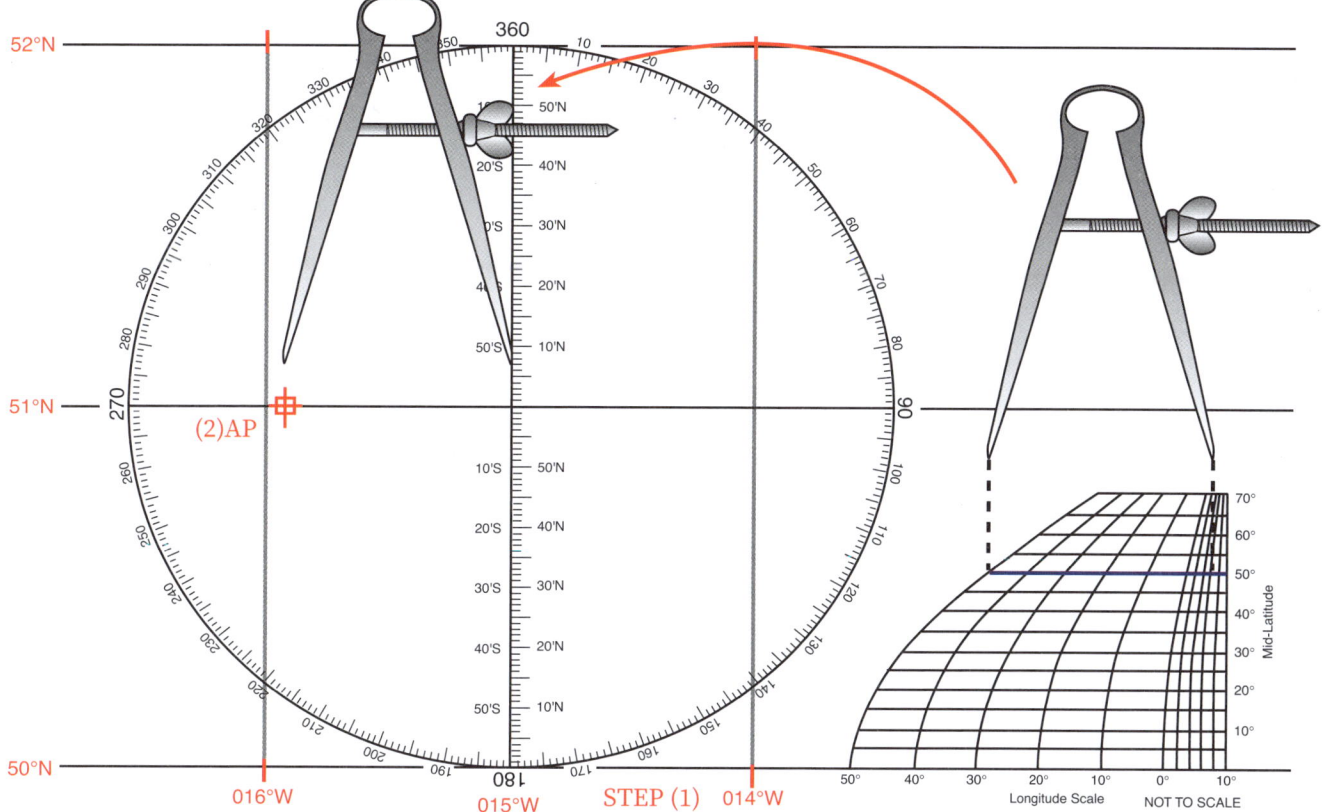

Figure 129

Step 2 Plotting our assumed position

We now plot our assumed position (made up of assumed latitude and assumed longitude, as shown in Figure 129). We're making this our starting point because it's from this position that the calculated sextant altitude Hc was calculated. It takes on the appearance of a waypoint. To see how we measure longitude using the scale in the bottom right-hand corner please consult Appendix 7.

Step 3 Plotting the bearing of the sun

If you cast your mind back, we said that if you were actually on the assumed position, you would get the same true sextant altitude (Ho) on the vessel as the calculated sextant altitude (Hc). We also said that this is highly unlikely, and we use the difference between the two sextant angles (Ho compared with Hc) to produce an intercept. The intercept is telling us how far from the assumed position we are. Knowing how far leads to the next question: In which direction? That's where the bearing of the sun comes in. We now plot the bearing on to the sheet.

(1) - Mark Longitude scale according to present latitude.
(2) - Mark assumed position (AP) (Made up of assumed latitude & assumed longitude.)
(3) - Draw on Azimuth (Zn) (direction of Sun indicated with arrows).
(4) - Mark intercept - reference to the AP - either towards the sun from AP or away.
(5) - Extend the intercept perpendicular to the azimuth (Zn) forming a 'line of position' (which if extended would form a position circle). You are *definitely* somewhere on this line.
(6) - Mark on original DR (Lat and Long) and transfer onto LOP to DR1.

(7) - Draw on RUN from line of position (preferably from your 'probable position').
(8) - Transfer the 'line of position' (becomes 'transferred position line'). Marked with two arrow heads.
(9) - Point 9 becomes DR2. Used for a 2nd Sun Sight if a mer pass wasn't possible
(10) - Draw on Meridian Passage.
(11) - Now, we are *definitely* on the transferred line of position and *definitely* on the mer pass. Therefore the only place we can be is at their intersection - our Fix.

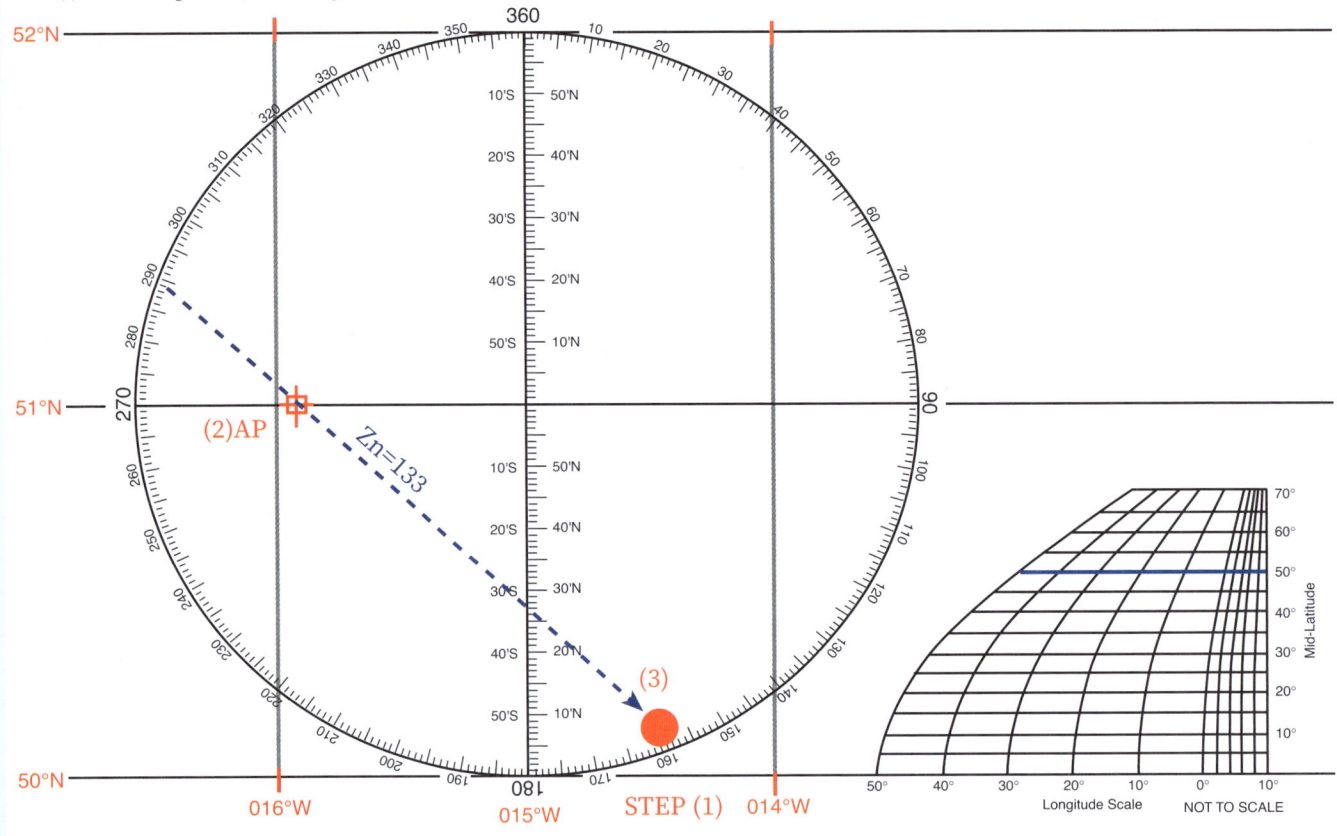

Figure 130

The true bearing or azimuth bearing (Zn) has only a temporary use for us, therefore it's better to make it a dotted line to avoid cluttering up the plotting sheet – see Figure 130.

It's better to draw the Zn through the assumed position AP, ie across the whole sheet in both directions. Although our completed proforma tells us whether we're towards or away, doing this helps us to take things one step at a time and often avoids confusion further on.

An arrow is drawn at the end of the bearing to show the sun's direction. We wouldn't normally draw a picture of the sun, but it often helps.

At this stage it's worth sense checking the azimuth bearing (Zn). It is, of course, a bearing of the sun and if you took a bearing of the sun at the time of the sight, you should be able to check that the numbers are similar. Also, the following is worth keeping in mind: if you've taken the sight in the morning the sun should be east of you; likewise, afternoon sights should put the sun west of you. This also double-checks that we did the Z to Zn conversion correctly, as errors are common when undertaking this.

(1) - Mark Longitude scale according to present latitude.
(2) - Mark assumed position (AP) (Made up of assumed latitude & assumed longitude.)
(3) - Draw on Azimuth (Zn) (direction of Sun indicated with arrows).
(4) - Mark intercept - reference to the AP - either towards the sun from AP or away. (Example below is 'towards').
(5) - Extend the intercept perpendicular to the azimuth (Zn) forming a 'line of position' (which if extended would form a position circle). You are *definitely* somewhere on this line.
(6) - Mark on original DR (Lat and Long) and transfer onto LOP to DR1.
(7) - Draw on RUN from line of position (preferably from your 'probable position').
(8) - Transfer the 'line of position' (becomes 'transferred position line'). Marked with two arrow heads.
(9) - Point 9 becomes DR2. Used for a 2nd Sun Sight if a mer pass wasn't possible
(10) - Draw on Meridian Passage.
(11) - Now, we are *definitely* on the transferred line of position and *definitely* on the mer pass. Therefore the only place we can be is at their intersection - our Fix.

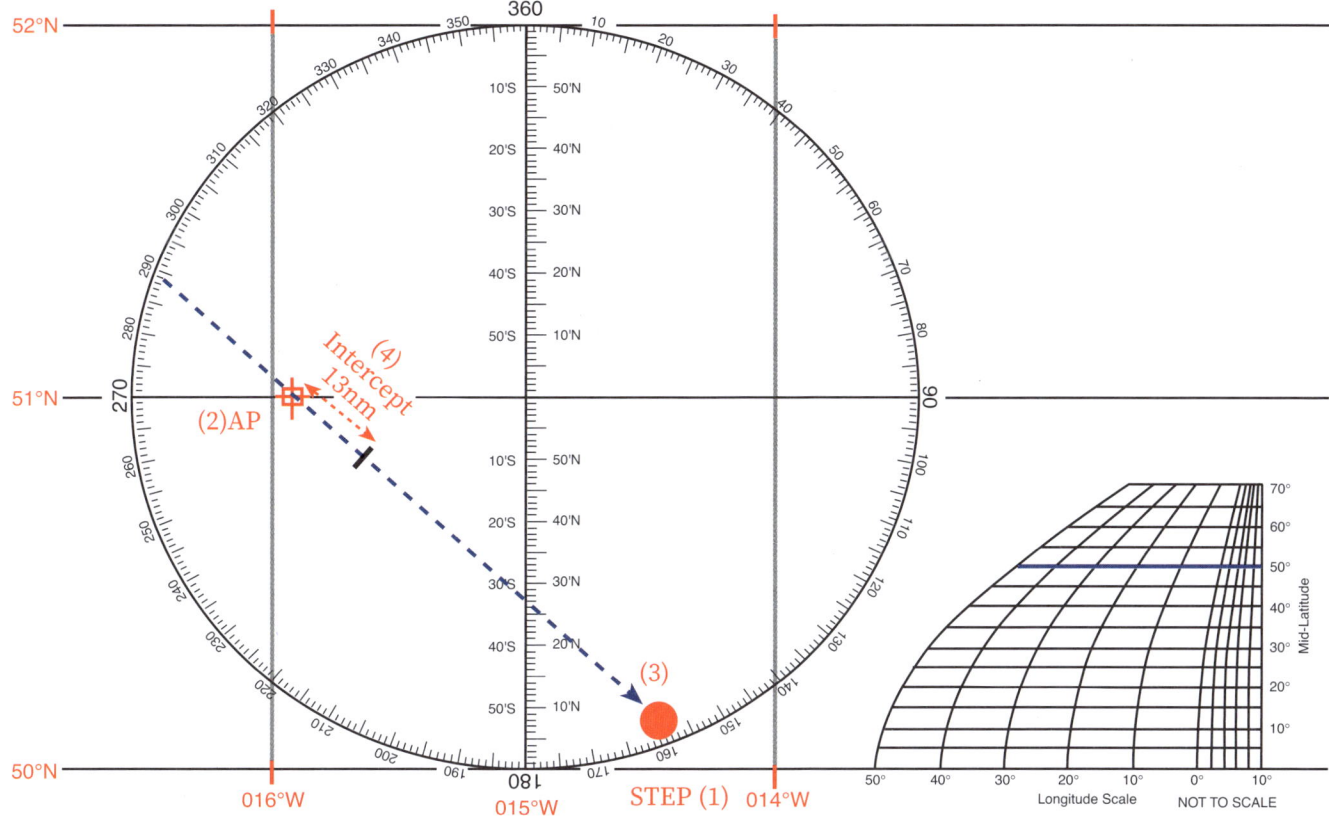

Figure 131

Step 4 Measuring our distance from the assumed position

We know we're not on the assumed position, so where are we? As we've said, it's our intercept that tells us that. In this scenario we are 13nm **towards** the sun. With our dividers, we measure off the latitude scale 13' (because 13' = 13nm) – see Figure 131. Measuring off the longitude scale is a common mistake to make. Unless you're on the equator, it will make your distance measured smaller.

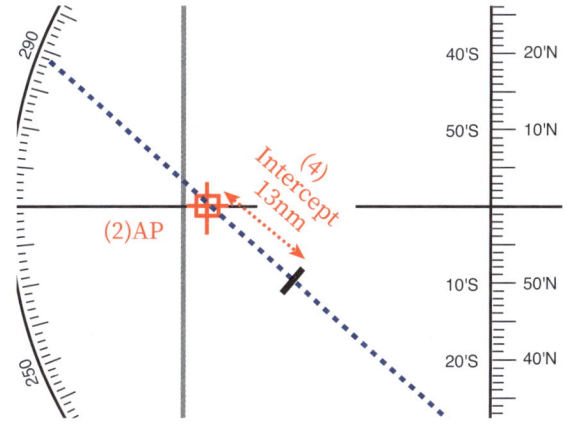

Figure 131a

(1) - Mark Longitude scale according to present latitude.
(2) - Mark assumed position (AP) (Made up of assumed latitude & assumed longitude.)
(3) - Draw on Azimuth (Zn) (direction of Sun indicated with arrows).
(4) - Mark intercept - reference to the AP - either towards the sun from AP or away. (Example below is 'towards').
(5) - Extend the intercept perpendicular to the azimuth (Zn) forming a 'line of position' (which if extended would form a position circle). You are *definitely* somewhere on this line.
(6) - Mark on original DR (Lat and Long) and transfer onto LOP to DR1.
(7) - Draw on RUN from line of position (preferably from your 'probable position').
(8) - Transfer the 'line of position' (becomes 'transferred position line'). Marked with two arrow heads.
(9) - Point 9 becomes DR2. Used for a 2nd Sun Sight if a mer pass wasn't possible
(10) - Draw on Meridian Passage.
(11) - Now, we are *definitely* on the transferred line of position and *definitely* on the mer pass. Therefore the only place we can be is at their intersection - our Fix.

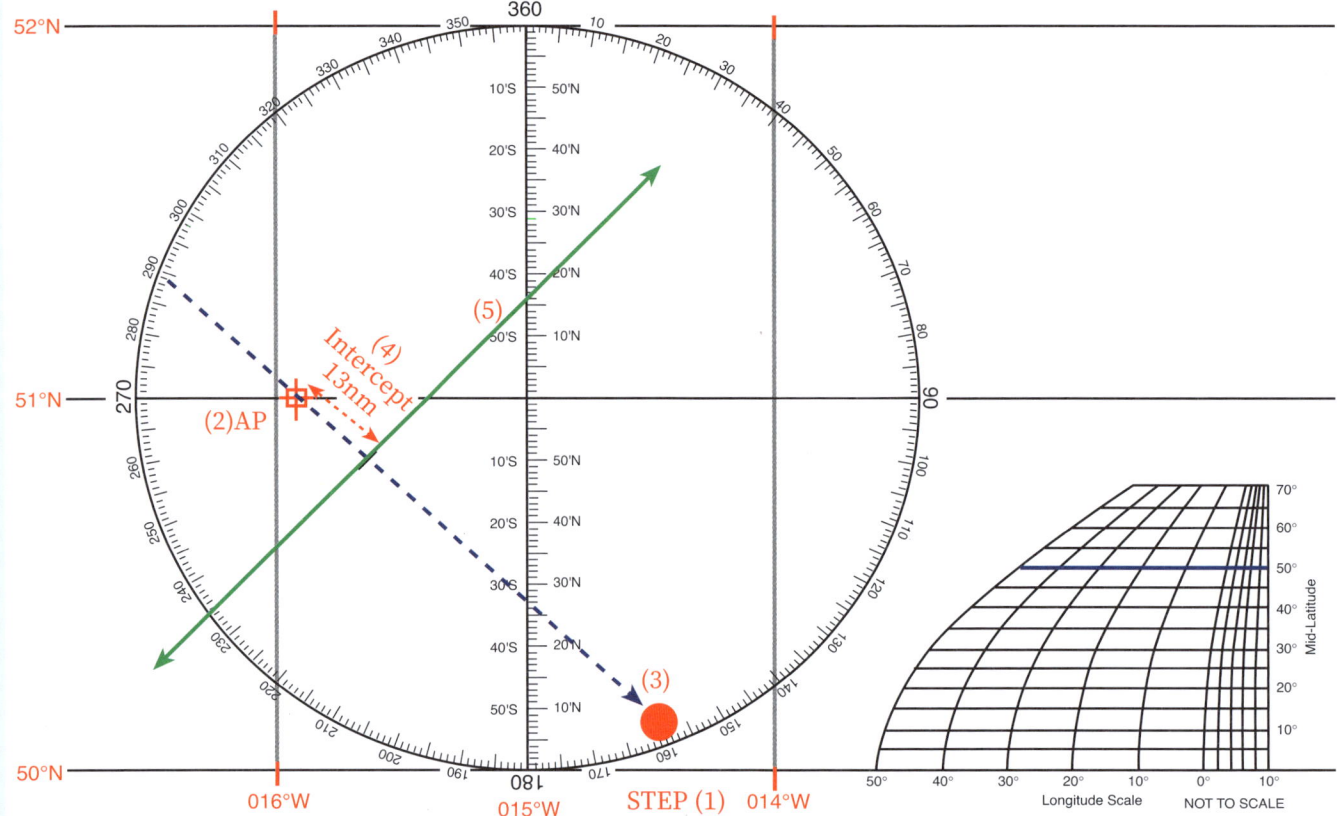

Figure 132

Step 5 Extending the intercept into an LOP

We now need to extend the intercept into a line of position (LOP), just like the green one we saw in Figure 62 on page 45. The LOP is drawn perpendicular (ie at 90°) to the bearing of the sun (Zn), as shown in Figure 132.

It may help if you remember that this LOP is just part of a position circle that surrounds the sun's GP. Although we plot this as a straight line, when actually it should be very slightly curved, it's such a small part of the position circle that any error is insignificant. We draw arrow heads on the ends of the LOP. This reflects the fact that this line forms part of a position circle.

But the following *is* significant: we have now established that we are *definitely* somewhere on the green line (LOP). We have completed the first part of a *Sun Run Sun*.

But whereabouts on the green line are we likely to be? This question gets answered in the next steps.

(1) - Mark Longitude scale according to present latitude.
(2) - Mark assumed position (AP) (Made up of assumed latitude & assumed longitude).
(3) - Draw on Azimuth (Zn) (direction of Sun indicated with arrows).
(4) - Mark intercept - reference to the AP - either towards the sun from AP or away. (Example below is 'towards').
(5) - Extend the intercept perpendicular to the azimuth (Zn) forming a 'line of position' (which if extended would form a position circle). You are *definitely* somewhere on this line.
(6) - Mark on original DR (Lat and Long) and transfer onto LOP to DR1.
(7) - Draw on RUN from line of position (preferably from your 'probable position').
(8) - Transfer the 'line of position' (becomes 'transferred position line'). Marked with two arrow heads.
(9) - Point 9 becomes DR2. Used for a 2nd Sun Sight if a mer pass wasn't possible
(10) - Draw on Meridian Passage.
(11) - Now, we are *definitely* on the transferred line of position and *definitely* on the mer pass. Therefore the only place we can be is at their intersection - our Fix.

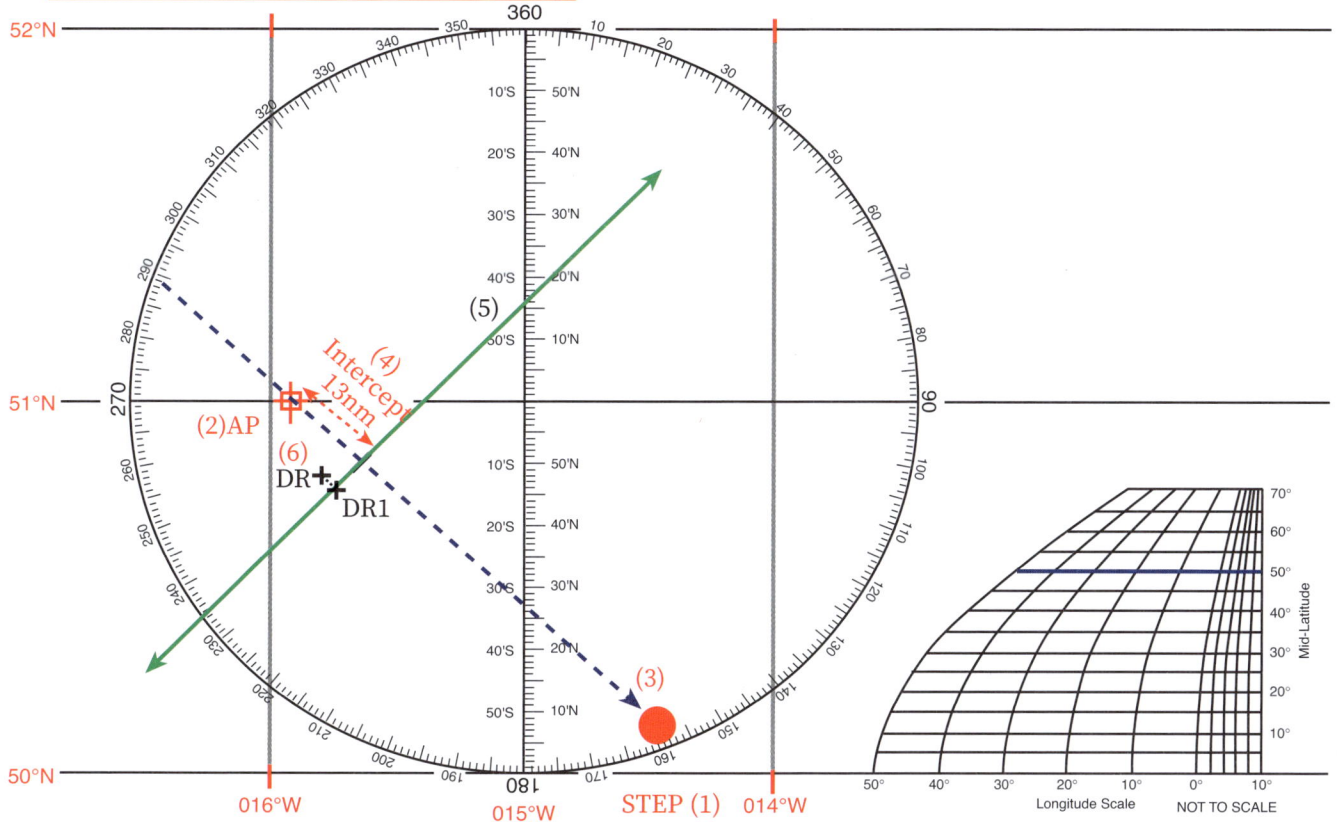

Figure 133

Step 6 Plotting and transferring our DR position

Now, we know we're **definitely** somewhere on the green LOP, but **whereabouts** on the LOP are we? The most logical way of solving this is to plot our original DR position and then transfer it on to the LOP to DR1, as shown in Figure 133. The shortest way of connecting the DR position to DR1 is perpendicular to the LOP or, easier still, parallel to the Zn.

In summary, we know our original DR position is not that accurate, but it's still more accurate than closing our eyes and guessing where we are along the LOP. Therefore, at this point, we're **definitely** on the LOP, and we're *probably* at DR1.

WHAT'S GOING ON ABOARD?

We're working our way towards a fix, but before continuing, let's take stock of what will have actually occurred on the vessel and on the day in question.

The sight we've just plotted was taken in the morning at 10hr 43min 24sec UT (note the sun is both south and <u>east</u> of us). We would have continued on our intended course and probably found out at what time the meridian passage could be observed, in the hope we could catch it. Let's say in this scenario the gods were kind to us, there was no cloud cover and we managed to observe the sun again on the meridian. As we've already seen, this noon sight will give us a new horizontal position line.

But we have a slight problem! Let's say we took the meridian sight at 13h 02m UT. (The mer pass on this day occurred on the Greenwich Meridian at 1159 UT. However, we are approximately 015° West and therefore our noon was approximately an hour later.) In other words, we took the noon sight 2hr and 18min after the morning sight. Clearly our vessel is no longer somewhere on the first green LOP in Figure 140. Therefore, we need to work out where the vessel has moved to during this time: we call this the *Run*. Once we've established what the run has been, we can move the LOP to compensate. This is where recording the details of the ship's log comes in. We should have done this as part of taking the morning sight.

Let's say, after examining the log again, we see that the vessel has travelled 38nm on a heading of 080°T. This may be excessive but it will help give clarity to the plotting.

(1) - Mark Longitude scale according to present latitude.
(2) - Mark assumed position (AP) (Made up of assumed latitude & assumed longitude.)
(3) - Draw on Azimuth (Zn) (direction of Sun indicated with arrows).
(4) - Mark intercept - reference to the AP - either towards the sun from AP or away. (Example below is 'towards').
(5) - Extend the intercept perpendicular to the azimuth (Zn) forming a 'line of position' (which if extended would form a position circle). You are *definitely* somewhere on this line.
(6) - Mark on original DR (Lat and Long) and transfer onto LOP to DR1.
(7) - Draw on RUN from line of position (preferably from your 'probable position').
(8) - Transfer the 'line of position' (becomes 'transferred position line'). Marked with two arrow heads.
(9) - Point 9 becomes DR2. Used for a 2nd Sun Sight if a mer pass wasn't possible
(10) - Draw on Meridian Passage.
(11) - Now, we are *definitely* on the transferred line of position and *definitely* on the mer pass. Therefore the only place we can be is at their intersection - our Fix.

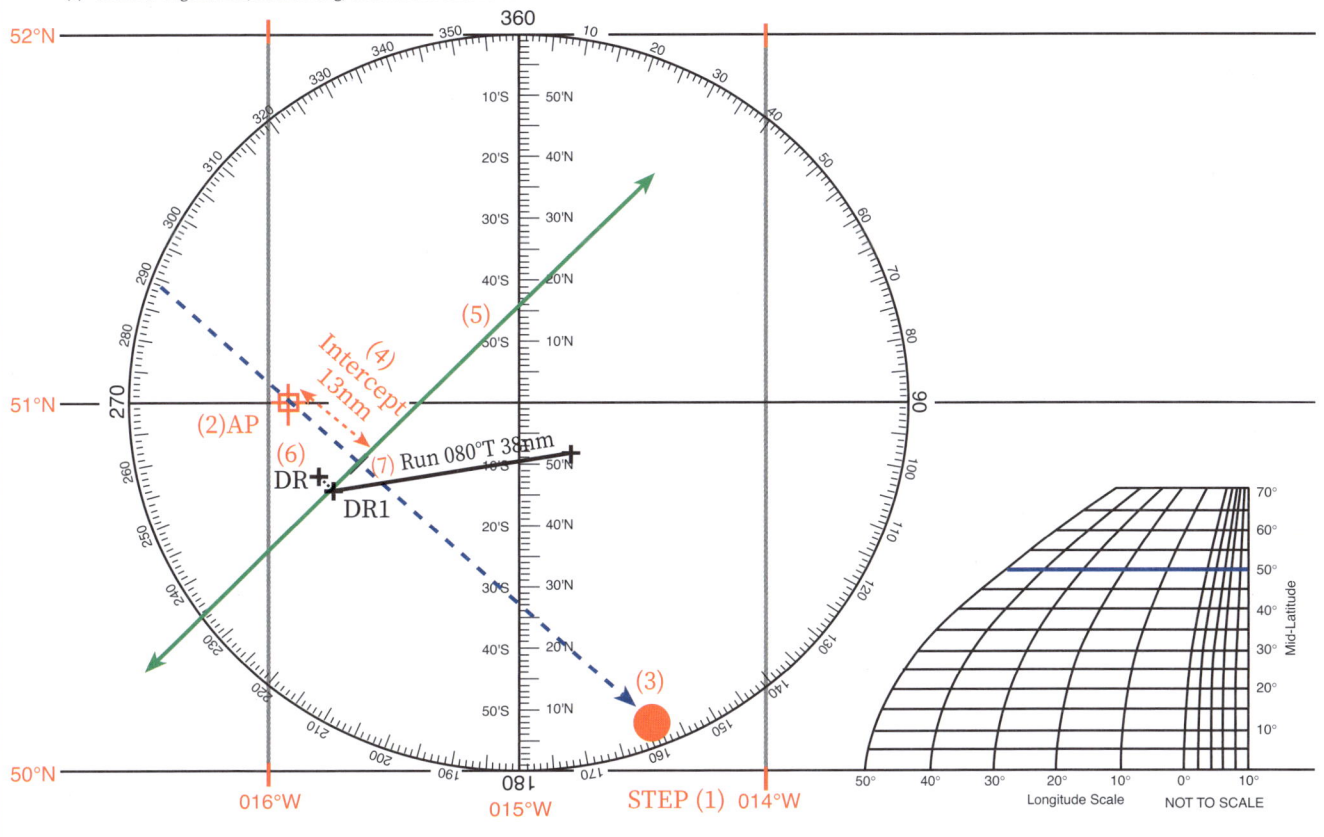

Figure 134

Step 7 Plotting our run

We plot our run as shown in Figure 134. Geometrically it doesn't matter where on the LOP we start the run from, but logically we would start it from DR1, because we're *probably* there.

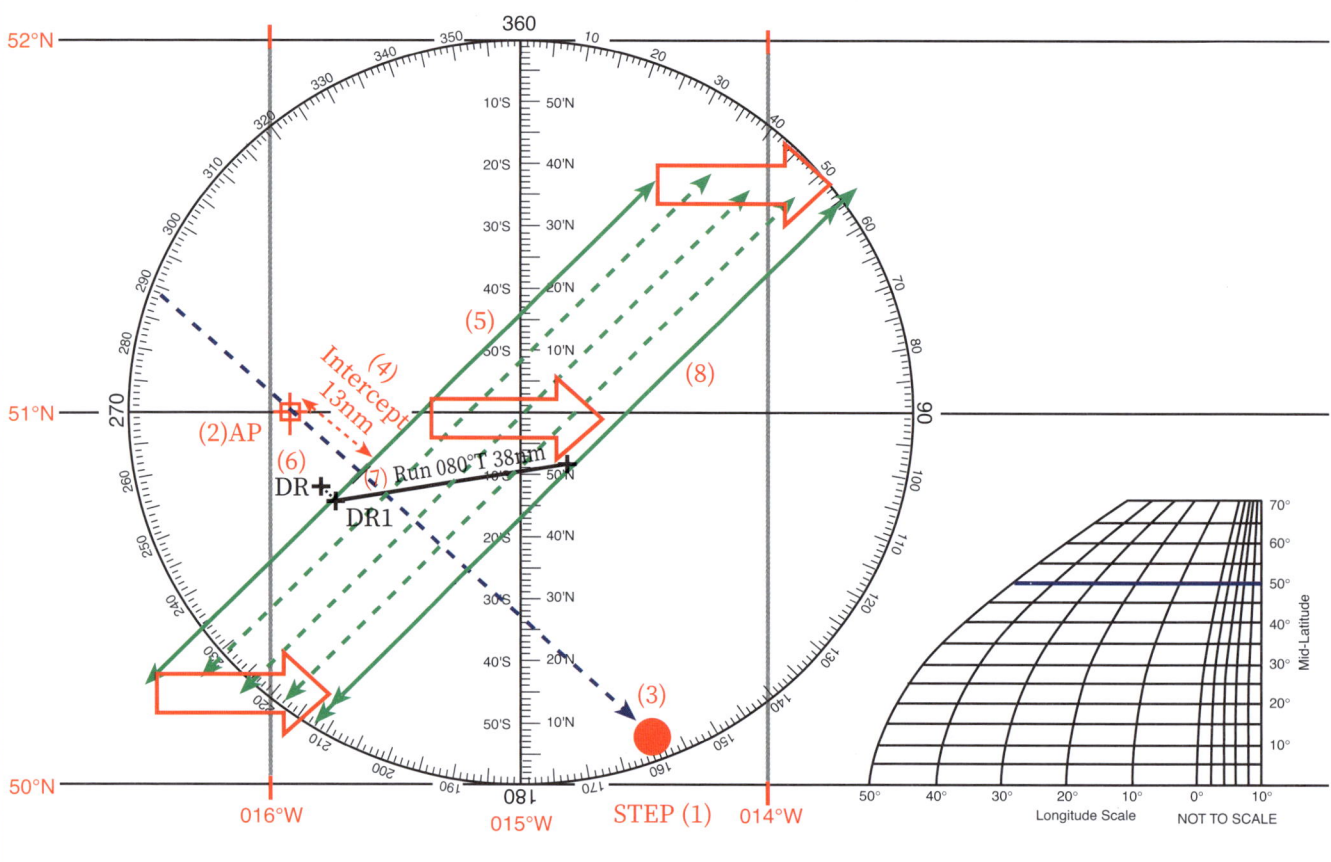

Figure 135

Step 8 Transferring the LOP

In order to see where we are at the time of the meridian passage, we simply *transfer* or move our original LOP to the end of our *run* – this second *transferred* LOP being parallel to the first (see Figure 135).

We would normally do this with a parallel rule, but we can improvise with a Portland plotter if necessary. The result of this should look like Figure 136. Note that the transferred LOP has two arrow heads to indicate what it is.

(1) - Mark Longitude scale according to present latitude.
(2) - Mark assumed position (AP) (Made up of assumed latitude & assumed longitude.)
(3) - Draw on Azimuth (Zn) (direction of Sun indicated with arrows).
(4) - Mark intercept - reference to the AP - either towards the sun from AP or away. (Example below is 'towards').
(5) - Extend the intercept perpendicular to the azimuth (Zn) forming a 'line of position' (which if extended would form a position circle). You are *definitely* somewhere on this line.
(6) - Mark on original DR (Lat and Long) and transfer onto LOP to DR1.
(7) - Draw on RUN from line of position (preferably from your 'probable position').
(8) - Transfer the 'line of position' (becomes 'transferred position line'). Marked with two arrow heads.
(9) - Point 9 becomes DR2. Used for a 2nd Sun Sight if a mer pass wasn't possible
(10) - Draw on Meridian Passage.
(11) - Now, we are *definitely* on the transferred line of position and *definitely* on the mer pass. Therefore the only place we can be is at their intersection - our Fix.

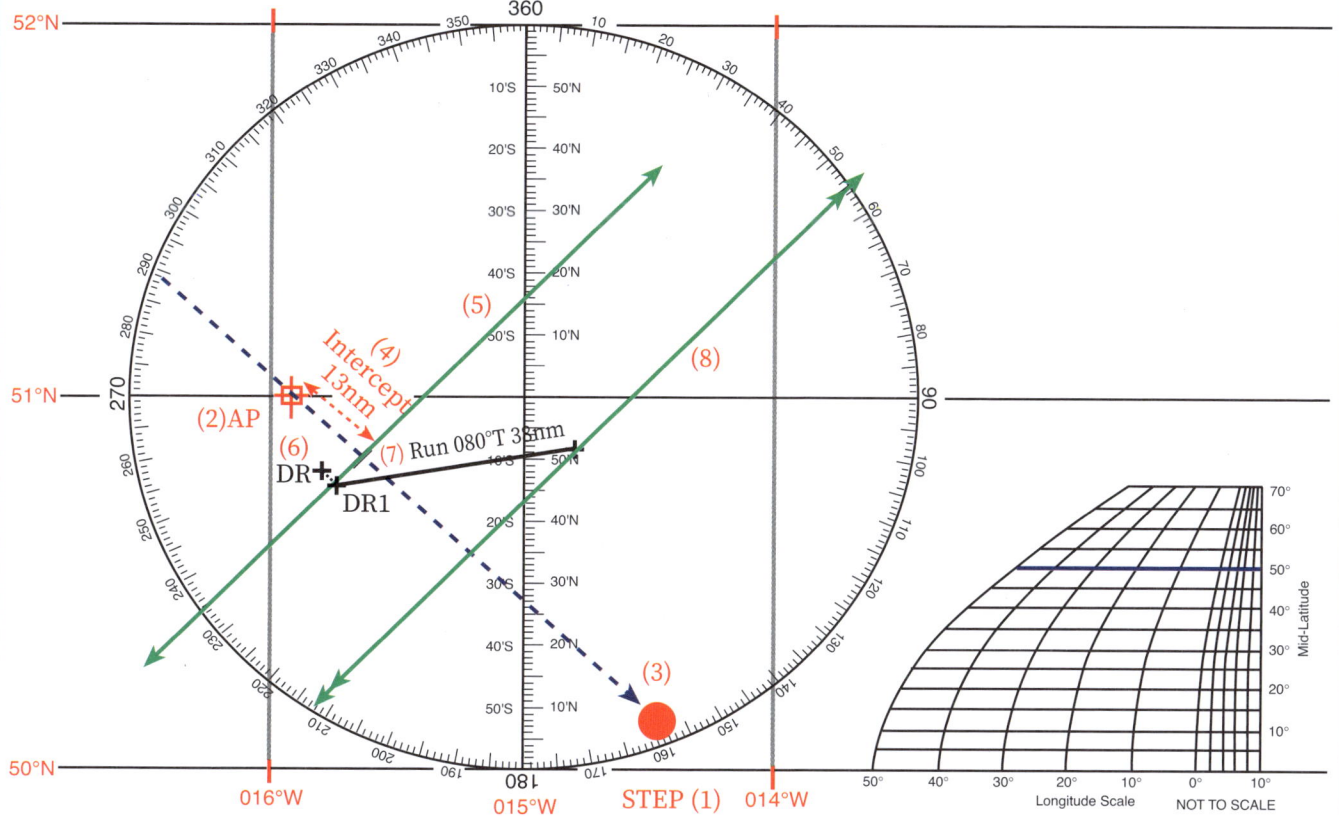

Figure 136

(1) - Mark Longitude scale according to present latitude.
(2) - Mark assumed position (AP) (Made up of assumed latitude & assumed longitude.)
(3) - Draw on Azimuth (Zn) (direction of Sun indicated with arrows).
(4) - Mark intercept - reference to the AP - either towards the sun from AP or away. (Example below is 'towards').
(5) - Extend the intercept perpendicular to the azimuth (Zn) forming a 'line of position' (which if extended would form a position circle). You are *definitely* somewhere on this line.
(6) - Mark on original DR (Lat and Long) and transfer onto LOP to DR1.
(7) - Draw on RUN from line of position (preferably from your 'probable position').
(8) - Transfer the 'line of position' (becomes 'transferred position line'). Marked with two arrow heads.
(9) - Point 9 becomes DR2. Used for a 2nd Sun Sight if a mer pass wasn't possible
(10) - Draw on Meridian Passage.
(11) - Now, we are *definitely* on the transferred line of position and *definitely* on the mer pass. Therefore the only place we can be is at their intersection - our Fix.

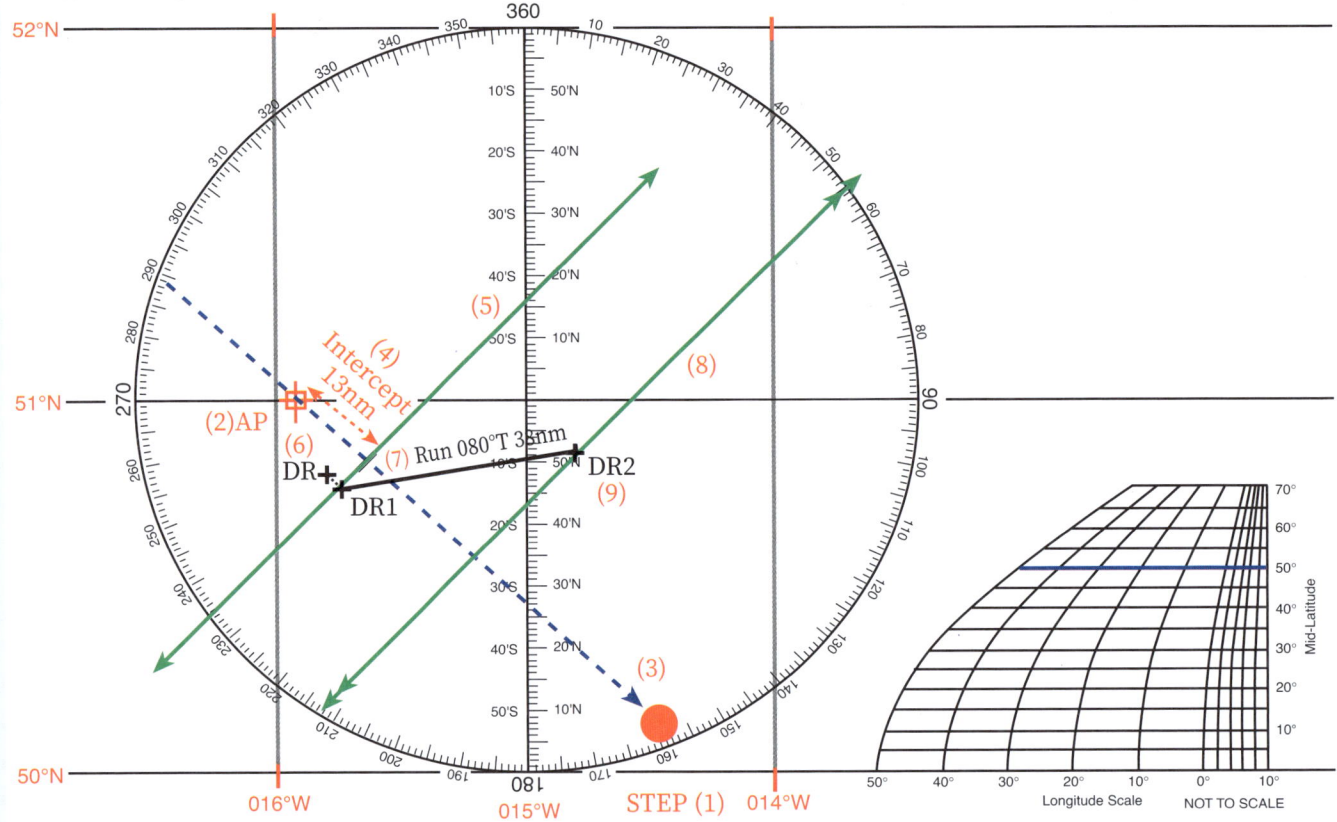

Figure 137

Step 9 Marking DR2

At the end of the run we mark on DR2, as shown in Figure 137. Prior to undertaking the run, we were *definitely* on our first LOP and *probably* at DR1. Therefore, having undertaken our run, it stands to reason to say we are *definitely* on the transferred LOP and *probably* at DR2.

NEARLY THERE: QUICK RECAP

By now we have:

- Undertaken our morning sight
- Taken our meridian passage 2hr and 18min later
- Plotted our morning sight
- Transferred the morning's LOP to the end of our run

We're now *definitely* on the transferred LOP and *probably* at DR2. Now for the fix.

(1) - Mark Longitude scale according to present latitude.
(2) - Mark assumed position (AP) (Made up of assumed latitude & assumed longitude.)
(3) - Draw on Azimuth (Zn) (direction of Sun indicated with arrows).
(4) - Mark intercept - reference to the AP - either towards the sun from AP or away. (Example below is 'towards').
(5) - Extend the intercept perpendicular to the azimuth (Zn) forming a 'line of position' (which if extended would form a position circle). You are *definitely* somewhere on this line.
(6) - Mark on original DR (Lat and Long) and transfer onto LOP to DR1.
(7) - Draw on RUN from line of position (preferably from your 'probable position').
(8) - Transfer the 'line of position' (becomes 'transferred position line'). Marked with two arrow heads.
(9) - Point 9 becomes DR2. Used for a 2nd Sun Sight if a mer pass wasn't possible
(10) - Draw on Meridian Passage.
(11) - Now, we are *definitely* on the transferred line of position and *definitely* on the mer pass. Therefore the only place we can be is at their intersection - our Fix.

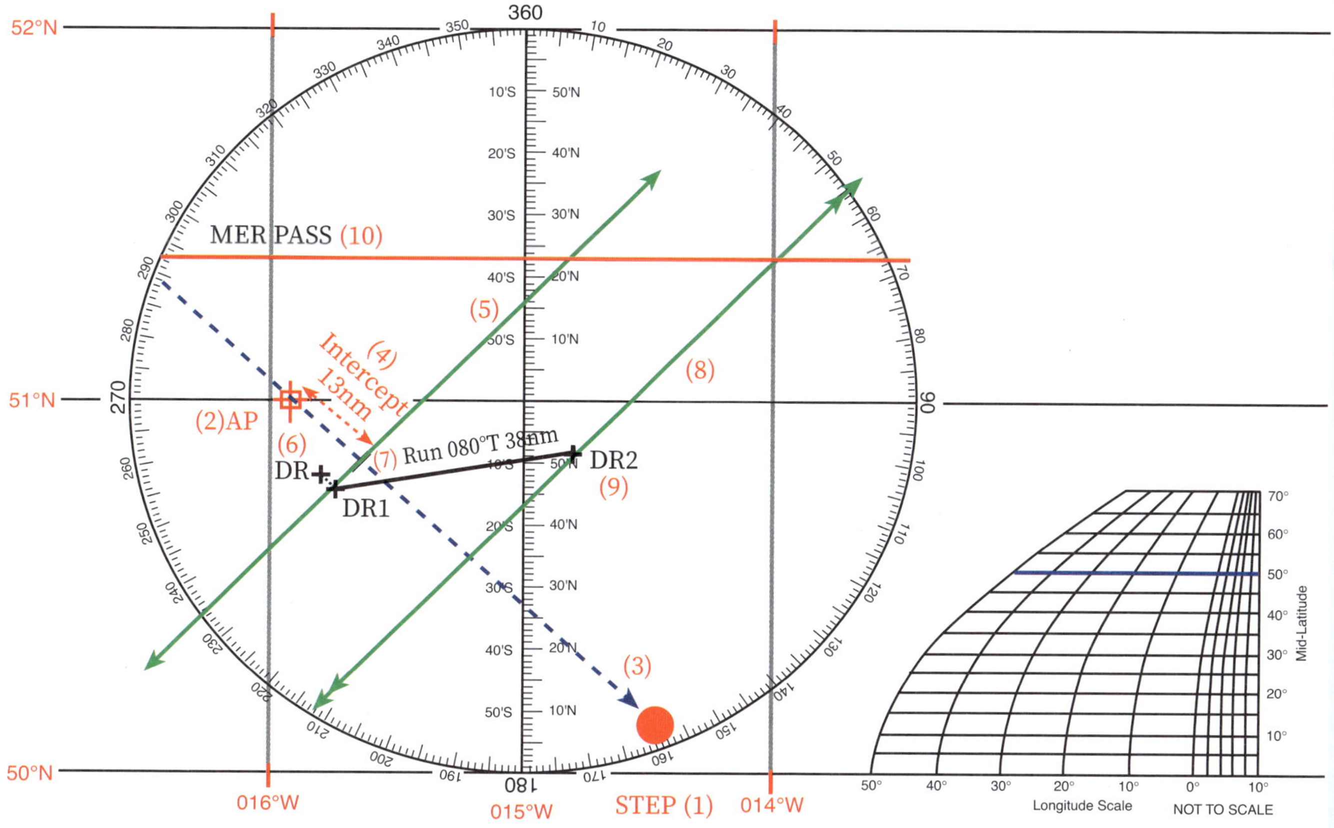

Figure 138

We now undertake our meridian passage calculations using the mer pass proforma and, as we've seen, this gives us our latitude.

Step 10 Plotting the latitude from the mer pass

We now plot our latitude obtained from the meridian passage, as shown in Figure 138 – our mer pass gave a latitude of 51° 23.7'.

CHAPTER TWELVE: PLOTTING

(1) - Mark Longitude scale according to present latitude.
(2) - Mark assumed position (AP) (Made up of assumed latitude & assumed longitude.)
(3) - Draw on Azimuth (Zn) (direction of Sun indicated with arrows).
(4) - Mark intercept - reference to the AP - either towards the sun from AP or away. (Example below is 'towards').
(5) - Extend the intercept perpendicular to the azimuth (Zn) forming a 'line of position' (which if extended would form a position circle). You are *definitely* somewhere on this line.
(6) - Mark on original DR (Lat and Long) and transfer onto LOP to DR1.
(7) - Draw on RUN from line of position (preferably from your 'probable position').
(8) - Transfer the 'line of position' (becomes 'transferred position line'). Marked with two arrow heads.
(9) - Point 9 becomes DR2. Used for a 2nd Sun Sight if a mer pass wasn't possible
(10) - Draw on Meridian Passage.
(11) - Now, we are *definitely* on the transferred line of position and *definitely* on the mer pass. Therefore the only place we can be is at their intersection - our Fix.

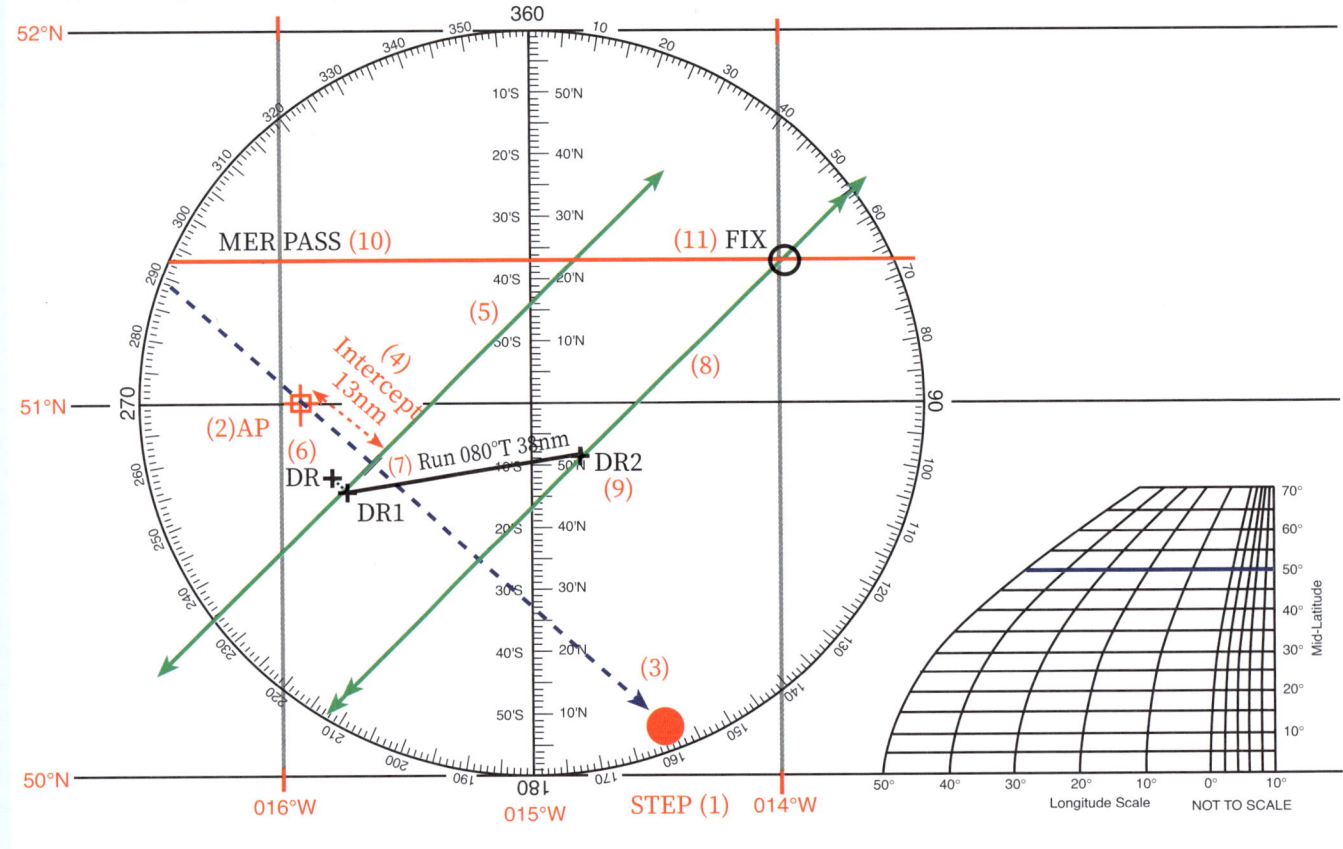

Figure 139

Step 11 Determining our position

OK, we're there. But where are we? At this moment we know we are definitely on the green transferred LOP and we're definitely on our red mer pass. Therefore, the only place we can be is where they intersect, ie our fix, shown in Figure 139

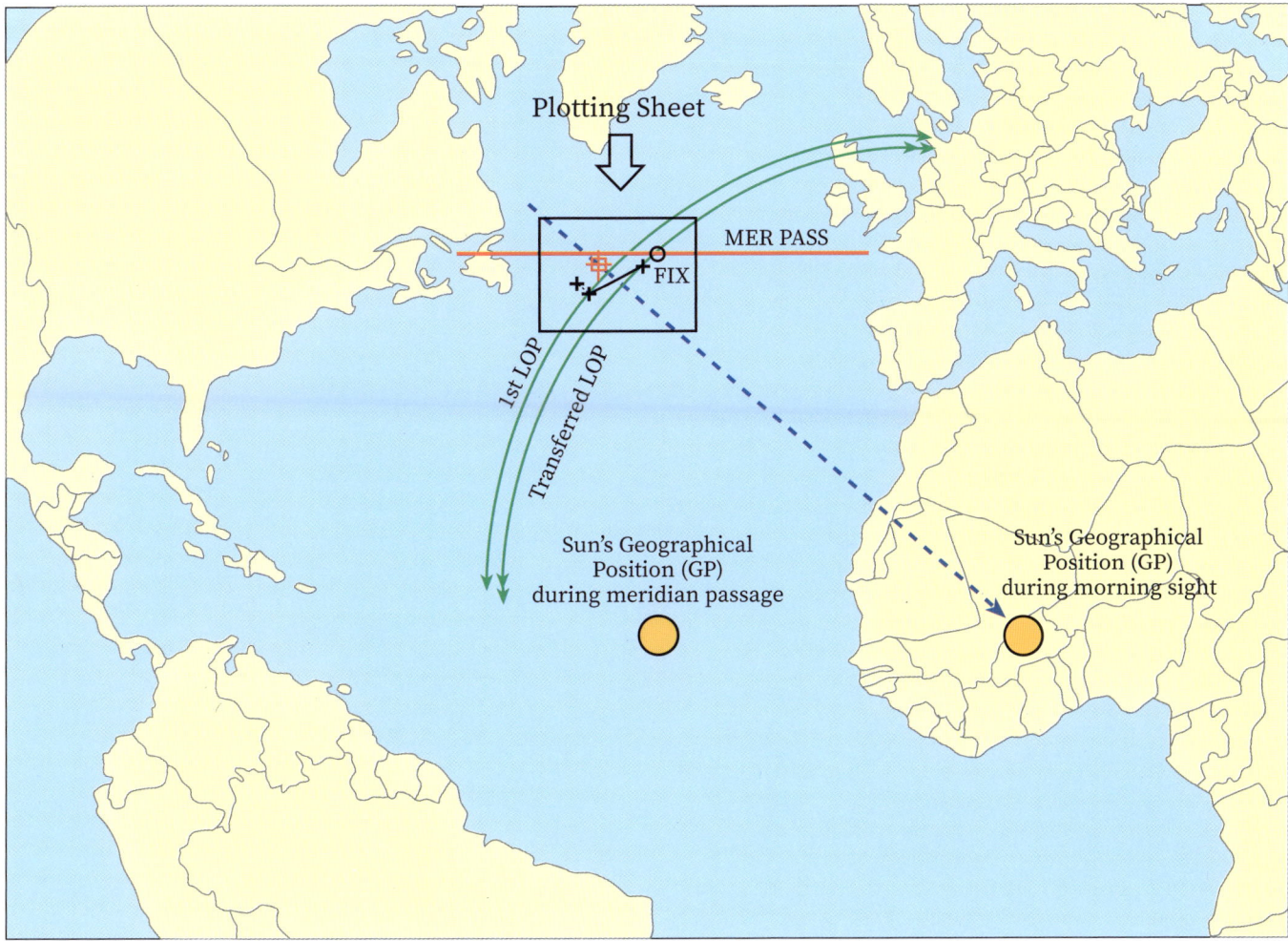

Figure 140

At this point some of you may be losing sight of what we've created. Figure 140 may help put things back into perspective. Obviously, this is not to scale.

SUN RUN SUN: MORNING SIGHT AND AFTERNOON SIGHT

So, we've successfully taken our morning sight, but then a large cloud comes over just as we're going to take a sight of the meridian passage! What are we going to do now? Don't worry, all is not lost. We simply take another sight of the sun when it becomes possible.

The plotting can become a bit confusing. It may help to think of the following steps:

PLOTTING STEPS FOR TWO SUN SIGHT REDUCTIONS

First, run through steps 1 to 6 for the morning sight.

Take second sight.

Calculate the run, plot the run, transfer the LOP and obtain DR2 (Steps 7 to 9).

Undertake the second sun sight reduction using DR2 for your DR position on the proforma.

Repeat steps 2 to 5.

(1) - Mark Longitude scale according to present latitude.
(2) - Mark assumed position (AP) (Made up of assumed latitude & assumed longitude).
(3) - Draw on Azimuth (Zn) (direction of Sun indicated with arrows).
(4) - Mark intercept - reference to the AP - either towards the sun from AP or away. (Example below is 'towards').
(5) - Extend the intercept perpendicular to the azimuth (Zn) forming a 'line of position' (which if extended would form a position circle). You are *definitely* somewhere on this line.
(6) - Mark on original DR (Lat and Long) and transfer onto LOP to DR1.

(7) - Draw on RUN from line of position (preferably from your 'probable position').
(8) - Transfer the 'line of position' (becomes 'transferred position line'). Marked with two arrow heads.
(9) - Point 9 becomes DR2. Used for a 2nd Sun Sight if a mer pass wasn't possible
(10) - Draw on Meridian Passage.
(11) - Now, we are *definitely* on the transferred line of position and *definitely* on the mer pass. Therefore the only place we can be is at their intersection - our Fix.

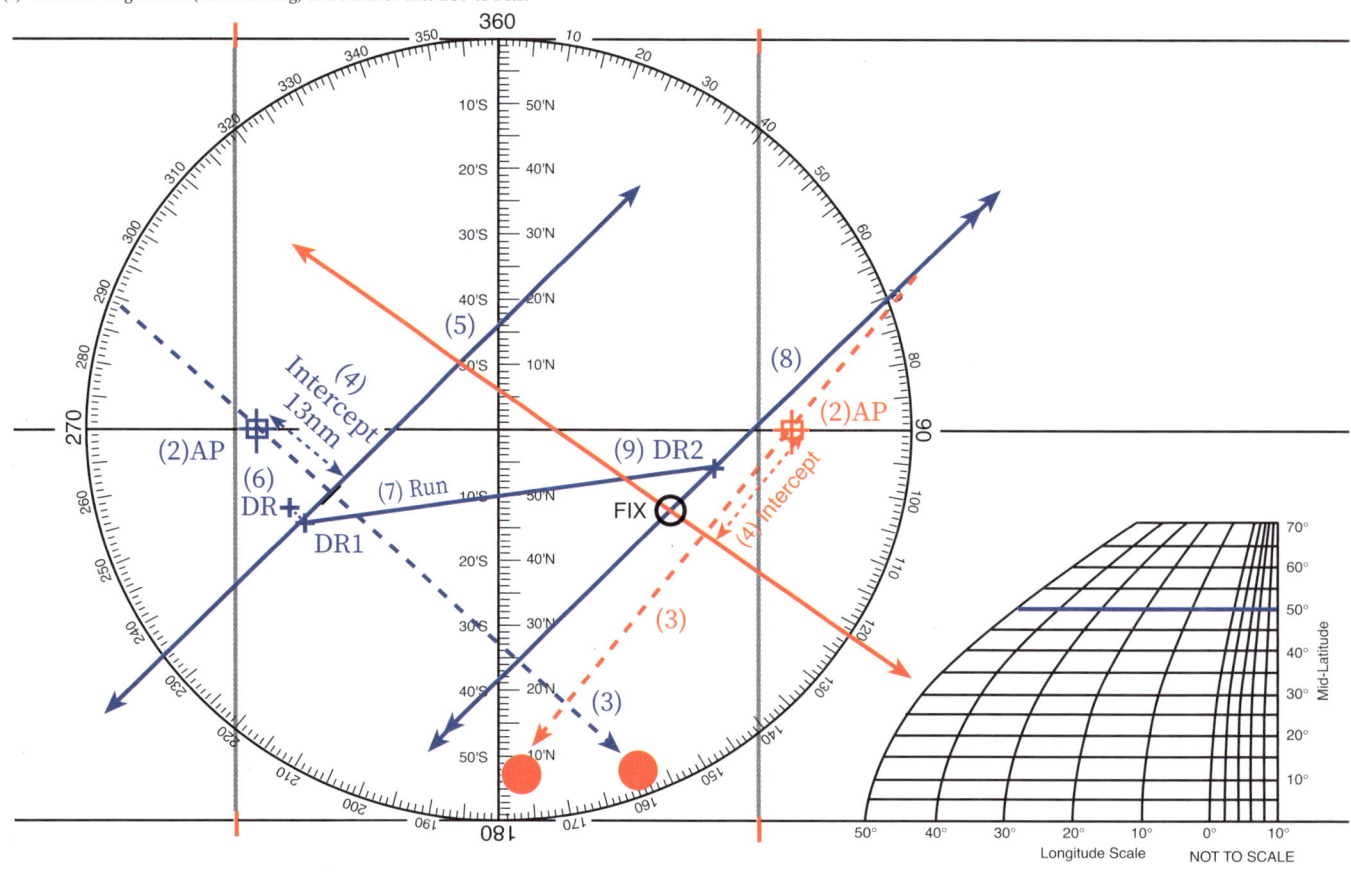

Figure 141

When repeating steps 2 to 5 for the second sight, it's best to try and ignore everything that is currently on the plotting sheet, which is easier said than done. Figure 141 shows the plotting of the second sight in red.

Now, we're *definitely* on the blue transferred LOP and we're *definitely* on the new red LOP. The only place we can therefore be is on their intersection, our fix.

Figure 142 may help put things back into perspective. Again, it is not to scale.

SUN RUN SUN: MERIDIAN PASSAGE AND AFTERNOON SIGHT

Now, it is possible to do a sight of the meridian passage followed by an afternoon sight. This involves transferring the meridian passage, which for some reason, confuses the heck out of people. This is often due to the fact that if our vessel is heading in a more or less easterly or westerly direction, even though we may travel some distance, the movement of the mer pass (when we transfer it) is relatively small. In the scheme of things, this scenario is pretty unlikely. After all, what are the chances that you've been

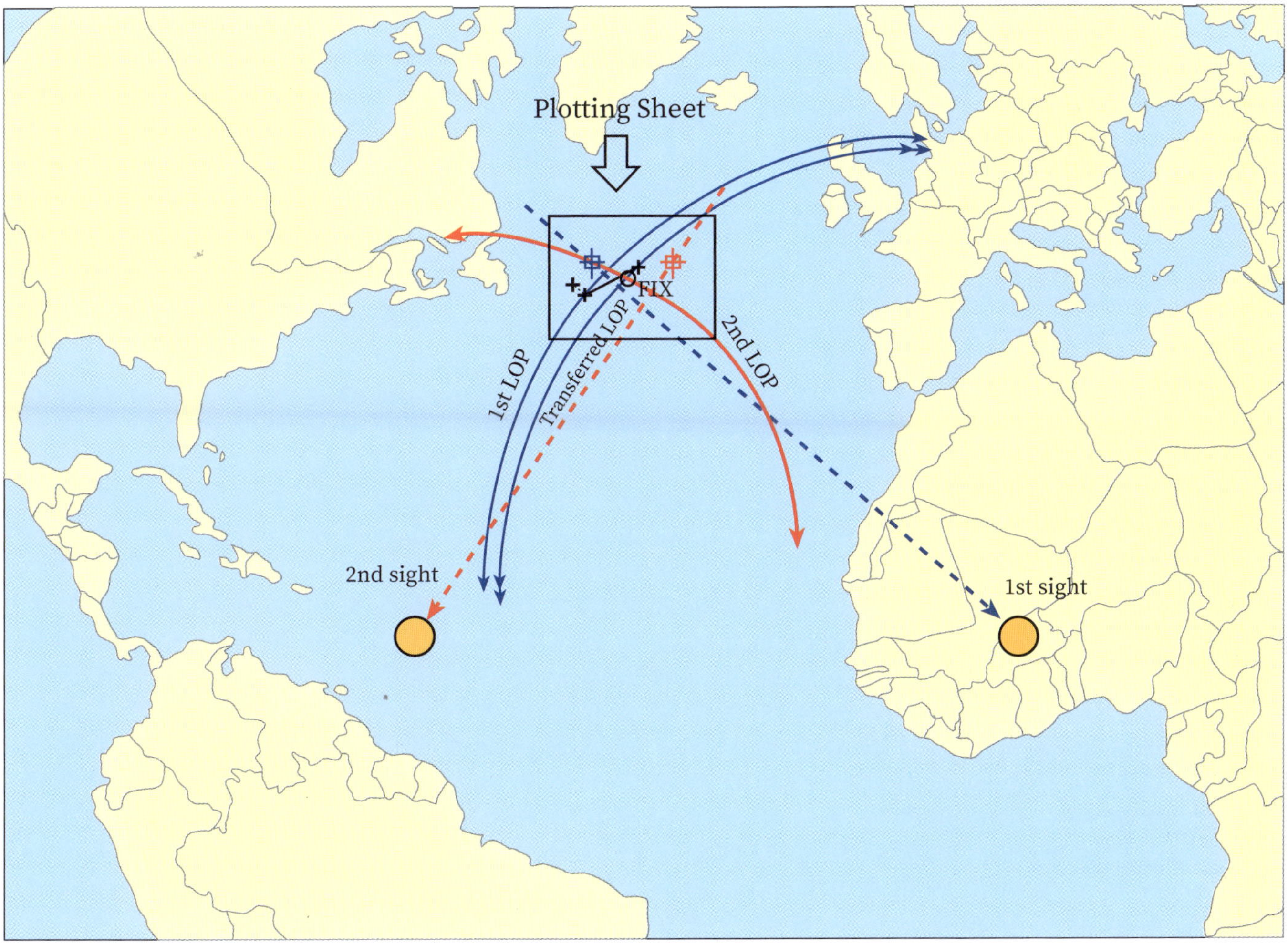

Figure 142

trying to take a sight all morning and then miraculously, just at the time of the meridian passage, the sky clears?

Because this is a less likely scenario, we're not going to dwell on it. Figure 143 demonstrates the plot for those that are interested.

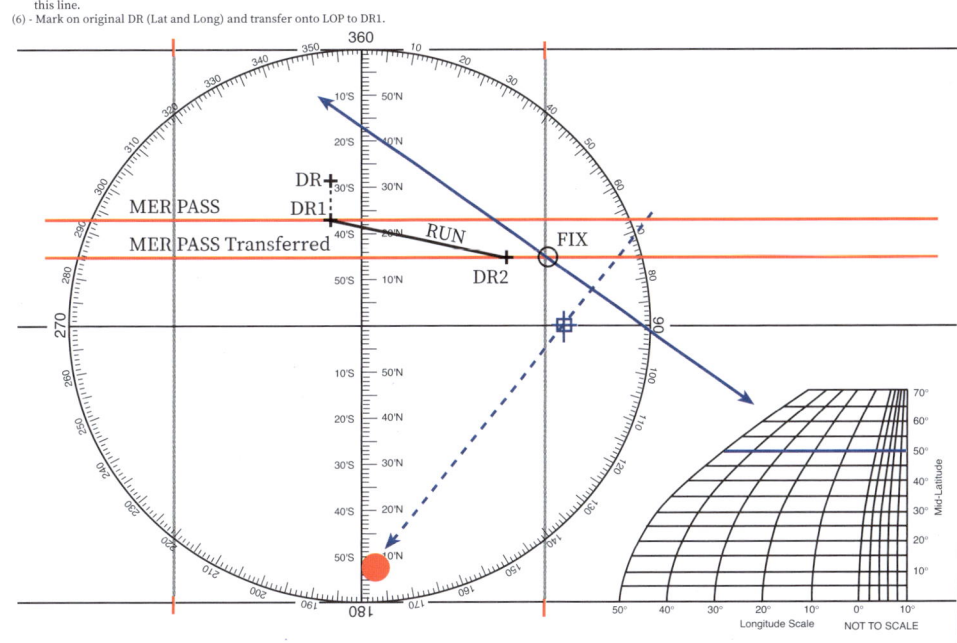

Figure 143

CHAPTER THIRTEEN

Compass checking

There's probably no argument that the most fundamentally important navigation tool we have on board is our compass. Day to day we might use a suite of navigation aids, but when all else fails, we'll fall back on our compass because it will operate without outside assistance.

Of course, when resorting to celestial navigation, the compass will play a key role. Our DR position will be based on distance and direction run, and it's the compass that will give us this direction. Without it, things would get very complicated indeed.

So, what do we need to check? Well, we have two compass errors, that of *variation* and *deviation*.

VARIATION

Variation should be a known quantity. It is the difference between *true* north and *magnetic* north.

When we say it's a known quantity, we should be carrying on board this information. Figures 144 and 145 make this known to us.

Figure 144

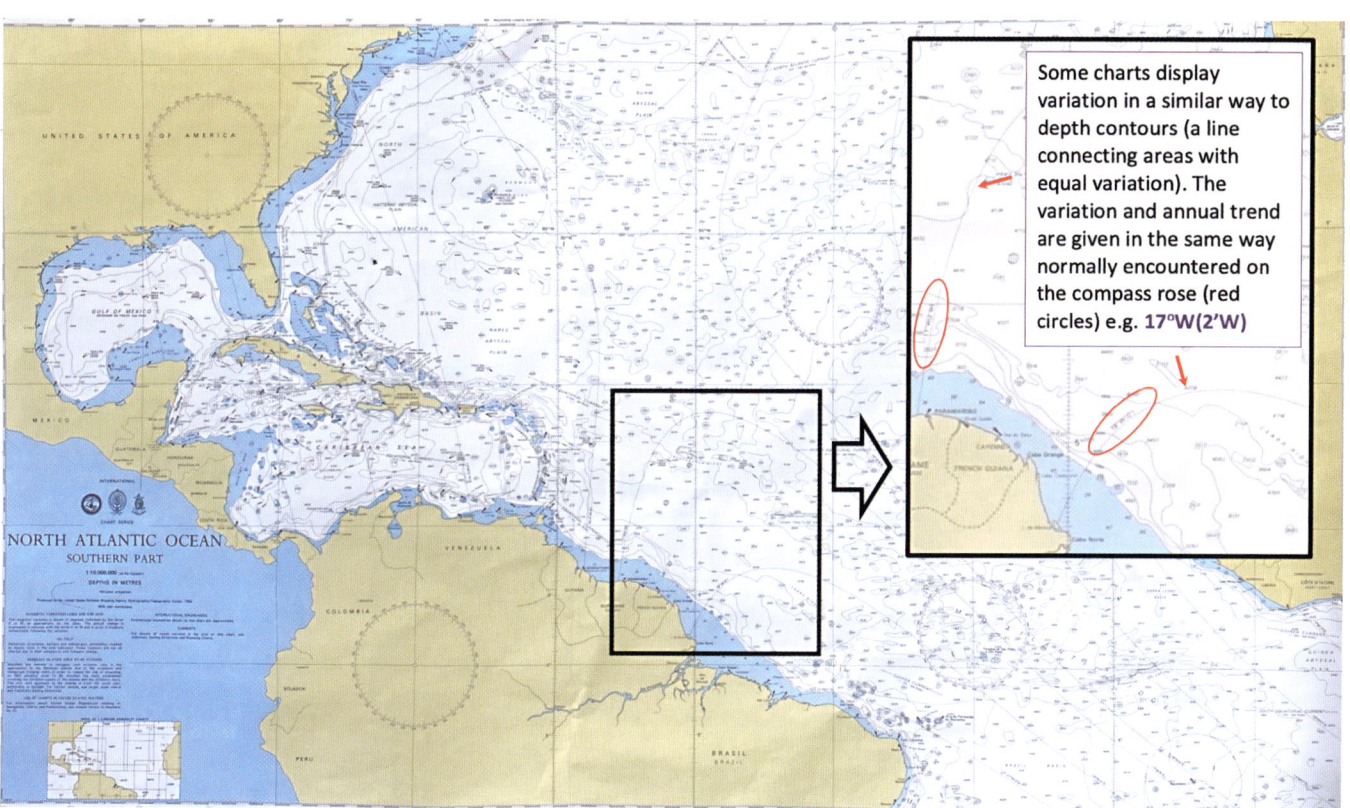

Some charts display variation in a similar way to depth contours (a line connecting areas with equal variation). The variation and annual trend are given in the same way normally encountered on the compass rose (red circles) e.g. **17°W(2'W)**

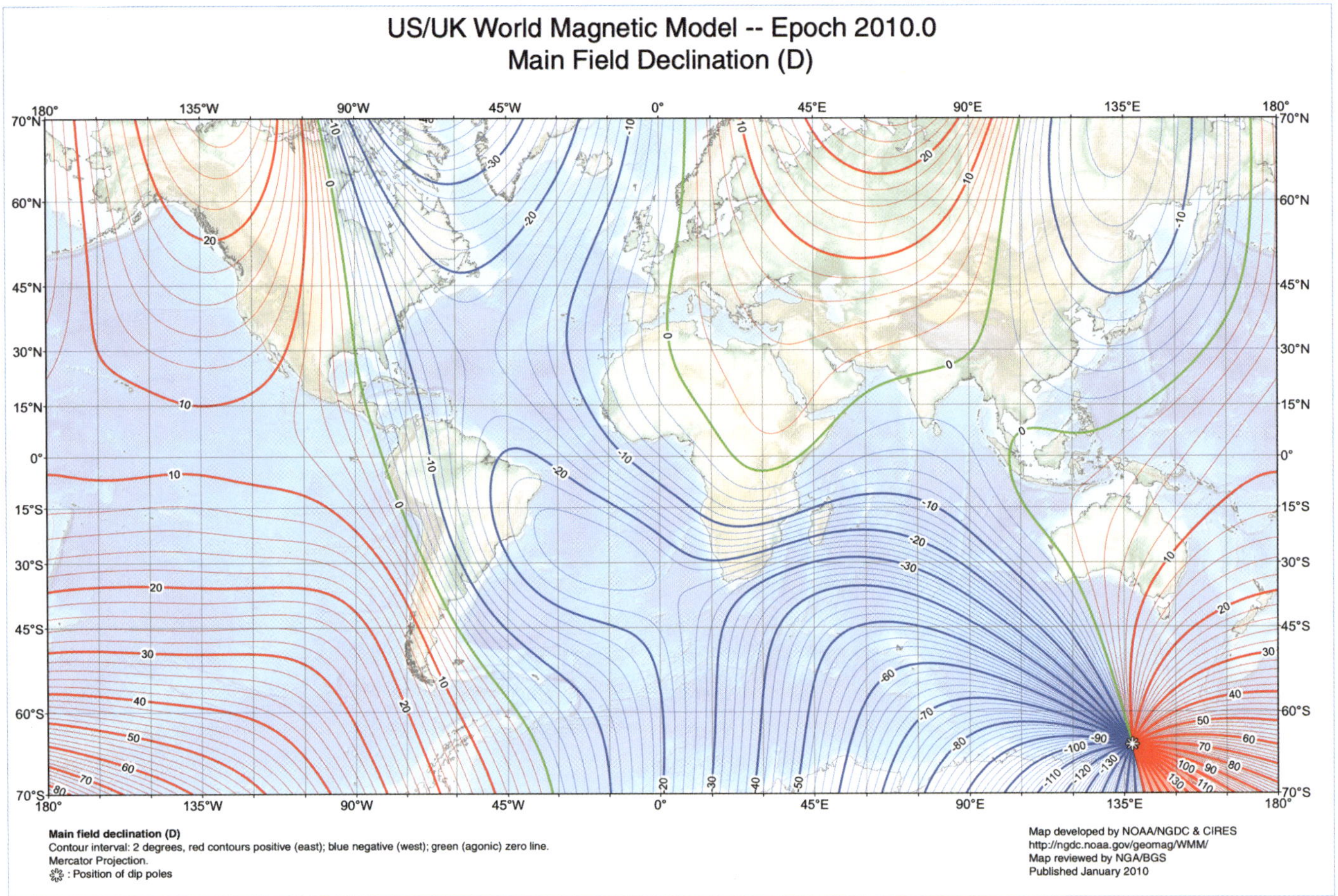

Figure 145

If you've sailed predominantly in the UK or Mediterranean, you'd be forgiven for thinking variation is so minimal that it can almost be ignored. However, you'll notice from Figure 145 that this is not the case worldwide.

DEVIATION

It's deviation that's likely to be the unknown quantity. This is the effect our own vessel has on the compass. Lots of factors can change this over time, and if we're suddenly going to be reliant on our compass, we should check it.

SIGHT REDUCTION FOR COMPASS CHECKING

The good news is we've already done this! Each sight reduction produces a Zn (true bearing of the

Figure 146

sun). And we can use this to check our compass. In fact, some compasses have a shadow pin for this very purpose, as shown in Figure 146.

Let's look at the proforma in Figure 147 and see what stages we require. Well for a start, we won't require the sextant or corrections. In fact, this is one of the few times we'll want the sun lower in the sky as it's advantageous when assessing the sun's bearing.

The other difference is when looking at the sight reduction tables, we will only require the *Z* and *Zn*.

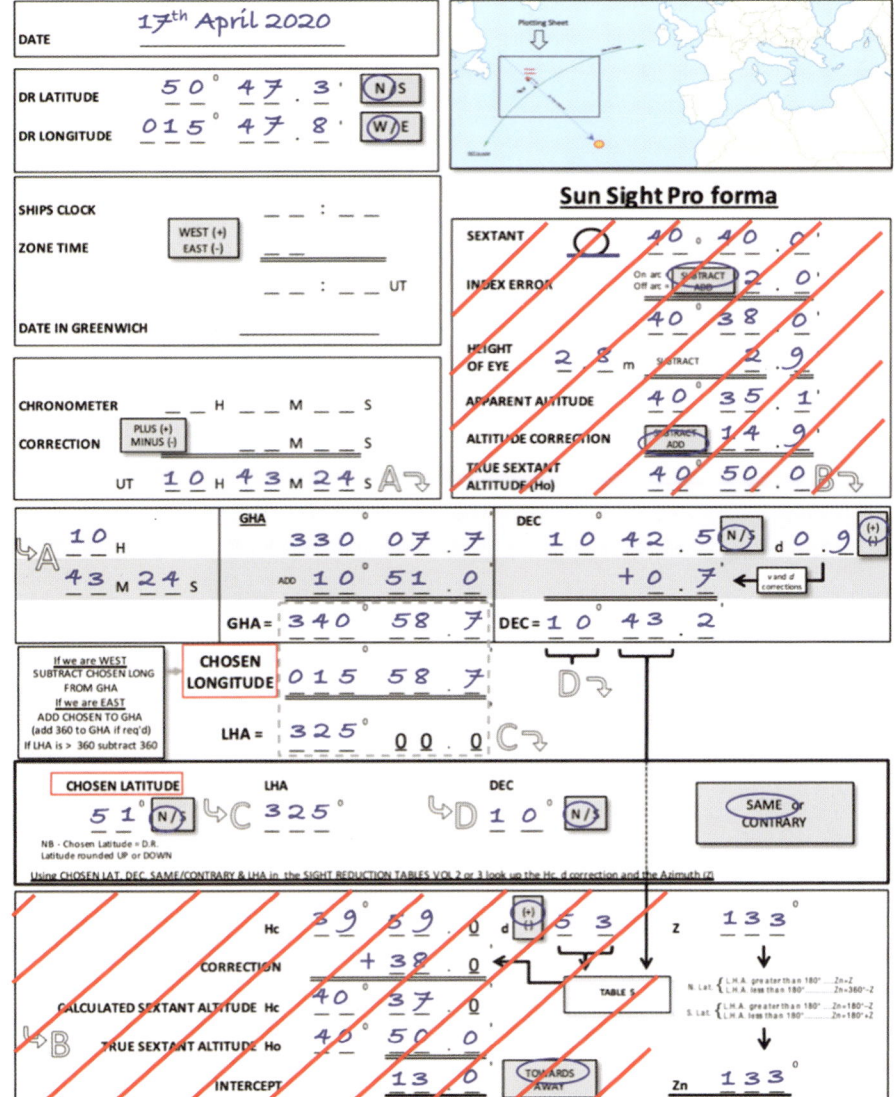

Figure 147

CHECKING FOR DEVIATION

In order to check the compass for deviation, we need to point the vessel at the sun, take a compass reading and make a note of the time (for the proforma).

Then, using the proforma, we need to complete a sight reduction, as per Figure 147, in order to obtain the Zn (true bearing of the sun).

There are a number of mnemonics that help us remember the process of determining the variation and deviation, we'll stick with a commonly taught method.

You may be familiar with Figure 148. It has the accompanying rhyme:

Variation/deviation **WEST** compass **BEST** (biggest)

Variation/deviation **EAST** compass **LEAST** (smallest)

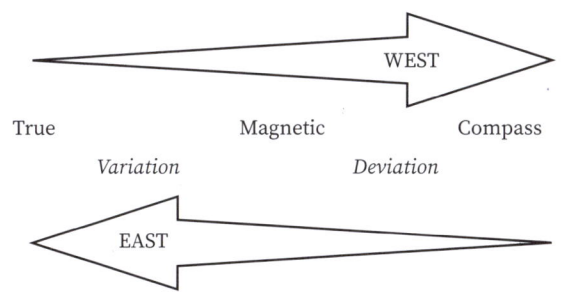

Figure 148

In essence, what the rhyme is saying, is that if the variation or deviation is **west**, the value will increase from true to magnetic, or from magnetic to compass.

And if **east**, the opposite will apply. Figure 149 shows an example.

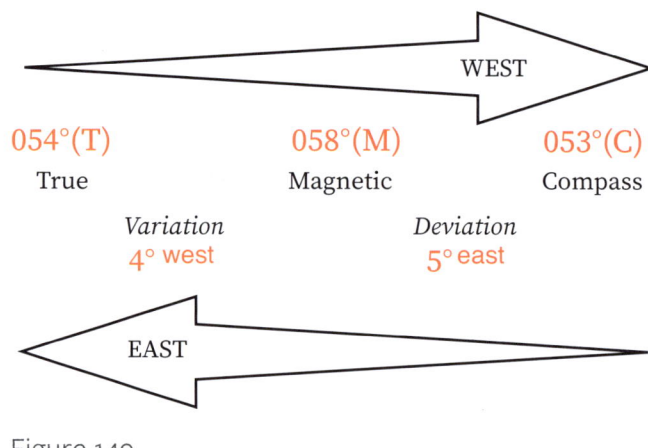

Figure 149

WORKED EXAMPLE

Let's say on a given day, we pointed our vessel at the sun and, using the ship's compass, observed its bearing to be 132°(C). We then undertook a sight reduction and found the Zn to be 133°(T). We will now need to establish what the variation is in our location; let's say it's 10° west.

The best way to proceed is to write out what we know as shown in Figure 150.

Now, we can't find the deviation yet, but we can now find the magnetic bearing, as shown in Figure 151.

We can now calculate the deviation. The difference between *magnetic* and *compass* is 11°. And, following our rhyme, it's east (see Figure 152).

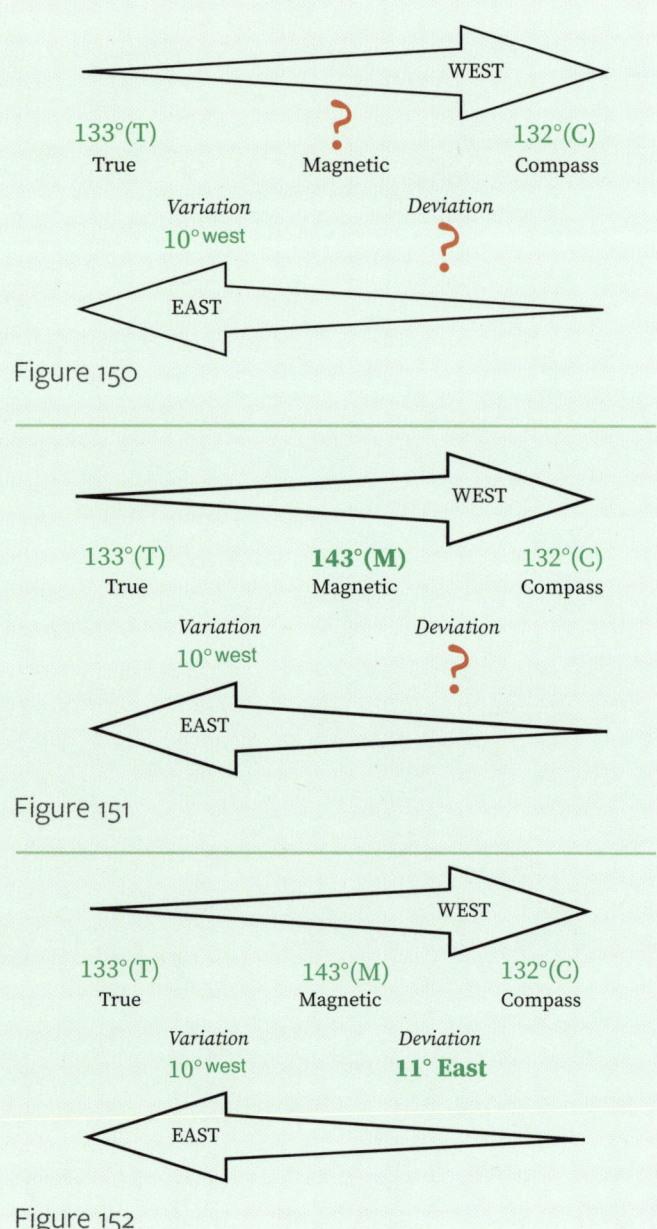

Figure 150

Figure 151

Figure 152

In the example above, we pointed our vessel at the sun. That's OK if we happen to be on that heading already, but what we really want is to establish the deviation on our current heading. In order to do that, we will have to factor in the relative bearing of the sun. Larger vessels may carry a pelorus, as shown in Figure 153.

If we're not carrying a pelorus, we can improvise with a Portland plotter, some blue tack and a matchstick, as shown in Figure 154.

Figure 153

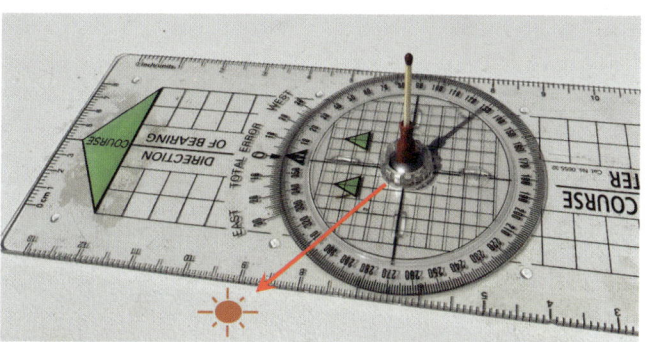

Figure 154

Norway's Are Wiig uses a sextant on his boat *Olleanna* in Les Sables d'Olonne Harbour, on June 30 2018, ahead of the Golden Globe Race ocean race in which sailors compete without high technology aides such as GPS or computers.

CHAPTER FOURTEEN

Time

When discussing time, it's easy to get lost down a number of rabbit holes. Of course, the time we keep reflects the rotation of the earth around its own axis, and its rotation around the sun. Unfortunately, when talking about very accurate measurements of time, the earth behaves slightly erratically. This leads to allowances and corrections that must be made.

Without going into too much detail, here's a quick overview:

> ### UT AND UTC
>
> Universal Time (UT) is based on the time it takes for the earth to rotate through one complete revolution in relation to the sun. Due to a number of factors, this is not exactly 24 hours. This is where the term *mean* time originates, where the term *mean* means average.
>
> Coordinated Universal Time (UTC) is a time based on the atomic clock. This is highly accurate, to one second over a period of 100 million years.
>
> From our perspective we can treat them as equal. Every 18 months or so, corrections are made to the atomic clock to bring it back in line with UT. As a result, the difference between UT and UTC is kept below one second.

So, on board our vessel we need an accurate timekeeping device or chronometer. It was Harrison's ability to design and construct such a device that revolutionised navigation at sea and led to Harrison's eventual claiming of the Longitude Prize.

Ideally, we should have one dedicated chronometer on board set to UT. After all, the nautical almanac times are in UT. This will also prevent having to make unnecessary time adjustments or risk accidentally introducing errors when changing the time for a given time zone.

TIME ZONES

General timekeeping when crossing oceans is a case of personal preference. We can run the ship on UTC if we wish. However, this can be confusing for crew having darkness during the daytime and mealtimes out of sync. The often preferred option is to run the ship as we do on land with the use of time zones. This means we have our local noon at around 1200hr local time, mealtimes follow normal times and it's dark at night. It also makes crew watch-keeping routines easier to manage.

The time zones we use at sea are linked to our longitude on board the vessel. There are 24 time zones and the time we establish is commonly

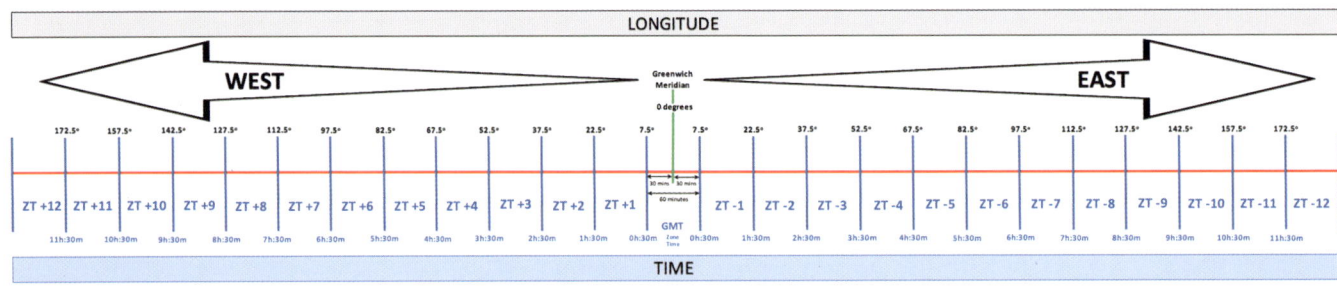

Figure 155

referred to as **Zone Time** (ZT), not to be confused with Zulu Time used in the military and aviation.

Figure 155 shows the structure of the time zones. It helps to look at zone time zero (originally Greenwich Mean Time) in order to calibrate ourselves (see Figure 156).

We see that zone time zero or GMT spans the Greenwich Meridian. It is 15° wide (as are all of the zones) and starts 30 minutes west of Greenwich and finishes 30 minutes east. In other words, if we are anywhere between 7.5° west and 7.5° east we are in this time zone. We can therefore use our longitude to establish how to set our ship's clock, or use it to return to UT.

You'll notice the zones east of the Greenwich Meridian are minus and those west are plus. Think of this as how we get back to UT, eg We're in time zone -2 east of Greenwich and our zone time (ship's time) is 1400hr. The time in UT will be 1200hr.

Why do we need to know this?

Well apart from the advantages mentioned above, it is possible that on board we may have a date different to that of Greenwich. In this case we need to establish what the Greenwich date is (because that's what the nautical almanac uses).

If we do need to establish the Greenwich time and date from our ship's clock, this is where the proforma can help.

In the scenario in Figure 157, the date *on our ship* is 22 June and our DR longitude is 131° west.

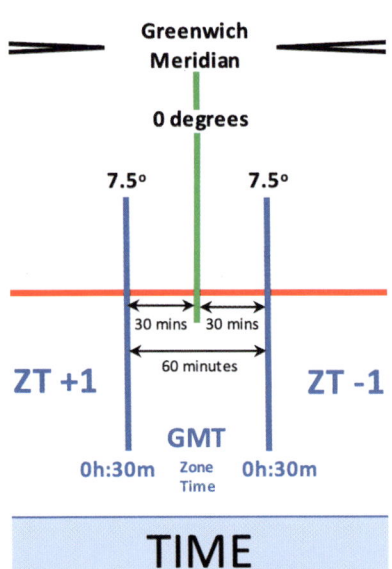

Figure 156

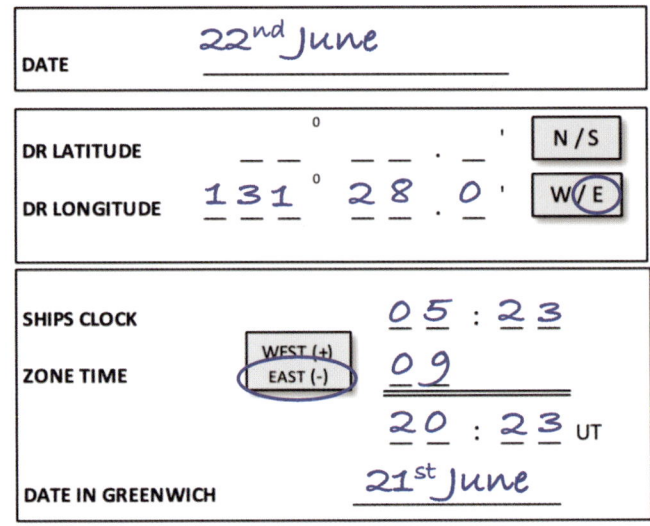

Figure 157

We use the proforma to apply the time zone to our ship's clock and establish a UT time of 2023hr. In doing this we have gone back through midnight. Therefore, it's still the 21 June in Greenwich.

Frankly, it's better to have a dedicated chronometer on board that also gives us the Greenwich date.

CHRONOMETER

The remaining time box on the proforma is for chronometer corrections (if we know how much our chronometer is running fast or slow) – see Figure 158.

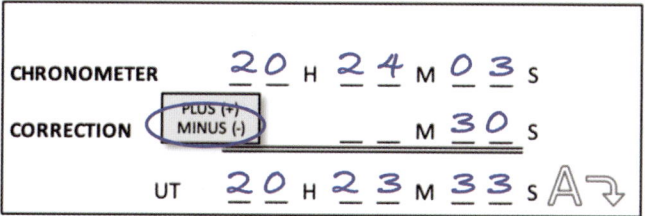

Figure 158

Traditional mechanical chronometers do not keep perfect time. Even modern certified Swiss chronometers have an allowed tolerance of -4 to +6 seconds per day. That may seem a lot, but that's still 99.994% accuracy! The point to note is that for a given chronometer like this, it may gain 2 seconds per day, but it will gain 2 seconds every day – day in and day out. So it's a known quantity.

Even modern quartz watches aren't perfect. Typically, they are accurate to within 15 seconds per month, so may still need checking.

Be careful of GPS time, GPS does not have the periodic time corrections mentioned earlier. As a result, in 2017 GPS time was 18 seconds ahead of UTC. It could be used in an emergency, but remember each four seconds equals one nautical mile. Obviously, we're talking about ongoing regular correcting of our chronometer here, because if we were resorting to celestial navigation it's probably because we've lost GPS navigation.

A PRACTICAL SOLUTION FOR ACCURATE TIMEKEEPING

In order to ensure we have the correct time at sea, we have a number of solutions. Nowadays, there are very affordable *radio-controlled* watches and clocks. These receive low frequency radio signals, transmitted from various base stations around the world, that update the timepiece when in range. Some of these stations have ranges up to several thousand kilometres. When not in range, they revert back to quartz-based timekeeping.

An HF (high frequency) receiver, sometimes referred to as SSB (single side band) or a longwave radio, is another useful means of obtaining accurate time. Although often referred to as HF, these sets will also receive radio stations around the world that transmit on LF (low frequency). Low frequency or 'longwave' signals have exceptional transmission distances. Propagation increases at night with achievable distances up to 11,000 miles. These radio stations transmit public information broadcasts such as news and public affairs. The BBC's World Service is one of the world's biggest. Sent out in over 40 different languages, it has an audience of more than 200 million people. The BBC, like many other stations, transmits the Greenwich Time Signal or *pips* every hour. Care must be taken if listening on DAB or online as delays of up to 30 seconds can be experienced.

INTERNATIONAL DATE LINE

One last point regarding date. At 180° longitude is the *International Date Line*. We will need to change the date if crossing this as shown in Figure 159.

Figure 159

Star Clipper sailing cruise ship *Terre de Haut*, Guadeloupe.

CHAPTER FIFTEEN

Sextant: Practical aspects of sight taking

Figure 160

The sextant is a device for measuring very accurate angles between two objects. In celestial navigation we use it for measuring the angle (altitude) between the horizon and a given celestial body, in our case, the sun. It gets its name from the fact that the graduated arc (see Figure 164) spans 60 degrees or a sixth of a circle. Due to the relationship between the mirrors the sextant enables us to measure angles up to 120 degrees.

The sextant carries with it a major kudos. The owners of these mythical objects are often revered by passive observers as if they were carrying some sort of supernatural power.

However, the sextant is really the simplest of devices. Yes, there are some errors that need to be checked for, and it can take a bit of practice to get the hang of sight taking, but it's not difficult. Don't be intimidated by the error checking process, you won't break the sextant.

Broadly, sextants fall into two camps: plastic and metal. The plastic ones are cheaper and lighter but are affected by temperature and therefore require more frequent adjustment. Metal ones are superior, but beware of imitation ornamental replicas. This is not intended as a buyer's guide, but if you were to look along the lines of Davis Mark 15 or 25 (plastic), Celestaire (metal) or Freiberger (metal, top of the range), you wouldn't go far wrong.

The sextant should only live in one of two places: in its box or in the user's hands. Dropping a sextant is probably the worst fate it could endure. Unless lucky, this is likely to bend the sextant and render it useless. Because of this, many owners tie a lanyard on to the sextant to avoid accidents.

The sextant has two mirrors: 'B' the *horizon mirror* is fixed to the frame, while 'A' the *index mirror* is attached to a moving arm called the index arm.

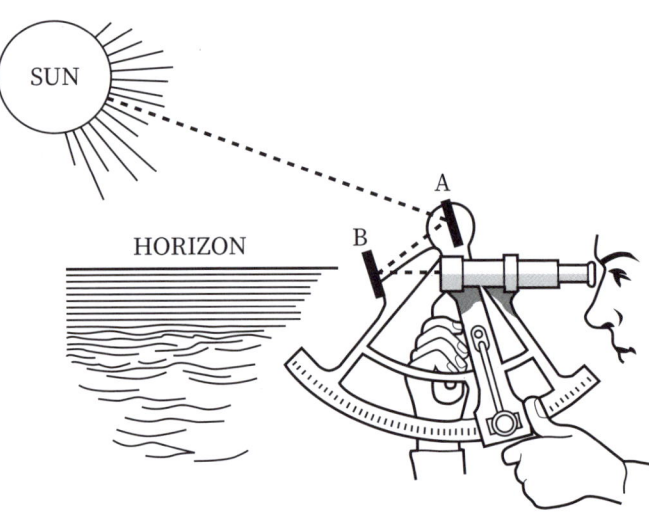

Figure 161

In Figure 161, the observer looks through the telescope. Light from the sun reflects off the index mirror 'A', then off the horizon mirror 'B' before being viewed by the observer. Different rays of light from the horizon pass straight through the horizon mirror 'B' into the observer's eye.

What is special about the horizon mirror B? Horizon mirrors basically come in two types:

Type one (often referred to as **all view**): These mirrors are semi-mirrored. In other words, they reflect light off them, but they also permit light to pass through them. The observer in Figure 161 would see an image as shown in Figure 162 if the sextant was fitted with an all view horizon mirror.

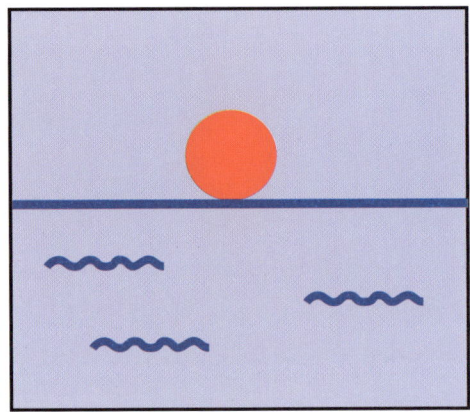

Figure 162

Type two (s*plit mirror)*: These mirrors are actually half mirror, half glass, as illustrated in Figure 163. The observer would see the horizon through the glass section, and the sun would appear on the right-hand side, mirrored section. The brain combines these two images, so the observer sees the sun hovering on the horizon.

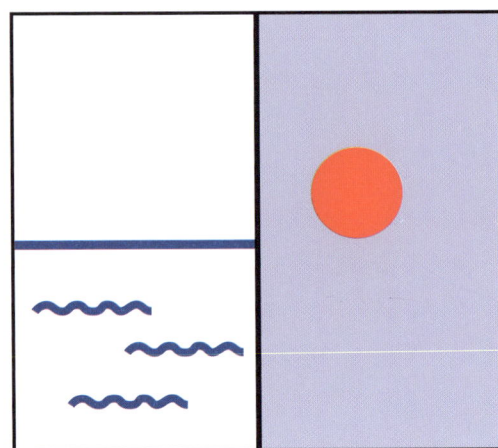

Figure 163

OVERVIEW

Figure 164 shows the components of the sextant. If the *locking device* is squeezed (as per the middle student in Figure 160), the *index arm* is free to move up and down the *graduated arc*. The *index mirror* is mounted on the index arm and it moves with it. When the locking device is released, the index arm locks on to the sextant frame. At this point small adjustments can be made using the micrometre drum (each revolution of the drum is 60 minutes, ie one degree). We'll look at this in more detail shortly.

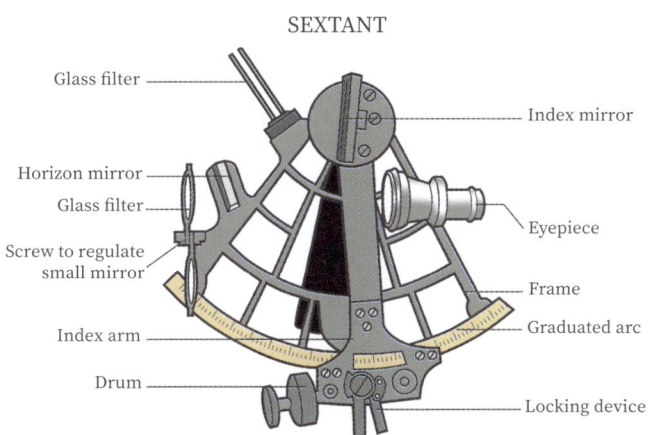

Figure 164

ERRORS

Before we can use a sextant, we need to check it for several errors. This will need to be done if the sextant is unknown to you, before every use if it's a plastic sextant and periodically if it's a metal sextant.

There are three errors we are interested in: perpendicularity, side error and index error.

PERPENDICULARITY

This check ensures the index mirror 'A' is perpendicular (at 90°) to the sextant frame. This check *must* be undertaken first.

In order to undertake this check, the sextant is held on its side. The index arm will need positioning so that an image is obtained similar to Figure 165, trial and error are key here. We want to achieve a view whereby we can see the graduated arc on the right-hand side of the index mirror and an apparent continuation of the arc on the index mirror itself. In this example, we see that there is a definite step.

Figure 165

Figure 166 shows the result we would want to achieve, ie the arc appears to continue in a straight line *without* a step between the graduated arc and its reflected image.

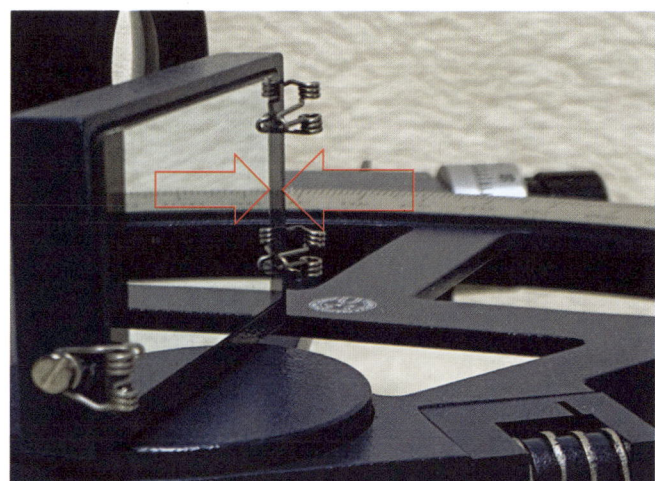

Figure 166

On the back of the index mirror there is one adjusting screw. Sometimes this is a knurled knob, other times a small tool is required as in Figure 167. Try in either direction to establish the desired effect on the alignment.

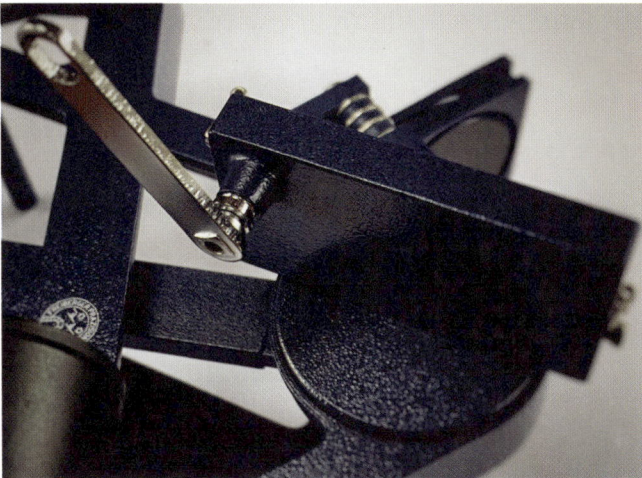

Figure 167

SIDE ERROR

Right, that's the index mirror aligned. The next adjustments concern the horizon mirror alignment. You will notice the horizon mirror has two adjustment screws.

For side error and index error, it is perhaps best to start with objects relatively close (relatively close compared with the sun, that is). It will make it easier because we won't have to deal with filters (yet). There's no need to use a nearby object every time the sextant is checked. However, it will help if the sextant you have obtained has large errors.

Identify an object as far away as possible. Set the sextant to zero, as shown in Figure 168.

Now, looking through the telescope, find the identified object. You should have a picture something like Figure 169.

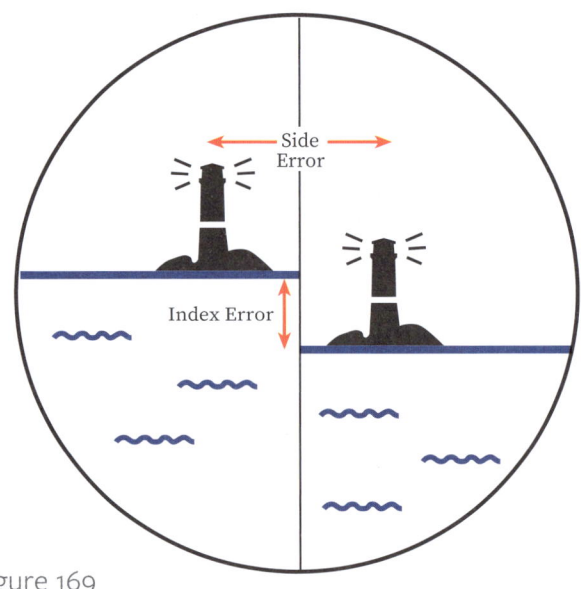

Figure 169

Using the outer screw, adjust to achieve something like Figure 170. Don't worry if it's not perfect!

Figure 168

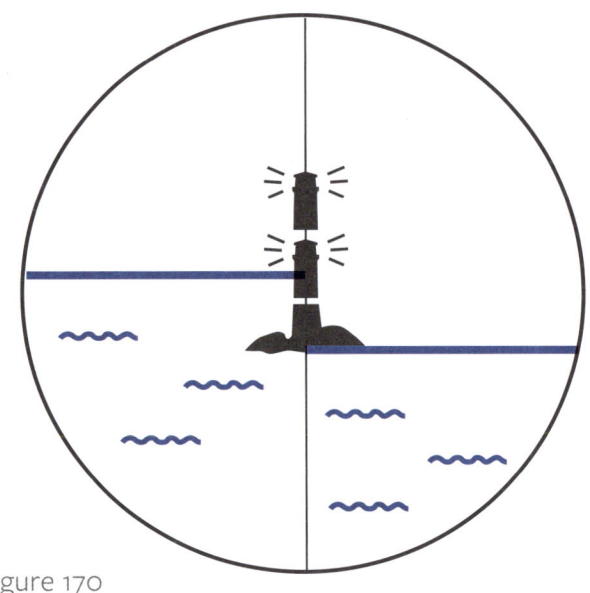

Figure 170

INDEX ERROR

Finally, we can correct the index error (vertical misalignment). If you remember, this was the first sextant correction we applied in Chapter 4.

This is an important error, as any misalignment here will have an impact on our sextant reading.

We are looking to achieve Figure 171 using the remaining screw – again, don't worry if it's not perfect!

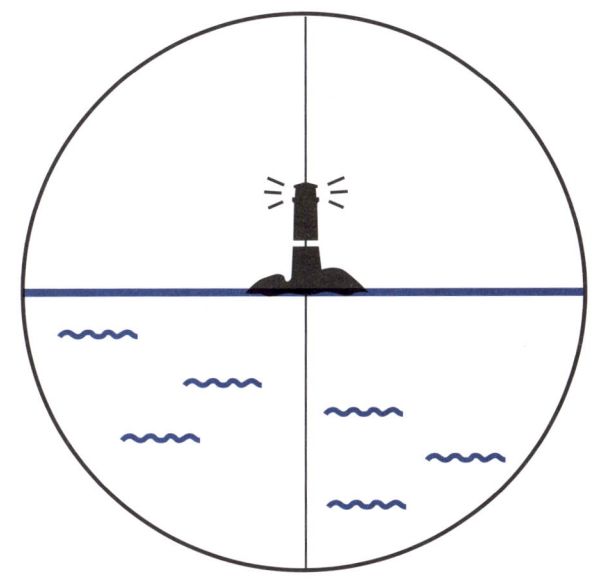

Figure 171

Never view the sun without the appropriate filters in place. Without filters serious eye damage could result.

Now we're pretty much there. However, it will be better if we use an even more distant object, like the sun. For this we're going to need the filters. Just like welding masks, these will protect our eyes.

Initially, as with all sights, we will start with the sextant set to zero. We will therefore be looking at two images of the sun at the same time (the direct one coming through the horizon mirror and the reflected one coming from the index mirror *and* horizon mirror). So we'll need two sets of filters.

If it's your first time of doing this, it may help to visit www.philsomerville.com for videos that will help.

We're going to start with all filters in place for both mirrors and then, one at a time, remove them to get the desired brightness of the sun.

To find the sun, the best technique is to point the sextant in the general direction and then zigzag left and right while tracking up and down (a bit like mowing the lawn). Go slowly, you'll be amazed how quickly it flashes by.

Once we've found the sun it is likely that we'll see two.

On split-view sextants, it may be necessary to slowly go from side to side to see both suns. It will often be obvious that there are two different images because they'll have slightly different colours, courtesy of slightly different filters.

Now, we're likely to have some misalignment again as shown in Figure 172. Don't worry if when undertaking the following that you can't perfectly align the two images.

We go through the same process as before using the adjusting screws. However, if we can't

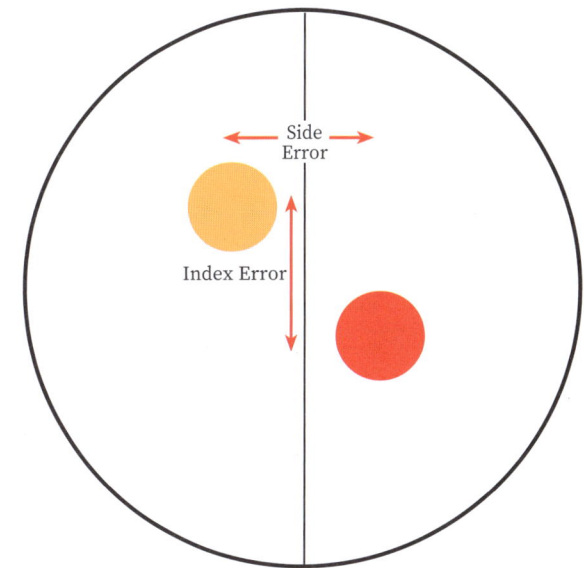

Figure 172

get the index error (vertical alignment) exact, we slowly wind the micrometre drum in either direction until the two images are perfectly aligned. Then, looking at the micrometre drum, we see how many minutes we have wound the drum through and make a note (this will make more sense when we have covered this topic shortly).

As shown in Figure 173 we also need to note if we have wound the drum on to the scale, ie *above zero*, called *on the arc,* or *below zero*, called *off the arc*.

We should really be aiming to get the index error below 10 minutes. With patience and a quality sextant we can often reduce the index error to zero using the adjusting screws.

Here we have 3 minutes of error *on the arc*

Here we have 4 minutes of error *off the arc.* (*Off* because we have gone below zero)

Figure 173

Undertaking a sight

Step 1 Find a stable position on the vessel. Sitting on or leaning against the superstructure may help.

Step 2 Set the sextant to zero and select suitable filters.

Step 3 Point the sextant at the sun and identify the two images. (If the sextant is perfectly aligned, only one image will be seen. In this case it may be worth winding the drum through 30 minutes to deliberately split the two images.)

Step 4 For stability, bracing your arms against your sides will help in this next step. As gently as possible, squeeze the locking device to release the index arm. This takes practice, the slightest movement will see the wanted image of the sun go flying out of view.

Figure 174

Step 5 Slowly bring the (right-hand) image of the sun downwards. This is often described as pushing the index arm away from you while gently rotating the sextant. In actual fact, the index arm practically remains stationary, while the body of the sextant is rotated – see Figure 174.

Step 6 As you approach the horizontal, release the locking device. The horizon filters should now be retracted to enable the horizon to be seen.

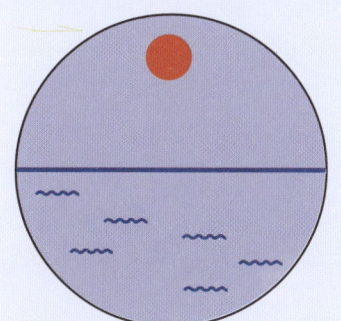

Step 7 You should now have an image that looks like Figure 175.

Figure 175

Step 8 Using the micrometre drum, bring the sun down to the horizon.

Step 9 Rotate the sextant slightly in each direction adjusting the sun so it just strikes the horizon at its lowest point, as shown in Figure 176. This is to ensure the observer is not holding the sextant at an angle.

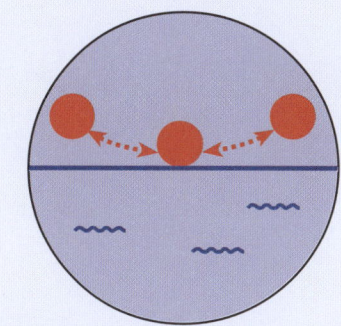

Step 10 Immediately make a note of the exact time.

Figure 176

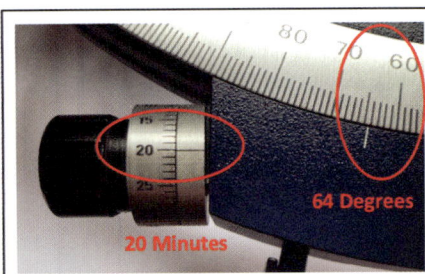
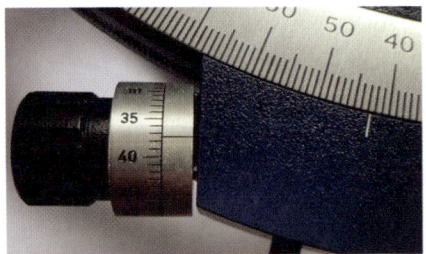
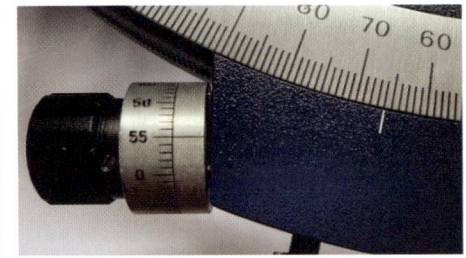

Figure 177

READING THE SEXTANT

Figure 177 shows a number of readings.

Many sextants have a vernier scale as in Figure 178. This enables the user to define down to tenths of a minute. Bearing in mind that one minute of arc translates into one nautical mile, unless you're already familiar with these vernier scales, it probably isn't worth the bother. There are too many other variables that make measuring down to tenths an arguable waste of time, not least taking sights on an unstable platform. If unsure, read off the minutes that are aligned with the *zero* marking.

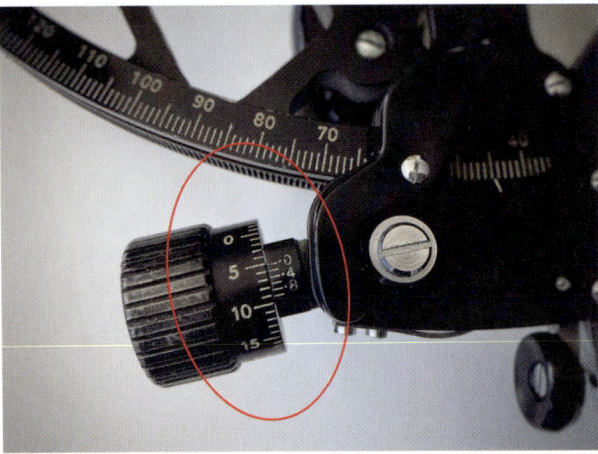

Figure 178

SIGHT TAKING CONSIDERATIONS

Avoid taking sights of the sun low on the horizon (less than 10°). Refraction will give false readings.

In rough weather, the sight should be taken on the crest of the wave. Then half of the wave height should be added to normal height of eye, as shown in Figure 179.

Figure 179

SEXTANT CARE

- The sextant should be kept only in one's hand or in its box.
- Use a lanyard.
- Only hold the sextant by its frame or handle.
- Wipe clean after use.
- Use silica gel in the box.
- Avoid excessive heat, moisture and vibration.

CHAPTER SIXTEEN

Troubleshooting

If our intercept seems exceptionally large (even if our original DR position was reasonably accurate in the first instance, it's still possible to have an intercept up to approximately 35nm) or our plotting seems adrift, there are a number of checks we can undertake:

- Have checks for sextant errors been undertaken recently? They should be made every time for plastic sextants.

- Was the sextant rocked during sight taking?

- Was the sextant reading correctly read? Easy to take the wrong degree reading if the minutes are greater than 30 minutes.

On the proforma:

- How accurate was the DR position used? The sight reduction process will accommodate this inaccuracy. Compensation will come in the form of a large intercept.

- Was the correct time recorded?

- Have the sextant corrections been undertaken correctly? It's a frequent mistake to add instead of subtract, or vice versa.

- Has the correct limb been taken? This can lead to an error of 30 minutes (30nm).

- Check GHA and declination were taken for the correct time and day – an easy mistake to make.

- Has the correct assumed longitude been established, ie is it as close to the original DR longitude as possible? It's not a show stopper but, if not, the process will compensate with a different LHA and large intercept.

- Compare your DR latitude and assumed latitude. If your DR latitude is roughly halfway between two degrees, you may have had to round up or down by nearly 30 minutes. If this is the case, the intercept will compensate with a large intercept.

- Have the correct pages in the Sight Reduction Tables been selected? It's easy to track up to the next degree of latitude when flicking through the pages.

- Has the correct Z to Zn conversion been undertaken? Remember the sun should be east for a morning sight and west for an afternoon sight. Likewise, if you're in the northern hemisphere, the sun is likely to be south of you and vice versa.

Appendices

1.	Sun sight proforma	130
2.	Sun sight proforma guide	131
3.	Meridian passage proforma	132
4.	Meridian passage proforma guide	133
5.	Plotting sheet	134
6.	Plotting guide	135
7.	Longitude scale plotting	136
8.	Z versus Zn	137
9.	Assumed longitude	139
10.	Adding and subtracting of 60ths	141
11.	Polaris	142

The proformas on pages 130-33 are available in PDF format from www.philsomerville.com.

1 Sun sight proforma

DATE _____

DR LATITUDE _ _ ° _ _ . _ ' N/S
DR LONGITUDE _ _ _ ° _ _ . _ ' W/E

SHIPS CLOCK
ZONE TIME _ _ : _ _   WEST (+) / EAST (−)

_ _ : _ _ UT

DATE IN GREENWICH _____

CHRONOMETER _ _ H _ _ M _ _ S
CORRECTION   PLUS (+) / MINUS (−)   _ _ M _ _ S
UT _ _ H _ _ M _ _ S →A

SEXTANT ○ _ _ ° _ _ . _ '
INDEX ERROR On arc = SUBTRACT / Off arc = ADD   _ _ . _ '
_ _ ° _ _ . _ '
HEIGHT OF EYE _ . _ m SUBTRACT _ _ . _ '
APPARENT ALTITUDE _ _ ° _ _ . _ '
ALTITUDE CORRECTION SUBTRACT / ADD _ _ . _ '
TRUE SEXTANT ALTITUDE (Ho) _ _ ° _ _ . _ ' →B

↓A _ _ H
_ _ M _ _ S

GHA _ _ _ ° _ _ . _ '
ADD _ _ ° _ _ . _ '
GHA = _ _ _ ° _ _ . _ '

DEC _ _ ° _ _ . _ ' N/S   d _ . _ (+)/(−)
← v and d corrections
DEC = _ _ ° _ _ . _ '   →D

If we are WEST SUBTRACT ASSUMED LONG FROM GHA
If we are EAST ADD ASSUMED TO GHA (add 360 to GHA if req'd)
If LHA is > 360 subtract 360

ASSUMED LONGITUDE _ _ _ ° _ _ . _ '
LHA = _ _ _ ° 0 0 . 0 ' →C

ASSUMED LATITUDE _ _ ° N/S →C
LHA _ _ _ ° →D
DEC _ _ ° N/S
SAME or CONTRARY

NB - Chosen Latitude = D.R. Latitude rounded UP or DOWN

Using ASSUMED LAT, DEC, SAME/CONTRARY & LHA in the SIGHT REDUCTION TABLES VOL 2 or 3 look up the Hc, d correction and the Azimuth (Z)

Hc _ _ ° _ _ . 0 '   d _ _ . _ (+)/(−)   **Z** _ _ _ °
CORRECTION _ _ . 0 '
TABLE 5
N. Lat. { L.H.A. greater than 180°.....Zn=Z
         { L.H.A. less than 180°.........Zn=360°−Z
S. Lat. { L.H.A. greater than 180°.....Zn=180°−Z
         { L.H.A. less than 180°.........Zn=180°+Z

CALCULATED SEXTANT ALTITUDE Hc _ _ ° _ _ . 0 '
↓B **TRUE SEXTANT ALTITUDE Ho** _ _ ° _ _ . _ '
INTERCEPT _ _ . _ ' TOWARDS / AWAY   **Zn** _ _ _ °

2 Sun sight proforma guide

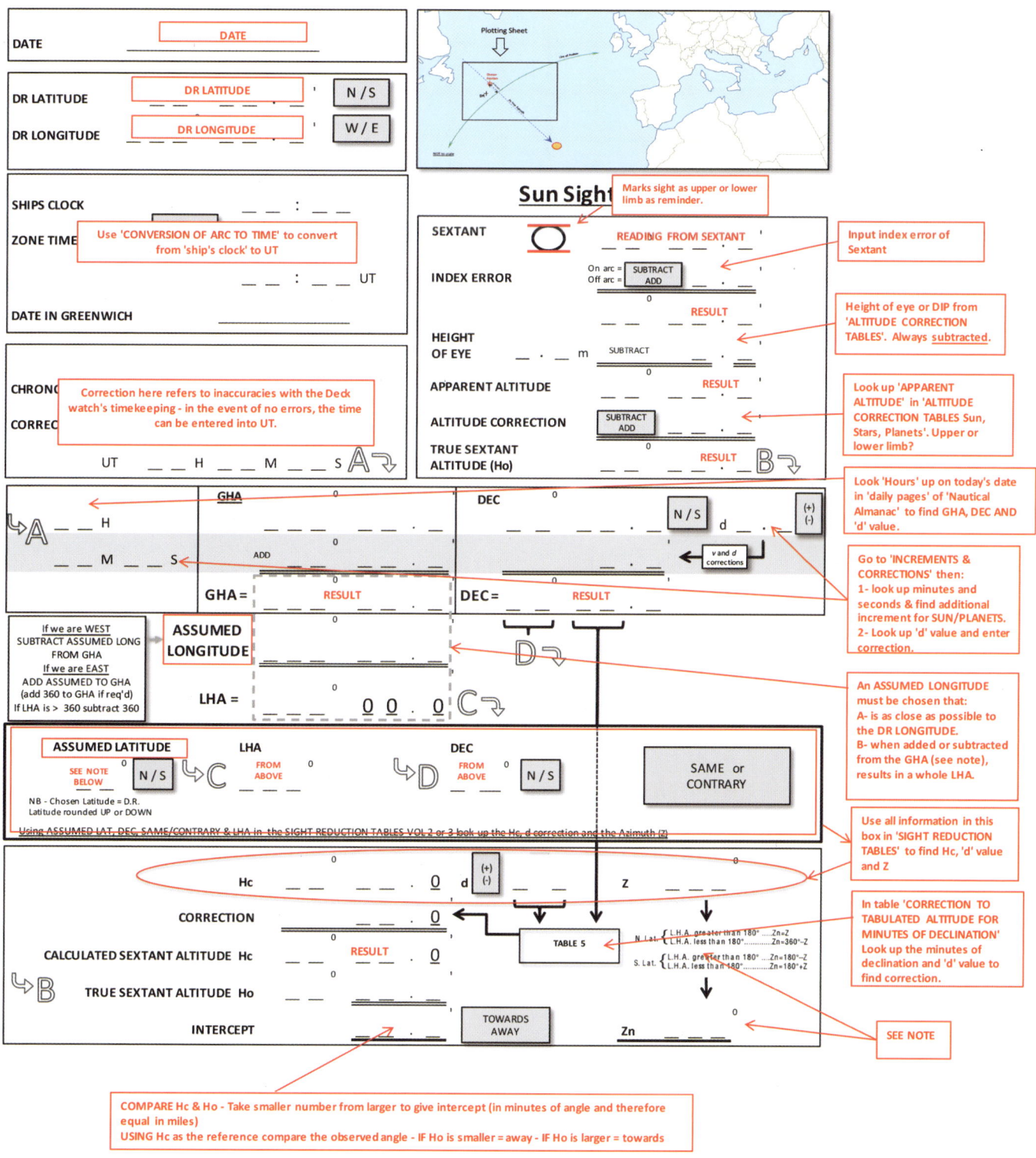

3 Meridian passage proforma

DATE _____

DR LATITUDE __ __ ° __ __ . __ ' N/S
DR LONGITUDE __ __ __ ° __ __ . __ ' W/E

ARC TO TIME CONVERSION (time difference between our vessel and Greenwich)

DR LONGITUDE 'degrees' __ __ __ ° = __ __ H __ __ M
DR LONGITUDE 'minutes' __ __ . __ ' = __ __ . __ M

         __ __ H __ __ . __ M A ↴

TIME OF MER PASS AT GREENWICH (UT)   __ __ H __ __ M
ARC TO TIME CORRECTION ↳A (+) if Longitude West / (−) if Longitude East   __ __ H __ __ M
TIME OF MER PASS AT VESSEL (UT)   __ __ H __ __ M B ↴

Meridian Passage Pro-forma

SEXTANT ALTITUDE ○   __ __ ° __ __ . __ '
INDEX ERROR On arc = SUBTRACT / Off arc = ADD   __ __ . __ '
                     __ __ ° __ __ . __ '
HEIGHT OF EYE __ . __ m SUBTRACT   __ __ . __ '
APPARENT ALTITUDE   __ __ ° __ __ . __ '
ALTITUDE CORRECTION SUBTRACT/ADD   __ __ . __ '
TRUE SEXTANT ALTITUDE (Ho)   __ __ ° __ __ . __ '   C ↴

↳B __ __ H
     __ __ M

DEC __ __ ° __ __ . __ ' N/S   d __ . __ (+)/(−)
        __ __ . __ '   v and d corrections
        __ __ ° __ __ . __ ' D ↴

↳C **TRUE SEXTANT ALTITUDE (Ho)**   8 9 ° 6 0 . 0 '
                                    __ __ ° __ __ . __ '   SUBTRACT
ZENITH DISTANCE (ZD)   __ __ ° __ __ . __ '
↳D **DECLINATION**   __ __ ° __ __ . __ '
LATITUDE   __ __ ° __ __ . __ '

Lat = Dec + ZD — Same Hemisphere - Latitude GREATER than Declination

Lat = Dec − ZD — Same Hemisphere - Latitude LESS than Declination

Lat = ZD − Dec — Opposite

WORKING AREA
__ __ ° __ __ . __ '
__ __ ° __ __ . __ '
__ __ ° __ __ . __ '

4 Meridian passage proforma guide

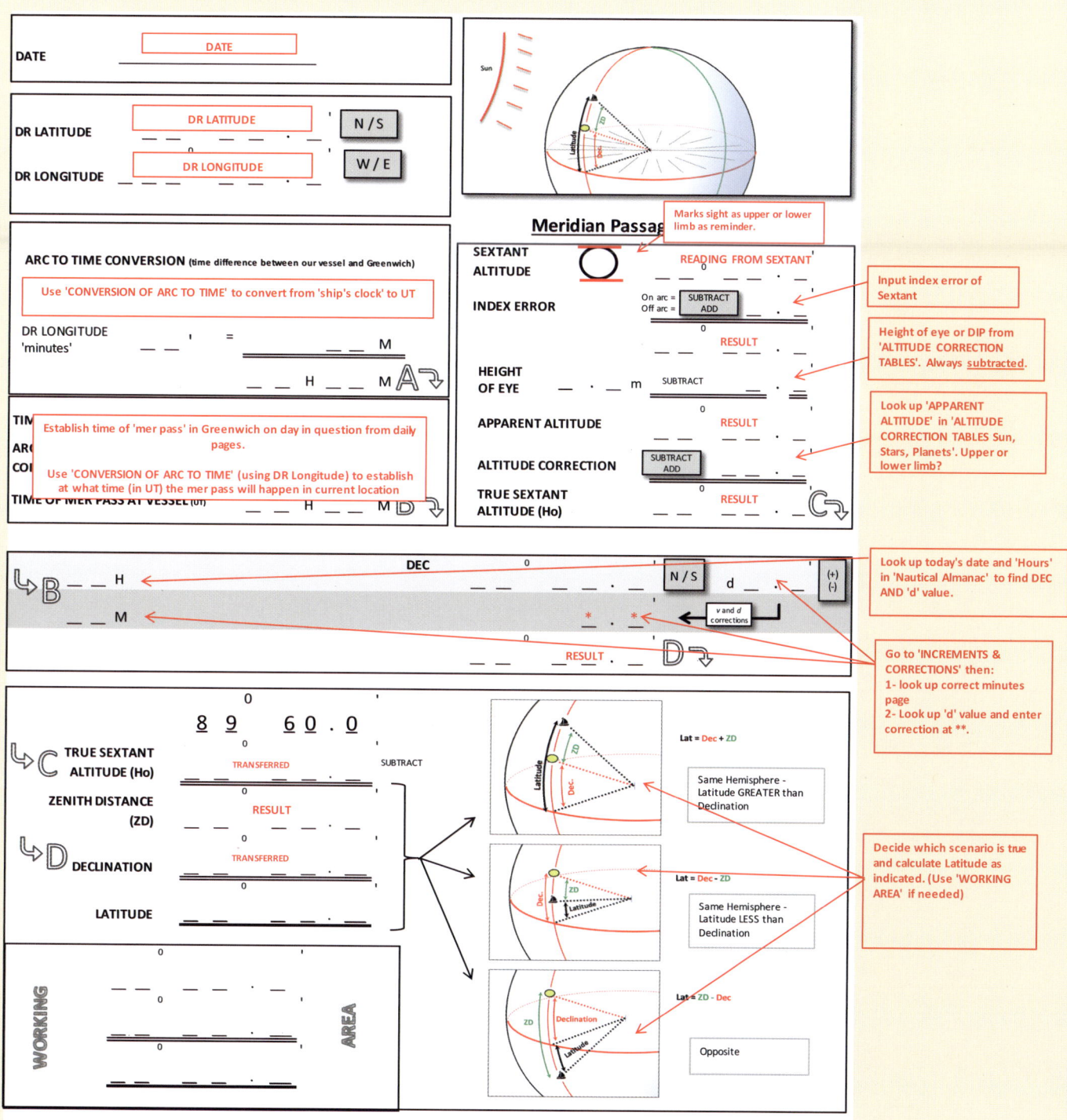

The proformas on pages 130-33 are available in PDF format from www.philsomerville.com.

5 Plotting sheet

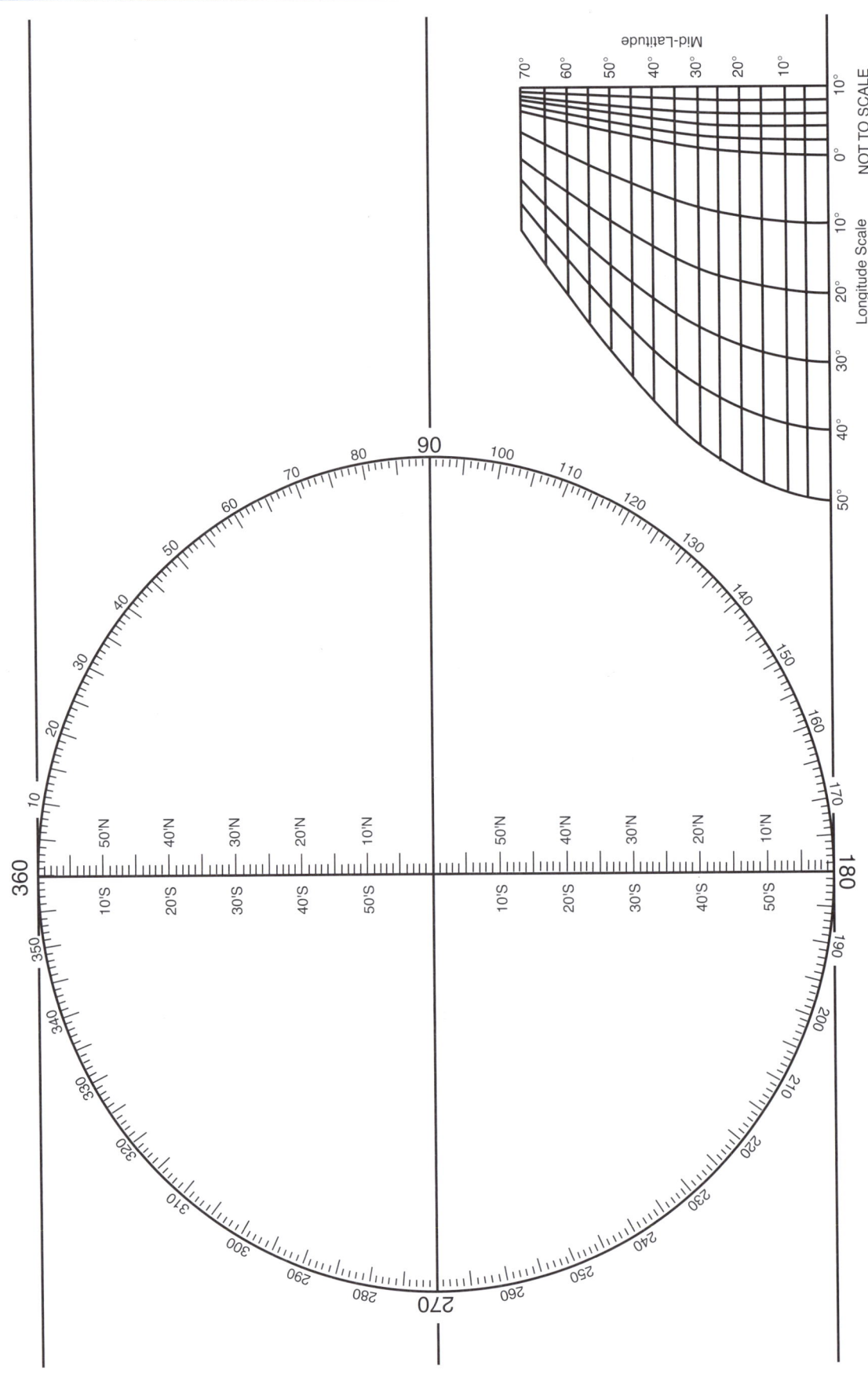

6 Plotting guide

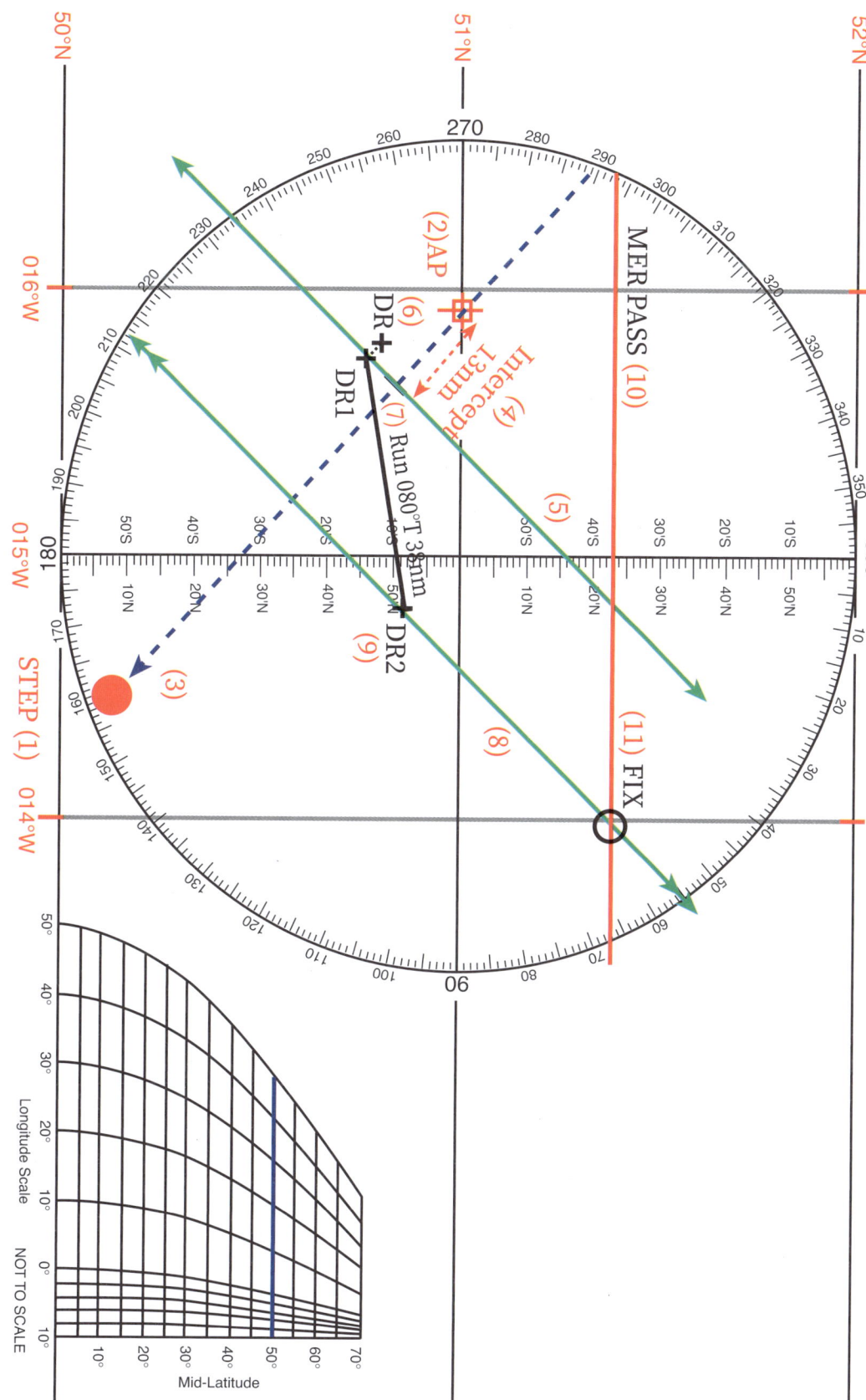

(1) - Mark Longitude scale according to present latitude.
(2) - Mark assumed position (AP) (Made up of assumed latitude & assumed longitude.)
(3) - Draw on Azimuth (Zn) (direction of Sun indicated with arrows).
(4) - Mark intercept - reference to the AP - either towards the sun from AP or away. (Example below is 'towards').
(5) - Extend the intercept perpendicular to the azimuth (Zn) forming a 'line of position' (which if extended would form a position circle). You are *definitely* somewhere on this line.
(6) - Mark on original DR (Lat and Long) and transfer onto LOP to DR1.
(7) - Draw on RUN from line of position (preferably from your 'probable position').
(8) - Transfer the 'line of position' (becomes 'transferred position line'). Marked with two arrow heads.
(9) - Point 9 becomes DR2. Used for a 2nd Sun Sight if a mer pass wasn't possible
(10) - Draw on Meridian Passage.
(11) - Now, we are *definitely* on the transferred line of position and *definitely* on the mer pass. Therefore the only place we can be is at their intersection - our Fix.

7 Longitude scale plotting

Using our dividers, we measure off the distance indicated by the red line and transfer this to our plot.

Conversely, we do the opposite if measuring off the plot and want to establish minutes of Longitude for a given position.

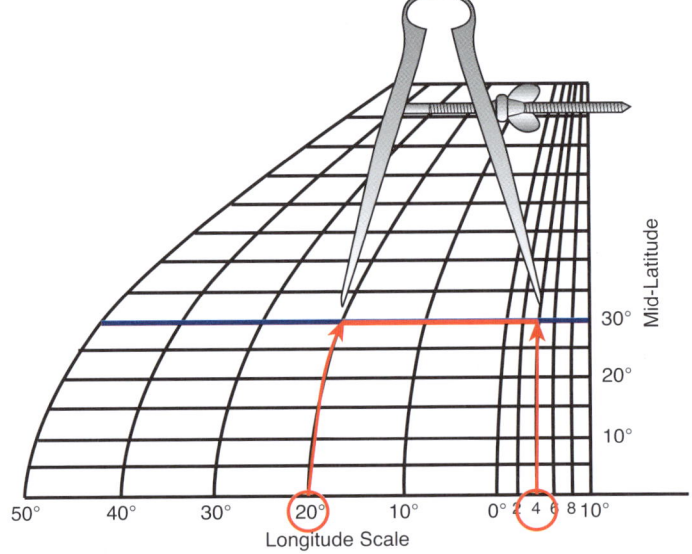

In this example our Chosen Latitude = 30° and we want to measure 24.0' of Longitude.

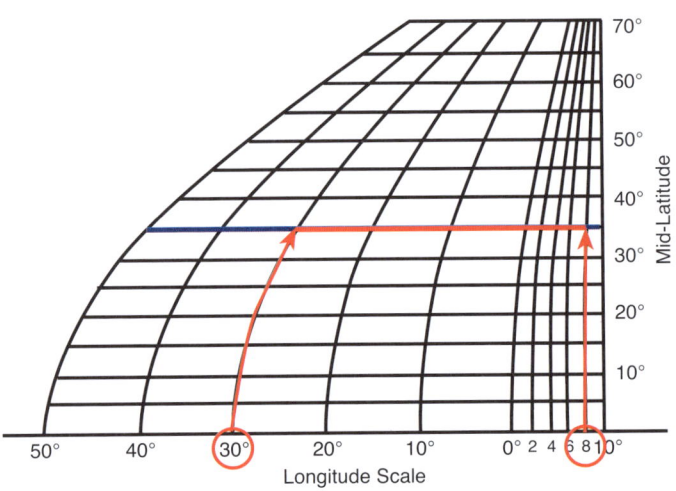

In this example our Chosen Latitude = 35° and we want to measure 38.0' of Longitude.

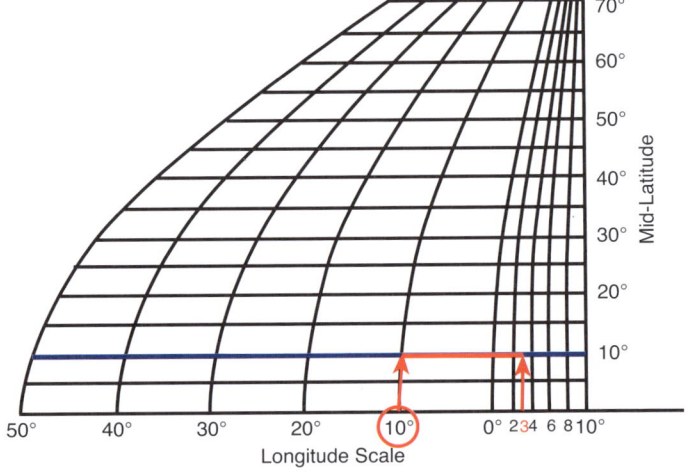

In this example our Chosen Latitude = 10° and we want to measure 13.0' of Longitude. (For 3 minutes we estimate halfway between 2 and 4.)

8 Z versus Zn

Here we tackle another instance where the tables have been cleverly reduced in size to eliminate unnecessary content. Unfortunately, that does lead to an extra action during the sight reduction process.

Now, we don't need to understand the concept, but for those who want to, here's a brief explanation.

Z is known as the **azimuth angle** and can be thought of as a relative bearing (but not a compass bearing) of the sun from our vessel. What do we mean by this?

Let's say we obtain a *Z* value from the tables of 080°T. The bearing we get from the tables could be either of the angles shown in Figure 180, putting the sun either east or west of our position. (In actual fact, Z could be one of four angles, including a mirror image of Figure 180. For simplicity of explanation, let's stay with the simplified picture.)

On the other hand, *Zn* is the **azimuth bearing** or true compass bearing and that's what we really want. As we know, the compass goes in a clockwise direction from 0° to 360°.

If we were in a scenario where the sun was east of us, the *Z* would already be a compass bearing, as shown in Figures 181 and 182. Therefore, we would find in the tables the statement: **Zn = Z**

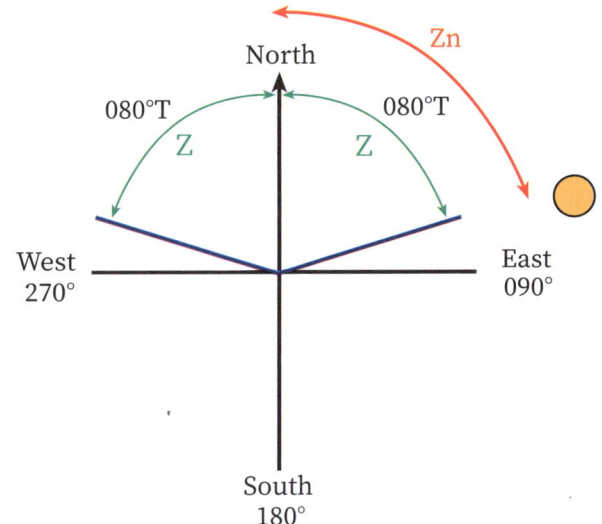

Figure 181

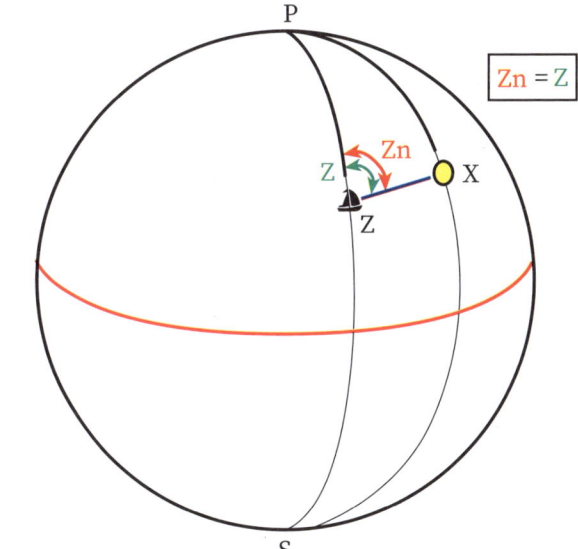

Figure 182

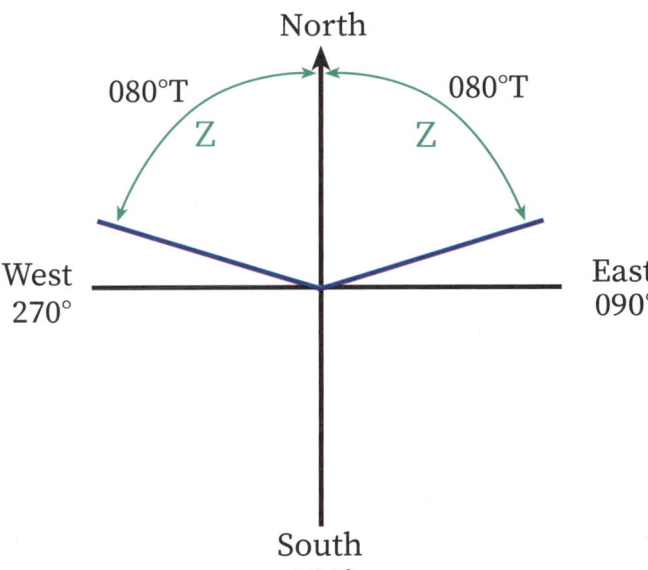

Figure 180

However, if we were in a scenario where the sun is west of us (this is the PZX triangle arrangement we have used extensively throughout the book), Z would *not* be a compass bearing.

In order to obtain a compass bearing from Z, we would need a picture as in Figure 183.

In this instance, we would have found the statement: *Zn = 360° - Z*

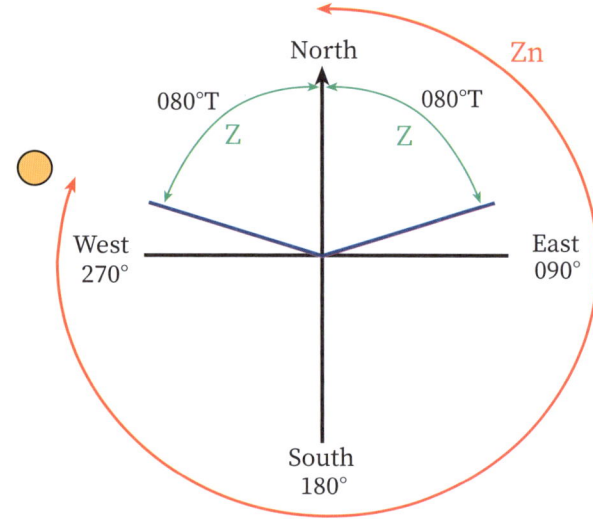

Figure 183

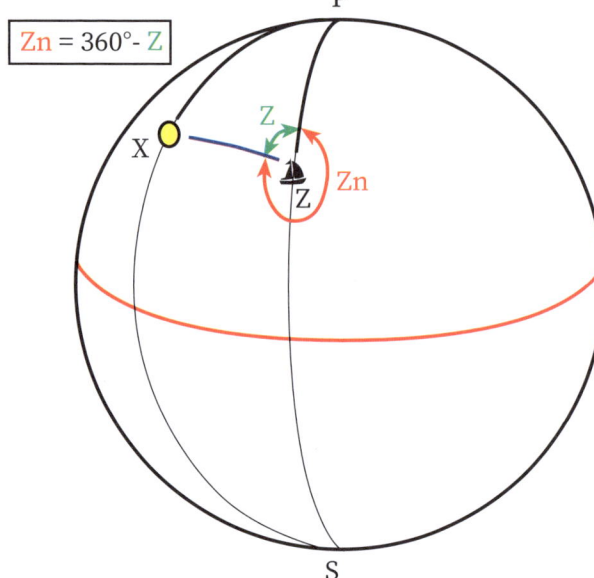

Figure 184

We've investigated two scenarios. In actual fact, there are four.

How do the tables determine which is correct? They use the *keys* we've gathered:

- Northern or southern latitude
- Same or contrary
- LHA less than or greater than 180° (LHA less than 180°: the sun must be west of the vessel. LHA greater than 180°: the sun must be east of the vessel)

Although it's not necessary to remember all of the connotations, for those that are interested, Figure 185 explores the variations. As a reminder, Z is given to us by the tables and Zn is the compass bearing that we will require.

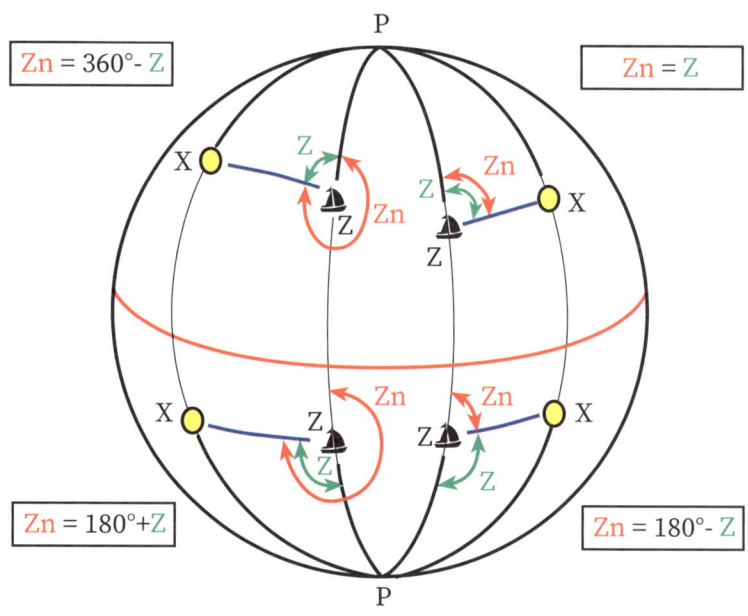

Figure 185

9 Assumed longitude

We've seen that in order to use the tables, we have to modify our DR position slightly to create an *assumed position* (consisting of *assumed latitude* and *assumed longitude*). Assumed latitude is easy: we simply round our DR latitude, *up* or *down*, to the nearest full degree.

Let's look at another longitude scenario:

Our DR position is 033° 15.8' west. We have a GHA as shown in Figure 186.

it won't make a huge difference in which direction we go. However, we should still choose the closest; in this case, the closest is 032° 48.6'.

When considering the minutes, it may seem a strange analogy, but it can help to imagine these minutes of longitude on a clock face (Figure 188). It often makes it obvious whether to move *up* or *down*.

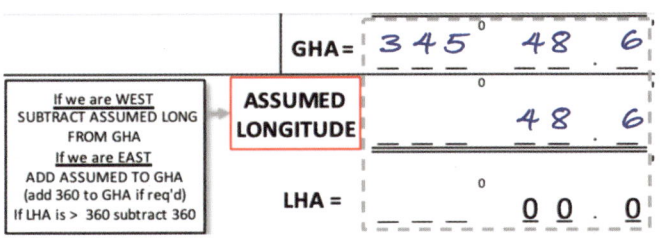

Figure 186

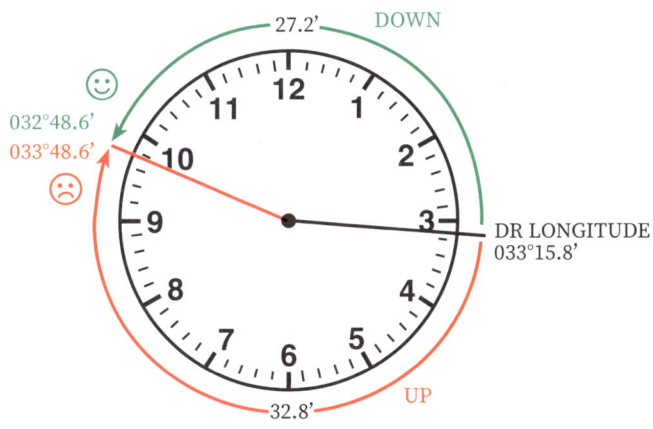

Figure 188

The picture would look like Figure 187.

Here, the picture is tricky. Our DR position is about halfway between options. Because of this,

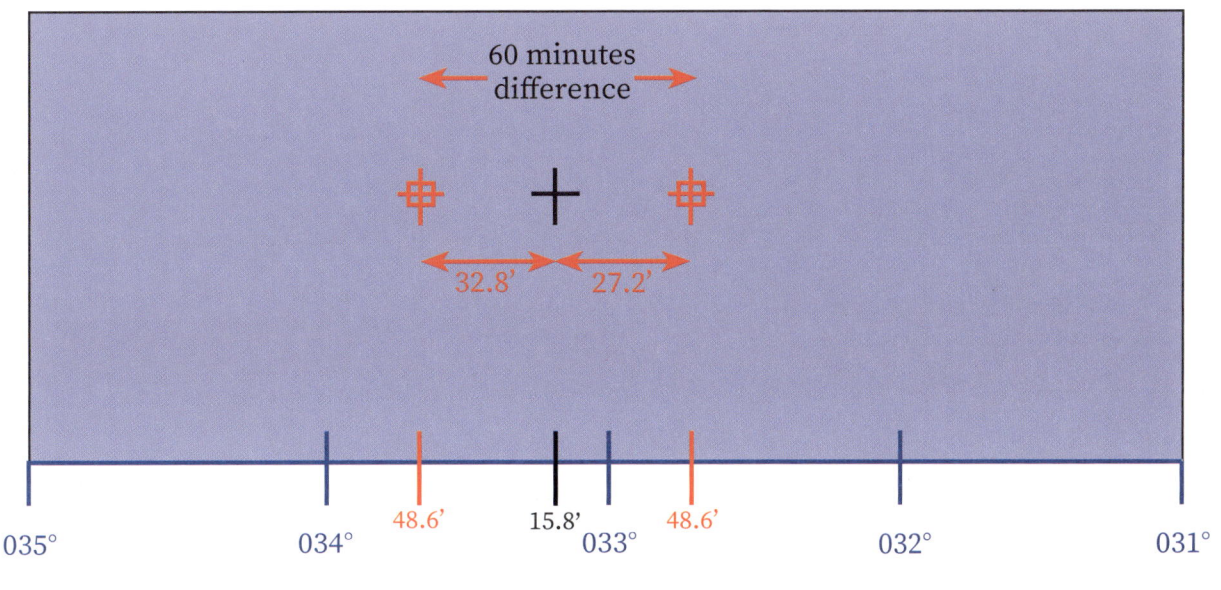

Figure 187

A FEW MORE VARIABLES

What if we had the following scenario shown in Figure 189?

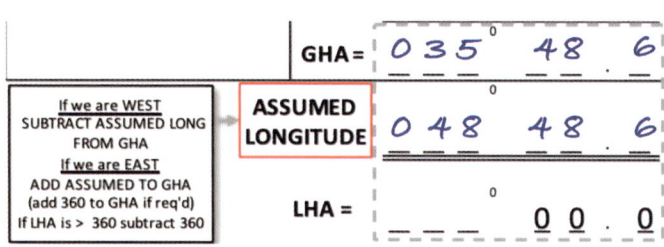

Figure 189

Now, we can't subtract 48° from 35°. Be careful here, the temptation is to subtract 35° from 48°, but this would *not* be correct!

The guidance box (left-hand side) tells us what we should do. We add 360° to the GHA as shown in Figure 190.

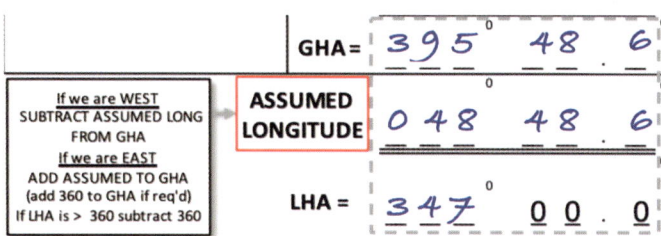

Figure 190

LONGITUDE EAST

So far, all of our scenarios have seen us (our DR longitude) west of Greenwich. What happens if we are east?

Well, we would have the picture as per Figure 191. In other words, in this instance, we will need to *add* our assumed longitude to the GHA.

It's fairly straightforward, but there are a couple of points to note, as shown in Figure 191.

The first thing to be aware of is that we are now asking ourselves: What do we need to *add* to 14.7' to leave zero? Well, obviously we can't make it zero, but if we make it add up to 60 minutes, doing this will make a full degree, one that we can carry over into the degree column.

This leads on to the second point, don't forget to carry it over.

We must remember to carry one degree into the degree column, as per Figure 192.

ie 70 + 15 + 1 = 86

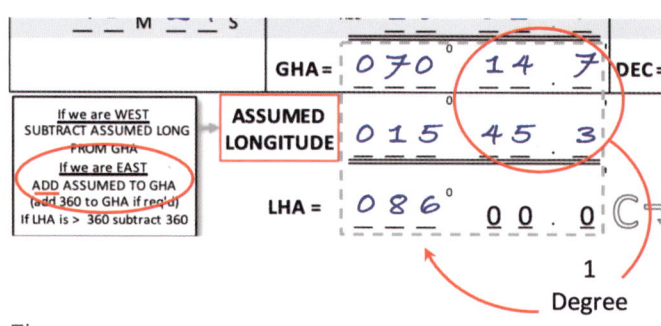

Figure 192

When east and adding the GHA to the assumed longitude it is possible that our LHA will exceed 360°. If this is the case, simply deduct 360° from the result.

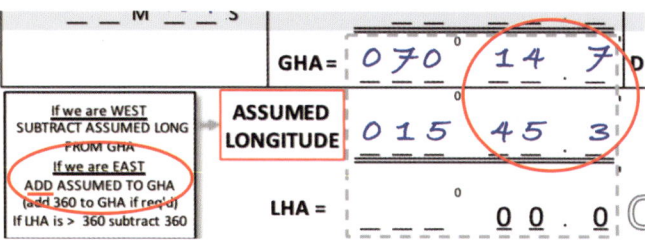

Figure 191

10 Adding and subtracting of 60ths

In everyday life, with the exception of time, we mostly use the decimal system. This can lead to problems with adding and subtracting.

Below are examples of tackling this issue which will help eliminate errors.

Let's say we want to add 123° 42.0' to 63° 27.0', as shown in Figure 193:

> We arrange the figures in the normal way. Then using a calculator, separately add the minutes up and then add the degrees up.
>
> ```
>        123 °  42.0
> plus    63 °  27.0
>        ───────────
>        186 °  69.0
> ```
>
> Then we assess the result. Clearly we can't have 69 minutes! So we carry over 60 minutes and add one degree. The use of a calculator helps minimise mistakes.
>
> ```
>        187 °  09.0
> ```

Figure 193

The trick comes into its own with subtraction. Let's say we want to subtract 42° 47.0' from 127° 17.4', as shown in Figure 194:

> We arrange them in the normal way. However, we can't subtract 47 from 17.4!
>
> ```
>         127 °  17.4
> minus    42 °  47.0
> ```
>
> So, we borrow one degree and add 60 minutes. It looks strange but we're not adding to the overall value.
> This allows us to do a straight forward subtraction using a calculator.
>
> ```
>         126 °  77.4
> minus    42 °  47.0
>          84 °  30.4
> ```

Figure 194

11 Polaris

We stated that this book is all about the sun. However, there is one other star that deserves a mention. In fact, no book on celestial navigation would be complete without it.

Polaris, also known as the North Star, has had a very significant role over the centuries for northern hemisphere navigators. So much so it was also referred to as Stella Maris (Star of the Sea).

Polaris sits almost exactly over the North Pole. Because of this, if you were to observe the night sky in the northern hemisphere, you would see the whole night sky pivoting around this point.

So Polaris sits due north and can lend itself for compass checking purposes. However, it has another very important attribute, it can be used very simply to obtain one's latitude.

We see the unique geometry Polaris gives us (Figure 195). Because of the 90° angles, we have a situation whereby our corrected *true sextant altitude (Ho)* equals our *latitude.*

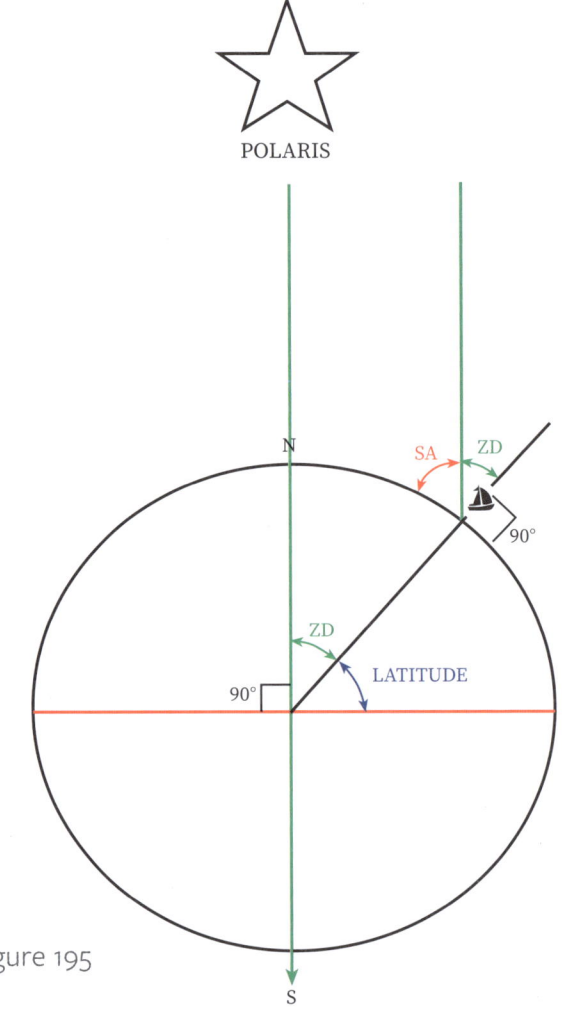

Figure 195

Unfortunately it's quite not as simple as this, because Polaris doesn't sit exactly over the North Pole and, due to this, some corrections are required. Looking at these corrections would lead us beyond the scope of this book. However, without corrections, we can still obtain our latitude to within approximately 40nm. Not bad on a vast ocean. And if we're lucky, on two occasions in every 24 hours, we can get our exact latitude. This is out of our control because the sight taking of Polaris is dictated by our sight-taking window at morning or evening twilight.

HOW TO FIND POLARIS

The easiest way to find Polaris is with Ursa Major, otherwise known as the Big Dipper, the Plough, the Great Bear and many more. This constellation is one of the prominent constellations in the northern hemisphere (see Figure 196).

As can be seen in Figure 196, the two stars at the end of Ursa Major point towards Polaris. If we gauge the distance between these two stars to be one unit, a further five units will locate Polaris.

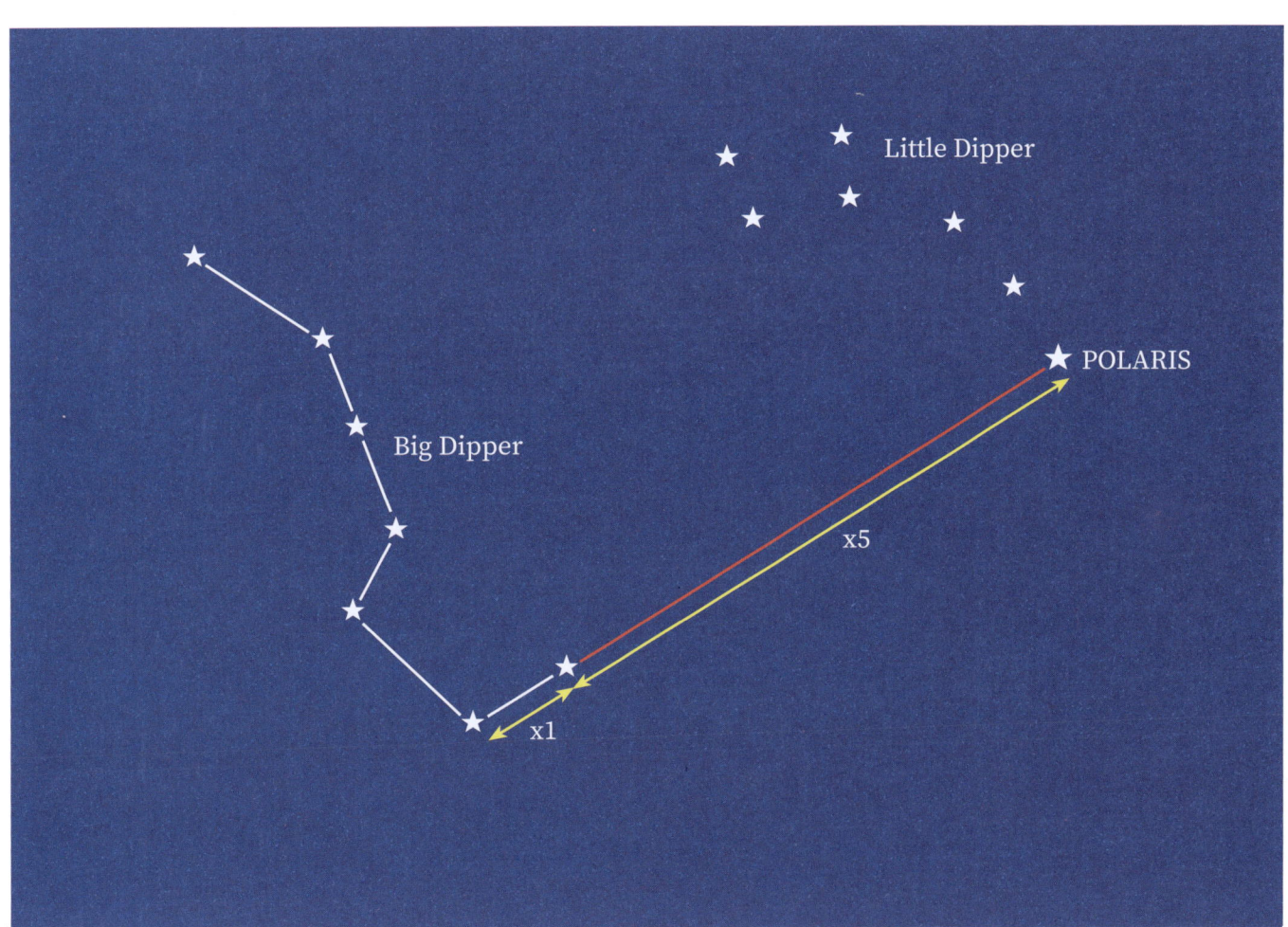

Figure 196

Glossary

Altitude – Used to describe the height of a celestial body above the horizon in terms of angle above the horizon, ie sextant *altitude*.

Assumed latitude – One of the *4 keys* required to unlock the sight reduction tables. In order to minimise the size of the tables, our DR latitude has to be rounded up or down to the nearest whole degree – in doing so it becomes known as our *Assumed Latitude*.

Assumed longitude – The Local Hour angle LHA is one of the *4 keys* needed to unlock the sight reduction tables. First, we establish the GHA, we then either add or subtract our DR longitude and the resulting angle is the LHA. However, in order to minimise their size, the sight reduction tables only accept LHAs with whole degrees. In order to achieve this, we have to modify our DR longitude, after which, it becomes known as our *Assumed Longitude*.

Assumed position (AP) – This is a position comprising assumed latitude and assumed longitude. This position, which we make as close to our DR position as possible, is used as a reference point from which we can establish a position line (or as we call them in the book, a Line of Position, LOP). Because our original DR position is by its very nature not that accurate, this modification has little impact.

Azimuth (Zn) – A true compass bearing of the sun, ie between 0 and 360 degrees.

Azimuth Angle (Z) – An angle of the sun measured from either the North Pole or the South Pole AND in either an easterly or westerly direction. We use the statements contained on the top or bottom of each page within the sight reduction tables to establish the Zn. This system is used to minimise the size of the tables.

Celestial body – A term used to describe any object in the sky, eg sun, stars and planets. Some publications refer to them as *heavenly* bodies.

Celestial navigation – A system of navigation whereby very accurate angles between celestial bodies (ie the sun) and the horizon are established. This information is then used to determine lines of position (or LOPs). Two or more lines of position give a fix.

Chronometer – An accurate timepiece. Traditionally this would have been an accurate mechanical watch or clock. Replaced by quartz watches.

Co-Dec – This is the 'compliment' of the declination.

    Declination + Co-Dec = 90°

    Therefore: Co-Dec = 90° − Declination

Co-Lat – This is the 'compliment' of the latitude.

Latitude + Co-Lat = 90°
Therefore: Co-Lat = 90° – Latitude

Compass rose – Protractor at centre of plotting sheet.

Contrary – This term originates from one of the 4 keys required for the sight reduction tables. One of the arguments that needs resolving is to choose either *same* or *contrary*. *Same* refers to the situation where our DR latitude is in the same hemisphere as the sun's declination, eg north latitude and north declination equals *same*. However, when these are opposite, they are referred to as *contrary*, eg north latitude and south declination equals *contrary.*

Course – The direction undertaken by the vessel.

d value – Referring to the d value for declination. This is the amount that the declination will change by during one hour of time. (June & December – almost zero; March & September – approximately 1 minute of angle per hour.) Referring to the d value for calculated sextant altitude Hc. This is the amount that the calculated sextant altitude Hc will change by for each given degree of declination.

Daily pages – The pages within a nautical almanac that give day-by-day information.

Dead reckoning position – A position derived from the heading of the vessel (as indicated by the ship's compass), combined with the distance travelled (as indicated by the log). Comprising DR Latitude and DR Longitude.

Declination – The position of the sun in a north or south aspect. Can be thought of as the sun's equivalent of latitude.

Deviation – An error resulting from an 'on board' magnetic influence that causes the ship's compass to read incorrectly.

Dip – Refers to the height of eye of the observer when taking a sextant reading.

Dividers – Equipment used for measuring distance on a chart.

DR Latitude – dead reckoning latitude position (see dead reckoning position).

DR Longitude – dead reckoning longitude position (see dead reckoning position).

DR Plot – The plotting on a chart of the vessel's dead reckoning position.

DR Position – (See dead reckoning position).

Equator – A parallel of latitude that is positioned exactly halfway between the North and South Poles. The only parallel of latitude that is a great circle.

Equinox – Occurs when the sun's geographical position sits on the equator. This happens twice a year (in spring & autumn).

Fix – When the ship's position has been established, this position is known as a fix.

Geographical position – An imaginary point on the surface of the earth through which a single beam of light from the sun (or celestial body) would pass before travelling through the centre of the earth. The position is defined in terms of declination (north/south aspect) and GHA (east/west aspect).

GHA – (see Greenwich Hour Angle).

GMT – (see Greenwich Mean Time).

GP – (see Geographical Position).

GPS – Global Positioning System. More correctly stated as Navstar GPS, this refers to the satellite positioning system owned by the United States government. It is one of the Global Navigation Satellite Systems (GNSS) operated worldwide.

Great circle – Any circle drawn on the surface of the earth that shares its centre with the centre of the earth. By definition any great circle will have the circumference of the earth. Great circles utilised on a chart include all of the meridians of longitude and the equator.

Greenwich Hour Angle – The position of the sun in an east or west aspect. Can be thought of as the sun's equivalent of longitude (although GHA is measured from 0 to 360 degrees in a westerly direction). The 'hour angle' reflects the relationship between longitude and its link to time.

Greenwich Mean Time – Greenwich was adopted as the prime meridian (0° longitude) as early as the 15th century, when time started to be used as an aid to nautical navigation. When the sun is directly above this prime meridian, it is 1200 noon in Greenwich. Coordinated Universal Time (UTC) replaced Greenwich Mean Time (GMT) as the world standard for time. For celestial navigation purposes UT, UTC and GMT can be considered to be the same thing. Times in the nautical almanac are based on these.

Hc – Calculated Sextant Altitude. This is obtained using the 4 keys on the sun sight proforma and it is based upon the sextant altitude that would be observed from the Assumed Position if one was situated there.

Heading – The direction the vessel is pointing.

Height of eye – The distance between water level and the observer's eye.

Ho – Observed Sextant Altitude. This is the actual sextant altitude obtained with the sextant and the application of corrections.

Increments and corrections – Found in the back of the nautical almanac. The information contained in the daily pages change in 1-hour segments. The Increments and Corrections table is used to determine changes in GHA and declination for parts (or increments) of an hour.

Index error – Having checked and corrected the sextant for errors, *Index error* is the small vertical error left on the sextant. With patience and a quality sextant this can be virtually eliminated. However, a plastic sextant is sensitive to heat and therefore needs checking before every sight. Time spent trying to eliminate *index error* on a plastic sextant would be wasted. Because of its vertical nature, *Index error* will have a direct effect on the reading taken from the sextant. Therefore, a correction must be made to account for it.

Intercept – We mention in the book that we use the sextant as a range finder utilising the great circle relationship between angle and distance. The Calculated Sextant Altitude (Hc) can be thought to provide a *calculated* distance from the GP. The Observed Sextant Altitude (Ho) can be thought to provide an *observed* distance from the GP. The *intercept* is the distance between these two points.

Intercept Method – A method of celestial navigation used to fix one's position on the oceans. The method firstly establishes a position close to the vessel (Assumed position). Then, using tables, a *hypothetical* calculated sextant altitude (Hc) is determined from that position. This Hc is then compared with an actual sextant reading 'Observed Sextant Altitude (Ho)'. This difference enables the user to establish a position line on which the vessel is positioned. Repetition of the process provides a second position line, and a fix is obtained. Also known as the *Marcq St Hilaire Method.*

Knot (unit) – A unit of speed equal to one nautical mile per hour.

Latitude – The position of a vessel on the earth's surface from a north/south perspective.

LHA – (see Local Hour Angle).

Line of Position – Part of a position circle, obtained by *range* from a definable point. As opposed to a position line that is obtained by bearing from a definable point.

Local Hour Angle – This is a term used to describe the angular difference between our Assumed Longitude and the sun's GHA. To use less accurate but more easily understood words, it is the longitudinal difference between our position and the position of the sun.

Local Mean Time – Time of an event anywhere on the surface of the earth as indicated using Universal Time (UT) or Greenwich Mean Time (GMT).

Log – An instrument for measuring the speed of a vessel through the water. May also refer to a vessel's record (see Logbook).

Logbook – A vessel's record of a voyage.

Longitude – The position of a vessel on the earth's surface from an east/west perspective.

LOP – (see Line of Position).

Lower limb – When undertaking a sun sight, the image of the sun is brought down to the horizon until the lower edge of the sun just touches the horizon.

MCA – Maritime and Coastguard Agency (Flag registration authority of the United Kingdom).

Meridian – North/south lines on a globe that travel through the North and South Poles. If extended, these form great circles.

Meridian passage – Otherwise known as the noon sight. This occurs when the sun sits on exactly the same meridian as the observer. At this point in time the LHA is zero. This gives a simplified picture when compared to the picture at any other time of day. From this picture we can find our latitude (our latitude being a horizontal position line).

Micrometer drum – Part of a sextant used for the adjustment of small angles. Each revolution equates to 60 minutes (one degree).

Nautical Almanac – A yearbook containing astronomical information for navigators utilising celestial navigation.

Nautical mile – A unit of measurement. Historically defined as one minute (1/60th of a degree) of latitude. Today the international nautical mile is defined as exactly 1,852 metres.

Polar Distance – (see Co-Dec).

Position Circle – (Using an isolated lighthouse as an example.) If we found we were 5 miles away from the lighthouse, we would be able to draw a circle around the lighthouse with a radius of 5nm. The resulting circle would be a *position circle,* somewhere upon which we would be positioned.

Position Line (or Line of Position) – A line or part of a circle drawn on a chart that is based on a bearing or distance to a known object. Two lines give a position fix.

Proforma – A proforma is a template used to undertake the sight reduction process. If sight reductions are undertaken regularly, proformas are probably not required. However, they serve as a great reminder and guide when one is out of practice.

RYA – Royal Yachting Association (UK).

SA – (see Sextant Altitude).

Semi-diameter – Used to describe half of the sun's diameter. Ideally, when sight taking, the centre of the sun should be brought down to the horizon. However, this is difficult to judge, therefore we use the lower or upper limb. A correction is then made (found in the Altitude correction tables) amounting to approximately 15 minutes of angle.

Sextant Altitude – The angle established between a celestial body and the horizon using a sextant.

Side error – An error on the horizon mirror that results in the two images of the sun being offset on the horizontal plane (ie the two images appear side by side).

Sight reduction – This is the name of the process we undertake, that takes an Observed Sextant Altitude (Ho) and transforms it into a line of position on a chart.

Sight reduction tables – The tables we use in the sight reduction process using the Intercept or Marcq St Hilaire Method.

Sun run sun – Two sun sights (one of which can be a meridian passage) with the vessel's run sandwiched in between.

Tropic of Cancer – The most northerly latitude which the sun's declination reaches in June (approximately 23.5° North).

Tropic of Capricorn – The most southerly latitude which the sun's declination reaches in December (approximately 23.5° South).

UKHO – United Kingdom Hydrographic Office

Universal Time – This is based on the time it takes for the earth to rotate through one complete revolution in relation to the sun. (For celestial navigation purposes UT, UTC and GMT can be considered to be the same thing. Times in the nautical almanac are based on these.)

Universal Time Coordinated – Time based on the atomic clock. (For celestial navigation purposes UT, UTC and GMT can be considered to be the same thing. Times in the nautical almanac are based on these.)

Upper limb – When undertaking a sun sight, the image of the sun is brought down to the horizon until the upper edge just touches the horizon.

UT – See Universal Time.

UTC – See Universal Time Coordinated.

Variation – The difference between True and Magnetic North.

VRM (Variable Range Marker) – On a radar, this function enables the user to establish the distance from the vessel to any identified feature.

ZD – See Zenith Distance.

Zenith – The extension of an imaginary line starting at the centre of the earth, going up through the observer and into infinity.

Zenith Distance – The compliment of the sextant altitude, ie Ho + ZD = 90°.
   Therefore: ZD = 90° – Ho.

Zn – See Azimuth Angle.

Zone time – One of 24 time zones adopted on board our vessel according to our longitude. Adopting the relevant time zone for our ship's clock makes life on board comfortable, ie it gets light in the morning, noon occurs at approximately 1200 and it gets dark in the evening.

Index

A
adding 60ths 141
afternoon sight
   Sun Run Sun: meridian passage and afternoon sight 106–7
   Sun Run Sun: morning sight and afternoon sight 105–6
almanacs
   Altitude Correction Table 35, 36, 78, 79
   Conversion of Arc to Time 77
   Daily Pages 23–31, 79
   Increments and Corrections tables 29, 79
   position of the sun 18
altitude 144
   altitude correction 35
Altitude Correction Tables 35, 36, 78, 79
Aries 24
assumed latitude 55, 57, 139, 144
assumed longitude 55, 56, 139–40, 144
assumed position (AP) 55, 71, 139, 144
   measuring distance from 95
   plotting 93
away (from the sun) 65, 66
azimuth angle (Z) 63, 110, 137–8, 144
azimuth bearing (Zn) 63, 93–4, 110, 111, 137–8, 144

B
bearing-based position line 15

C
calculated sextant altitude (Hc) 47, 63, 71, 146
celestial navigation, definition of 144
chronometers 115, 117, 144
Co-dec 48, 145
Co-lat 48, 145
compass checking 109–13
   deviation 110–13
   sight reduction for compass checking 110
   variation 109–10
contrary 57–8, 145
Conversion of Arc to Time 77

D
Daily Pages 23–31, 73, 78–9, 145
dead reckoning (DR) position 4, 40, 44, 69, 109, 145
   inaccuracies in 55
   plotting and transferring your DR position 97
   and sextant altitude 44–6
declination (Dec.) 21–2, 23, 63, 145
   almanac data 25–31
   seasons and 25
   sight reduction tables 48
deviation 110, 145
   checking for 111–13
dip (height of eye) 34, 145
distance, measuring from the assumed position 95

E
earth rotation 6–7, 22–3, 25, 76–7, 115
equator 5–7, 8, 10, 87, 145
estimated position (EP) 40

F
fixes 2, 14–17, 44, 145
   DR and 55

G
geographical position (GP) 11–14, 16, 145
   defining 21–31
   finding using the proforma 28–31
   obtaining the sun's GP 18–19, 23–6
   and sextant altitude (SA) 39, 43
GOAT (Greater Observed Altitude equals Towards) 66
GPS 146
   GPS time 117
great circle 8–10, 12–14, 39, 40–1, 73, 146
   angle-distance relationship 13, 14, 17, 31, 39, 41, 43
Greenwich Hour Angle (GHA) 22–3, 25, 146
   almanac data 25–31
   and longitude 22–3
Greenwich Mean Time (GMT) 28, 116, 146
Greenwich Meridian 5, 6, 8, 22–3, 116
Greenwich Time Signal (pips) 117

H
Harrison, John 2, 7, 115
Hc (calculated sextant altitude) 47, 63, 71, 146
height of eye (dip) 34, 146
Ho (true sextant altitude) 34, 35, 38, 146
HoMoTo 66
horizon 43
   true sextant altitude (Ho) 34, 38, 146

I

Increments and Corrections 26, 29, 79, 146
index error 34, 123–4, 146
intercept 46, 55, 65, 146
   errors in 127
   extending into an LOP 96
intercept method 43–6, 146–7
International Date Line 118

J

Jupiter 24

L

latitude 5–6, 8, 147
   assumed latitude 55, 57, 69, 139, 144
   and distance from the equator 10
   and Local Hour Angle (LHA) 73–4
   plotting from the mer pass 103
   sight reduction tables 48
Line of Position (LOP) 14–19, 46, 73, 147
   extending the intercept into 96
   transferring 102
Local Hour Angle (LHA) 48–9, 54–5, 147
   and latitude 73–4
   sight reduction tables 48
longitude 5–6, 8, 147
   assumed longitude 55, 56, 69, 139–40, 144
   creating the longitude scale 90–2
   GHA and 22–3
   Local Hour Angle and 48
   longitude east 140
   Longitude Prize 2, 115
   longitude scale plotting 136
   sight reduction tables 49
   and the sun 73
lower limb 35, 38, 147

M

magnetic north 109
Marcq St Hilaire Method 46
Mars 24
mer pass *see* meridian passage
meridian passage 73–82, 147
   completing a meridian passage sight 84–5
   meridian passage and afternoon sight 106–7
   meridian passage proforma 132
   plotting 88
   quick start and recap 83–5
meridians 40, 73, 147

Moitessier, Bernard 4
morning sun sight
   plotting 88
   Sun Run Sun: morning sight and afternoon sight 105–6

N

nautical almanac 147
   Altitude Correction Table 35, 36, 78
   Conversion of Arc to Time 77
   Daily Pages 23–31, 79
   Increments and Corrections tables 79
   position of the sun 18
noon sight *see* meridian passage
North Pole 142, 143
North Star 142–3

P

parallax 35
parallax correction 11
pelorus 113
perpendicularity 121–2
plotting 87–107
   longitude scale plotting 136
   plotting guide 135
   plotting a Sun Run Sun 90–7
   for two sun sight reductions 105
plotting sheets 87, 88–92, 134
Polar Distance 48
Polaris 142–3
position 11–19, 21–31
   assumed position (AP) 55, 71, 93, 95, 139, 144
   dead reckoning (DR) and 44
   determining position 104
   measuring distance from assumed position 95
   plotting an assumed position 93
   plotting and transferring your DR position 97
position circle 14–16, 147
position line 14–19, 73–4, 148
proforma 26, 28–31, 148
   meridian passage 75–82, 132
   sextant corrections in the 37–8
   sight reduction process 52–67
   sun sight proforma 130–1
PZX triangle 39–41

R

radar 16
radio-controlled watches 117

range-based position line 15–16
refraction 35
run 98, 99

S
same 57–8
Saturn 24
semi-diameter 35, 148
sextant altitude (SA) 12, 13, 14, 148
   calculating (Hc) 44–6, 47, 63, 71
   and dead reckoning (DR) 44–6
   and distance from the GP 39, 43
sextants
   care of 126
   components of 33, 121
   corrections 33–8
   errors 119, 121–4
   practical aspects of sight taking 119–26
   reading 126
   sight taking 75
   types of 119–20
   undertaking a sight 125
Shovell, Sir Cloudesley 1–2
side error 122, 148
sight reduction 26, 148
   for compass checking 110
   completing a sun sight reduction 69–71
   sight reduction tables 24, 41, 47–9, 54, 58–62, 64, 148
   undertaking a full sight reduction 51–67
sights, undertaking 75, 125, 126
spherical trigonometry 40, 41
stars 24–5
subtracting 60ths 141
the sun 11
   declination (Dec.) 21–2, 23
   geographic position of (GP) 18, 21–6, 40
   Greenwich Hour Angle (GHA) 22–3, 25
   lower limb of 35, 38, 147
   meridian passage 73, 83
   plotting the bearing of the 93–4
   position of 18
   sight taking 75
   sun sight proforma 130–1
   sun sight reductions 69–71, 105
   as the zenith 12
Sun Run Sun 17, 46, 75, 148
   meridian passage and afternoon sight 106–7
   morning sight and afternoon sight 105–6
   morning sun sight and meridian passage 88
   plotting a 90–7

T
time 115–18
   accurate timekeeping 117
   time zones 115–17
towards (the sun) 65, 66
trigonometry 14, 40, 41
Tropic of Cancer 21, 22, 148
Tropic of Capricorn 22, 148
troubleshooting 127
true north 109
true sextant altitude (Ho) 34, 38, 146

U
Universal Time (UT) 28, 115, 148
Universal Time Coordinated (UTC) 115, 148
Upper limb 35, 38, 148

V
variation 109–10, 148
Venus 24
VRM (Variable Range Marker) 16, 148

Z
zenith 11, 12, 13, 63, 149
zenith distance (ZD) 13–14, 39, 149
Zone Time (ZT) 116, 149
zone time zero 116